uncultured

A Memoir

DANIELLA MESTYANEK YOUNG

with Brandi Larsen

ST. MARTIN'S PRESS

New York

First published in the United States by St. Martin's Press, an imprint of St. Martin's Publishing Group

www.stmartins.com

The Library of Congress Cataloging-in-Publication Data is available upon request.

ISBN 978-1-250-28011-4 (hardcover)
ISBN 978-1-250-28012-1 (ebook)

First Edition: 2022

10 9 8 7 6 5 4 3 2 1

To Mom: thank you for teaching me how to read

To all my teachers, in schools and in life:

thank you for teaching me how to think

The first rule of cults is you are never in a cult.

CONTENTS

■

PART II: THE SYSTEM

PART III: THE ARMY

AUTHOR'S NOTE

■

This is a true story of my lived experiences. On these pages, I share what I know about the groups I've joined and the ones I've been born into, and how I recognized the difference between culture and cults. However, some names and details have been changed.

PROLOGUE

■

You belong to us.

I can't hear the exact words being yelled, but the words don't matter. I know what the tone means:

We own you.

My hands reach toward the sky, knuckles white as I struggle to maintain my grasp on the duffel bag stuffed with pieces of gear I don't know how to use. My muscles scream as I force my arms to keep the bag aloft.

The voices grow louder. I don't know how many. I can see the fear and confusion on the faces of the fellow soon-to-be-soldiers around me, but I am not afraid. If the people shouting were going to hit me, they would have by now. They want a reaction, so I know not to give them one. Keep your head down. Don't make eye contact. Do what they say.

I know how to tune out, go outside my body. I know the trick of focusing on a meaningless detail. All I see is the drab-green bag in someone else's hands. I allow it to fill my vision, my mind. I make it the centerpiece of my world.

The yelling started the moment the bus full of recruits came to a stop at Fort Jackson, South Carolina. Everyone in our group shot to their feet, shuffling down the aisle, bodies colliding with one another, held vertical by the mass of people pressing up against them. We had no idea why we were in trouble, what we had done to earn this verbal beating. But we all had the same instinct—we'd do anything to make it stop.

We fly into formation, standing shoulder to shoulder, staring straight ahead, unblinking, not daring to move even when drops of sweat slide from the base of our necks all the way down our backs and into the cracks of our asses. We clench tighter and try not to shiver. Don't move. Don't be the one who stands out. Don't become the failing one out of many.

The yells turn into words: *GRAB YOUR DUFFEL BAG! LIFT IT ABOVE YOUR HEAD AS HIGH AS YOU CAN!*

I know what is happening. I read about it online after signing my paperwork. This is how they shock your system. We'll be here for at least an hour, maybe two, straining our arms, dropping our gear, doing push-ups, jumping to our feet, hoisting the fifty-pound bags into the air. We'll grunt and gasp and sweat and cry.

They scream and we push. We force ourselves past the pain, nausea, and fear. We ignore the little voice saying, "Stop, this is crazy."

This is easy for me. It's a switch I can turn on and off. That little voice, silenced. My gut, ignored.

Soon, I will no longer exist. There will only be the group. There will be only army.

Most of these recruits have never left home. Seventeen is the average age of this summer's class; they could have been camp counselors instead of soldiers. They will finish basic training and then head back for their senior year of high school before reporting back full-time.

They are scared, but I am not. They are kids missing their mommies, yearning to go home. But I don't have a home, and my mother could never protect me from anything.

I spent my life playing at battle drills, getting ready for what to do when the Antichrist's soldiers showed up. I can't count the hours I spent as a child standing in lines, eating mass-produced food that tasted like cardboard, never quite getting enough to feel full. I was always next to a handler, sleeping and waking, always watched, always commanded. My mind couldn't wander, not even an inch. I know how to follow orders, how not to ask questions.

I was born a soldier.

I stand staring at the big blue sky, straining under the weight of my equipment, trying to block out the drill sergeants' shouts. I am suddenly nine years old again, standing on the Brazilian shore, eyes glued to the horizon, imagining I can see the shores of Angola across the Atlantic. As the waves wash the sand from my toes, I wonder what would happen if I started swimming, if I swam until I couldn't anymore. But there is a big white van parked a few yards up the shore, waiting to return us to the gray walls of the commune, the whitewash of the children's dorms, the home of my loneliness, hunger, and fear.

HIGHER! a voice yells. *GET YOUR BAG IN THE AIR!* The blue sky is a promise and a lie with no real portent of freedom for me, not since I signed on that dotted line. I let out a gasp, almost releasing my grip on the duffel and, with it, my tenuous hold in the group, as a sharp thought pierces my consciousness:

Did I just join another cult?

Part I

■

THE FAMILY

1

SPARE THE ROD, SPOIL THE CHILD

■

Petropolis, Brazil, 1993

From the end of the spanking line, I could see the paddle in Uncle Zephaniah's hand. The oldest kids, the twelve- and thirteen-year-olds, stood at the front. At five, I was the youngest and would take my punishment last. This was the worst—not only did you have the longest wait, but you endured it alone. Just you, an adult, and a paddle.

We stood single file in the center of our dorm, a room full of rough-hewn bunk beds stacked three levels high, yellowed sheets covering thin pieces of foam pretending to be mattresses, bare lightbulbs hanging from the ceiling. I felt the familiar fear creep over me. Don't make a sound. Don't look up. Don't let anyone see you shaking.

Then it started. I kept my eyes on the floor but I could still hear the smacking sound so loud, the thick, unbending slab of wood striking the skin of bare bottoms. We all knew not to cry because that would earn us more swats, so we kept our pain silent, our whimpers as tiny as possible. The older kids were better at controlling their tears; usually, the crying didn't start until the younger children's turns.

Suddenly, a high-pitched screech bounced off the tile and filled every crevice. *Who's doing that?* I wondered. They needed to stop. Somebody needed to make them stop. *Everybody knows you aren't allowed to cry like that.*

The other kids started turning around in line.

Everyone looked at me.

My friend Virginia lifted her finger to her lips, her eyes dire with warning. But I couldn't stop. The sounds burned my throat, hurt my ears. I knew I was in trouble, but I didn't understand why. The injustice of it all bubbled up inside me. *This isn't fair,* flashed through my mind, a thought that I knew if spoken out loud would earn me an even worse punishment.

Through my sobs, I remembered the fear I felt when I had woken up a few minutes earlier from a sound sleep on my trundle bed. My frizzy, dirty-blond hair had come loose from my braid and I didn't want to be chastised by the Aunties for messiness.

Nap time could be dangerous. All twenty-two of us kids were expected to maintain perfect silence, either sleeping or studying the Prophet's words, for the entire two-hour time period, always enforced by an Auntie-in-charge. If someone talked or asked to go pee, or did anything else that wasn't allowed, we all got punished.

Sometimes it was hard to know why we were getting punished. One thing might make the Aunties mad one day, and the next day they might not even notice. Some things made some of the Uncles mad, but not others. I tried so hard, but it was impossible to keep track.

I had heard the raised voices and loud stomping feet entering the dorm as the other kids frantically tried to get in position. I felt so relieved when I saw my mother that I forgot to fall in line like I should have, like I had been trained. I should have known better, but I ran to her to comfort me. The older kids, already in formation, tried to catch me to prevent a harsher punishment, but I flew past them, eyes only on Mom.

"Daniella, what are you doing?" she barked. "Get back in line. Everybody is in trouble. I've had it up to here with all of your horseplay during quiet time."

I looked up at her, confused. She was a different mother than the mother she could be when no one was looking. There was no warmth or friendliness in her eyes, her mouth drawn into a single thin line. It didn't make sense. I had been asleep, doing nothing wrong. I was doing what I was supposed to. I was being a good girl.

As older kids' hands shepherded me back to the line, I understood.

Mom would insist I get spanked, whether I was guilty or not. My mother, at that moment, was no longer Mom. She had become Auntie Kristy, the adult in charge of all of us. She couldn't treat me differently. If she played favorites, she might get punished too. I didn't know exactly how adults got punished, but I knew that sometimes they disappeared, got sent away to different communes, in different countries, because they needed to be humbled. Sometimes kids did, too.

The Uncle holding the paddle, Uncle Zephaniah, was my new stepfather, but I knew that wouldn't change my punishment. He said the same things all the adults always did: "If you aren't guilty this time, this is for all the times you *were* guilty and didn't get caught."

I struggled to get my sobs under control, trying to catch my breath. I could be quiet. I could be good.

The line got smaller and smaller as the other kids received their swats and returned to their bunks. It was up to whoever was swinging the paddle to determine the extent of the punishment to be doled out. In the system we kids had for ranking the Uncles' punishments, Uncle Zephaniah was one of the better ones. In a big group, he usually refrained from repeated swats. Probably because it took a lot of energy to spank more than twenty kids, and he had bad asthma.

As I counted the loud smacks reverberating throughout the room, I felt a kind of stillness. Thinking about the spanks as numbers made them less scary. Numbers were just ideas. Ideas couldn't hurt me. *One. Two. Three.* Next child. *One. Two. Three.* Next child. *One. Two. Three.* Next child. *One. Two. Three.*

Only three swats. What a relief! Some of the other Uncles gave ten or even twenty swats no matter the size of the offense. There were some, like Uncle Jerry, who we all knew enjoyed hitting us and calling it discipline for God. No matter who was doing the spanking, they always told us that it hurt them more than it hurt us. *What a lie.*

My stomach clenched and I tried to make myself tiny and invisible as it became my turn. Uncle Zephaniah was my new dad. Maybe he would go easy on me when he saw just how small and scared I was.

I stepped up all alone. From where I stood, he looked giant, his red hair and prickly beard standing on end—he'd probably been woken up from his own nap for this. He was breathing heavily and moving the paddle back and forth between his hands.

"For crying and running out of line, you will receive nine swats, instead of three," he pronounced.

My sobs broke free again. I glanced desperately over at Mom, hoping she would intervene on my behalf. *I was being a good girl*, I tried to tell her with my eyes. *I don't deserve to be hit nine times.*

But she didn't move. She was not my mother, I remembered. She was Auntie Kristy. And Uncle Zephaniah was not my new dad, he was today's punishment Uncle. They were leaders in the commune, so they knew better than anyone that you always put The Family before yourself, before your own family.

With shaky hands, I pulled up my hand-me-down dress and dropped my underwear to the floor, leaning over to expose my bare buttocks. Uncle Zephaniah was wheezing, sticky, and covered in sweat—even just three swats each had been hard work for him. I held my breath and braced for what was coming. With the pain of every swat came something else, something stronger. I could feel my face get hot, my teeth grinding into each other, my hands turning into fists. *This isn't fair*, I thought, anger surging through my body. *I will never forgive him. I'll never forgive any of them.*

This was wrong, and even though I was the one getting punished, somewhere deep inside I suspected the wrong thing wasn't me.

When it was over, I stood up, pulling my underwear back into place before forcing myself to move forward, to hug and thank Uncle Zephaniah for the discipline, the way each of us had been programmed, the way each child had performed before me. He exited the room in silence, each of us having returned to our beds, only a few muffled sobs coming from the scattered pillows and mattresses on the floor. Back to nap time. Just another day in the Children of God.

■

THE CHILDREN OF GOD was started in 1968 by the Prophet David Berg, a failed fifty-year-old preacher who finally found his calling by saving "lost souls searching for meaning" among the hippies gathering in California. The adults called him Dad and we kids called him Grandpa.

The counterculture movement had given the Children of God an opportunity to flourish, as many people—especially young people—were leaving organized religion in the name of finding their own relationship to spirituality and peace. Berg saw these young people as sheep, in need of a shepherd, and began to corral them into his flock. But the thing nobody ever tells you about the shepherd analogy is that shepherds always eat their sheep in the end.

To join the group, all adults forsook their worldly possessions and dedicated their lives to Jesus, as explained by the Prophet. They took on new names from the Bible, and David Berg rechristened himself Moses David, answering as Prophet, Father David, Mo, Dad, and, later, Grandpa to his followers. The group was full of idealistic seekers who deeply believed in the righteousness of their mission—young people gathered before the End Times to bring in souls for Christ, sharing and living together communally with love and acceptance. They called themselves Teens for Christ until a journalist derisively called them the Children of God, and they decided to adopt the moniker as their own. Internally, they referred to themselves as "The Family." They started proselytizing, launching communes throughout the world. By the mid-seventies an estimated thirty thousand people were on the active membership rolls of the Children of God from all over the US and the group had spread to at least fifteen countries.

Spotting a way to differentiate himself from all the other new religious movements sprouting up, Berg started preaching how much God loved sex, that the Devil was the one who had demonized it. He began writing prolifically, sharing his beliefs through thousands of publications he called Mo Letters, as well as comic books and, later, movies and music produced by a central ring of his followers. He taught my grandparents' generation—the First Generation—that it was their sacred duty to raise sexually liberated children and publicly declared how much he wished he'd been liberated enough to have sex with his own mother as a young teenager.

Berg also believed, like many Evangelicals of his day, in the

Christian idea that if you "spare the rod, you spoil the child," and as the Children of God began to have children of their own, the rod of correction was polished. The Prophet claimed that no child was too young for discipline, and that babies as young as six months old would benefit from spankings to teach them to behave. I can't remember a single day of my childhood that I wasn't hit. Hard.

Spankings weren't the worst way to get punished. Swats, knocks on the head, slaps on the hand, flicks on the mouth, backhands to the face, and other kinds of paddlings were things that happened every day in response to the hundreds of bad things we did—like stepping out of line, talking out of turn, complaining about food or hunger, or not respecting our elders. At five, I had been instructed for years on how to act, but I struggled to control my frustrations, almost always rolling my eyes when an adult corrected me. I got hit a lot for disrespect. But it didn't really bother me; it hurt for a minute and then it was over. Besides, I learned from the older kids that I could always tell on someone else, and then they might get hit too, and that would make me feel better for a little while.

This was the way I lived, and I, in turn, never knew who I could trust—one minute another child might be my friend, and the next she would be "convicted by the Lord" to report me, and the discipline cycle would start again.

There were as many different flavors of punishment as there were adults in whatever commune we lived in. Some liked to give us hard labor. Some enjoyed making us stand with our arms outstretched, holding the Bible on flat palms for what seemed like hours. Some of them hung signs around our necks, with sayings like DON'T TALK TO ME, I'M DISRESPECTFUL. Time-outs could last for hours, as any passing adult could place me in a corner somewhere and leave, and the person in charge of childcare that day couldn't be sure when it was okay to take me out again. If a home shepherd—someone in the leadership— put a child in time-out, he or she would be stuck there for the rest of the day, none of the rank-and-file adults willing to risk interfering with a punishment from an elder. Technically, parents could stop what was happening at any time, but that hardly ever happened. They were Children of God first, parents a far second, and none of us ever forgot that.

Washing our mouths out with soap was another form of punishment the adults favored, used to combat signs of the Devil in us like using foul language, taking the Lord's name in vain, gossiping, or exhibiting the "foolishness that is bound in the heart of a child." Each Uncle or Auntie had a unique mouth-washing style, but the process remained the same: I'd be taken into the nearest bathroom, alone or in a group, and the punisher would grab the nearest bar of soap, and then clean out my mouth. Some would rub the bar on their hands then shove their fingers into my mouth, spreading the suds around the insides of my cheeks and sliding them down my throat. Some adults would make me open wide and hold the bar of soap in between my lips, my tongue having no choice then but to either slide back and forth across it or sit still beneath it, gathering all that soap-flavored saliva. The worst ones would make me take a bite of the soap and chew it slowly, and the especially sadistic ones would make me swallow it. The sting stayed in my throat for hours, and particles of soap would wash up on my tongue and from the crevices in my teeth long after the punishment was over. I fantasized about biting down hard every time a grown-up's hand was shoved inside my mouth, but of course I never dared. Any visible reaction or tears would only bring on more punishment. I couldn't always help myself, but I tried never to cry.

Silence restriction, where children, young people, or even adults were banned from speaking aloud for hours, days, or weeks in some cases, and lengthy periods of isolation were reserved for the most serious offenses—like doubting or questioning the Bible, Grandpa's teachings, or any Children of God doctrines. From the time we were born, we were taught that David Berg was God's chosen Prophet and we could never, ever question anything he said, no matter how strange it seemed.

I learned to be grateful every time I got spanked or received one of the more minor forms of punishment, especially if it was administered by one of the less brutal adults. I learned to be grateful that it wasn't worse. Because it could always be worse.

It could have been Uncle Jerry, who enjoyed it too much, who got to do whatever he wanted. He loved giving group spankings, seemed to feed off the crying and screams. He loved to brag about how even Grandpa thought he was one of the best spankers in The Family. As bad as his spankings were when he was performing for the crowd, it was always worse when he would take you alone into his room and close the door. Worse because he liked to do all sorts of things besides spanking. Worse because you knew that nobody was ever going to come in and stop him.

2

A TALE OF TWO MOMMIES

■

Manila, Philippines, 1987

"But who is the father?"

The question resounded around the downtown Manila hospital. It wasn't unusual for a teenager to give birth without a man in sight, but the terrified, White, fifteen-year-old American girl surrounded by several women—laying their hands on her, speaking in tongues, and calling on Jesus—each of whom she called "Auntie," concerned the doctors.

Especially when the birth started to go wrong.

"Who's making the medical decisions for this pregnant child?"

No one seemed able to give them an answer.

The medical professionals weren't the first who had asked who my father was. Months earlier, after Mom had graduated from Teen Training Camp, where the Prophet trained her directly on how to be a "Bible Woman" who served at the feet of men and gave them everything they required, she, at fourteen, had been sent to another leadership commune, where she served a mission as one of the Prophet's secretaries by day and a symbol of God's love by night. As her young, lithe body swelled with pregnancy, a scandal also grew in The Family. Mom was the youngest of her generation to get pregnant by a full-grown adult, and everyone seemed surprised that a baby could result from a girl sent from bed to bed, expected to share God's love through sex with all the men in the commune.

Though there were many candidates, it seemed likely that the father was Uncle John, a forty-year-old lieutenant in the Prophet's inner circle, the only one who knew where all the money came from and went to, a man well-known for targeting the prepubescent girls and youngest teens, and one of Mom's regulars. Grandpa grew angry, paranoid that "the System" would not understand children having their own children, and that it could be used against us in times of persecution. In addition to sending Uncle John away for good, he dictated angry letters that Mom posted for his disciples. The new doctrine stated girls could no longer have full intercourse once they started menstruating, until they turned sixteen, when "the System" would understand if they became pregnant. The unspoken implication was that sex with girls was fine if they weren't yet old enough to bleed.

That was the world Mom was born into. Her father, Tom, joined the Prophet Berg in 1970 as his accountant and trusted advisor. He brought with him his then-girlfriend, Margarita, from Texas. Her mother was so thrilled to be rid of a troublesome teenage daughter that she donated her Dallas-area house to Berg. The location was just close enough to the Children of God's first commune, the famed Texas Soul Clinic, that it allowed Berg a luxurious haven for his leadership circle, while the rank-and-file members lived in survival mode on the compound. And it cemented our family's honored place in the Family's rank structure.

Tom and Margarita had trouble conceiving. Inspired by the Old Testament story where Hannah promises God her firstborn child, Margarita begged God for a baby and promised the same. Within a few years, my mother, Kristy, was born, and later, her two younger sisters. But as the Prophet's revelations became more sexualized, including religious prostitution, child brides, incest, and pedophilia for God, Margarita feared for her daughters. And she feared that Tom would obey his Prophet over any instincts to protect his children. She told Tom she was done.

This is where the story splits. I was told a tale of prayer and dedication to God, of how special my mother was, and how God had chosen her to stay in His service, to grow up in The Family. To do so, she had to forsake her mother. All my childhood, I prayed to God that he wouldn't make me forsake mine. Later, I would find out Margarita's side of the story: that Tom had kidnapped Mom and fled from Texas to a commune hidden deep in Switzerland, where the Children of God was already beginning to set up secret financial accounts and Tom was needed. He quickly remarried, and because of his role within the Family's leadership, he spent most of his life living in secret communes and traveling the world, while Kristy stayed with another family until she was twelve. The Prophet taught us that flesh-and-blood family was the least important connection to have—after all, we had The Family all around us. To favor a biological family was selfish and went against God.

On my mother's twelfth birthday, Tom toasted her with a glass of red wine. The Aunties then instructed her to make a list of all the Uncles with whom she wanted to have sex, her official initiation into the sexual sharing required of all the Family's women.

A year later, Kristy was honored to receive an invitation to Grandpa's house, alongside the preteen daughters of several other leaders, selected for their tender age and malleability. I remember hearing the stories of the romantic storybook wedding between the septuagenarian Prophet and a bevy of girls, ranging in age from fourteen to a toddler who was barely three. It was mere symbolism, we were told. A marriage to Jesus. A commitment to the faith. But, of course, there was "love up time" afterward, when the girls took turns alone with the old man.

At fourteen, my mom became pregnant with me. Even though Grandpa was furious about Mom's unexpected pregnancy, he instructed his followers: "God never makes mistakes, so we will love this baby."

God might not have made mistakes, but sometimes he did create emergencies to test our faith. That's how I came into the world in a hospital, which Grandpa permitted for births. I was breech, less than thirty-six weeks, and the doctors were worried.

It became clear that a cesarean might need to be performed, but the Aunties refused. They tried to coach Mom to let go and let God, reminding her he was always in control. But in the end, the doctor offered the choice to my mother directly, and though it was a betrayal of her faith, she said she wanted the operation. She yearned for the blissful promise of the kiss of anesthesia, the relief from her terrible pain. The Aunties tried to protest, but they had no legal standing. Mom was wheeled into the operating room, gloriously numb for the first time in her life—she'd deal with any consequences for asserting herself in a medical decision later.

But the consequences didn't come. Instead, her choice was declared as divine intervention: the cord had been wrapped around my neck. Neither Mom nor I would have survived natural childbirth. Berg could say that it was God's perfect will—even if he had used the Devil's doctors to perform it.

Mom got a quick peek at her baby as they rushed me off to an incubator in the NICU—silent, miniscule, and purple. A nurse hurried to tell the doctor that a father had arrived, but she couldn't tell if it was the mother's or the baby's. The doctor shook his head and left the room as my mom feared for my life.

An Auntie entered to tell my mother that her father, Tom, was the man in the waiting room. Relieved, she trusted he would take care of her and it would all be okay. He knew where Uncle John had been spirited off to in hiding, and he could tell him about his baby, little Daniella.

Mom felt a secret sense of joy as she thought of the name: *Daniella*. In a world where she'd never been allowed to make a decision for herself—not when to cut her hair, when she could eat, or whether she wanted to have sex or not—she had a human being of her own. At least she'd get to make some decisions about her baby. She would cut her bangs and teach her to read and swim. She would have someone to love, no matter what. She rolled the name over and over on her tongue. Daniella, little Dani, her first child. Nobody could have an issue with the name. It was biblical, it was beautiful, and it had meaning.

I was named Daniella, or "God is my judge," the perfect name for a baby born into a family that, for three generations, had followed a prophet who taught them that God—and by extension, he—were the only authorities to whom they ever had to answer.

■

AFTER I WAS born, I was handed off to the commune nursery. My mother would visit whenever the schedule said it was time for me to be nursed, if she could be excused from her work. Other times, I'd be nursed by another mom visiting the nursery, a common practice. For a short while, Mom got a break at night, and instead of Uncles, different Aunties shared her bed to help care for me while she recovered from her C-section, and so that she could keep her strength up to return to her secretary work during the day. As she healed and I became a toddler, her schedule became more demanding and she came to the nursery less and less, finally only allowed to see me for an hour a day, at dinner and Parent Time, before I was returned to the dorms for sleep each day. The only exception was Sunday—Parent Day, my favorite— when we got to spend almost the whole day together.

When I turned three, and we moved to our third commune, in Peru, after a few years in Japan, Mom decided to take a risk and add an extra hour to our days together.

"Daniella, wake up," said the soft, cautious voice that I recognized as Mom's.

I remember the fear that ran through me the first time she woke me up. What was she doing in the toddler room in the middle of nap time? Didn't she know she could get in trouble for causing a ruckus? I opened an eye and peered at the adult bed where the Auntie-in-charge lay, back to the wall, snoring softly. Mom motioned for me to get out of bed and go with her, finger to her lips in warning. Together, we tiptoed out of the room, my mind racing with possibilities. What was happening? Was I in trouble again? Had I done something that she had just learned about? Mom almost never spanked me, and if I'd done something truly bad, I was sure Auntie Margie would have sent for an Uncle, not Mom. In the dark hallway, I stared up at her, confused, and grasped her hand tighter. I'd never been out of bed when the commune was quiet before. Was everybody sleeping, all the hundreds of people I lived with? *Were Mom and I the only two people awake in the whole world?*

We stopped walking when we reached one of the living rooms, and I noticed some books under Mom's arm. "I decided that it was time for us to work on your reading," she said to me. "I've been waiting for this day since you were born." She smiled the gorgeous grin that made everyone in the commune fall in love with her. "But we're not going to tell anyone for now, okay?"

I could see in her eyes that she wanted me to understand something more, but I didn't know why we were sneaking around, how audacious and "individual" it was for a mother to teach her own child to read. Reading and learning, like everything else, was done with the group, at the group's pace. I nodded my head, bringing my own fingers to my lips in imitation of her earlier gesture. But in that moment, we snuggled together on the couch, and I ran the palms of my hands over the well-worn comfy cushions always reserved for high-ranking adults. I leaned back and nestled into Mom's side. I never got to be alone with her—no Merry, my baby sister who'd been born six months earlier, before we left the communes in Japan; no bustling Aunties in the kitchen singing songs to Jesus and working on the endless food prep; no Uncles stomping through the house, eyes sharp, looking for children committing infractions, hands on their belts in case one had to come off quickly. I wasn't sure how long this moment would last, but I wanted it to be forever. Mom was all mine.

I loved Mom fiercely, even though I didn't really know her. At three, I understood I was special and different from the other little girls I lived with and that it had something to do with who Mom was. I knew she, at eighteen, was younger than most of the other Aunties with kids my age. She'd also been born in The Family, not out in the System like the other kids' moms. I knew her dad was really important—he even lived with Grandpa, which is why we couldn't ever see him. Mostly, I knew she was special because she was the most beautiful woman in the whole world.

Why don't I look more like her? I thought to myself, comparing my freckled face and unruly blond tangles to her alabaster white skin and long, shiny dark hair. Grandpa always said that hair was the best jewelry a woman could have, but I thought maybe that was just because we didn't have any money for real jewelry. I hugged my mom tighter, noticing places where her white skin bruised just like mine did. Had she been bad too?

She opened one of the volumes she had on her lap. "This book is called *Peter and Jane,*" she said. "My dad taught me how to read with books like these when I was your age, so I was able to convince the home shepherds to let me buy a set. Now I'm going to teach you."

I was surprised to find out her dad had time to teach her to read. I wondered if he had to sneak her away from the Aunties too. But I also knew Mom didn't have a mother, so maybe she'd had special privileges. When my grandma became a backslider and rejected God, Mom never saw her again. That's how I knew that sometimes we had to "forsake all," even our own parents or children, if they didn't follow God's will.

"I already know the whole alphabet," I told her. "And all my numbers too! I can do uno, dos, tres, quatro . . ."

I rattled off all the facts I knew, proud of my new skill of counting in Spanish that I'd learned from Auntie Margie, an Argentinian disciple who had joined The Family. Even though she terrified me at nap time, I loved the bits of language she taught me.

"I know, baby! You are so smart," Mom said. "I read the progress reports from your teachers every day, and they say you are one of the smartest in your group. But you need to behave better and not be so naughty and loud all the time, okay?"

"Okay, Mommy, I promise to try," I said, really meaning it.

Alone with her, all cuddled up and warm in our own little world, it suddenly felt safe to ask questions. "What's reading for?" I whispered.

"Well," she explained, "it's for ideas. It's how we learn things. You know, when I was a little girl, I didn't go to Systemite school either. I lived in Switzerland and my teacher spoke mostly French before she joined The Family. It was okay, though, because once I learned to read, I could teach myself things. There are so many good lessons in the Mo Letters from Grandpa and that's why we don't need to go to school—he teaches us the right things. And you know Systemite schools teach the *wrong* things, right?"

I nodded. I wanted to learn how to read, but even at three, I wasn't sure if I agreed that we didn't need to go to school. All of the books I had ever seen for kids were black-and-white comics drawn by Uncles. They told us stories of Grandpa's life, his kids, and other things, like Bible stories and miracles. I'd never seen a book like *Peter and Jane* before, with its glossy colored pictures of Systemite children at the beach and stories that had nothing to do with the Bible or Grandpa's teachings. I realized that was why we were sneaking around. Even though Mom had been allowed these books, we could never be certain how long this arrangement would be permitted. If the right person got upset, this special time with Mom would vanish.

"The thing I want you to understand, Dani Baby," Mom said, suddenly looking right at me, her eyes big like mine, "is that you don't need school at all. The only thing that you really need in life is for someone to teach you how to read. Once you know how to read, you can teach yourself anything you want in the world—math, history, science . . ."

"Science like evolution?" I asked, repeating the two words I always heard adults mutter together. I wondered if I'd get in trouble for saying a bad word like "evolution."

"No, honey," Mom said as she laughed, but it wasn't her funny laugh. She looked over her shoulder and seemed relieved that no one else had overheard. "We don't believe in evolution. That's just a lie from the Devil. But lots of science is true. It explains how things work, like rain."

Mom explained more about rain and promised to find me on the rare chance that it happened so we could watch it together. I wanted to believe her, but I wasn't sure it was a promise she could keep. I never knew where she was at a given time during the long days, and, at nights, I only saw her at dinnertime and for an hour of Parent Time after that. What if she didn't know where I was either, the next time it rained?

I snuggled back down, determined to be good so Mom would never change her mind about reading with me. I knew adults didn't like it when I asked too many questions; it was something I got in trouble for all the time. But I couldn't help wondering—if books were so important, and learning how to read was so good, then why weren't we allowed to have real books, and why were we sneaking?

■

I HAVE COME to understand that my mother was a naturally sweet and sensitive woman raised in a world filled with people who'd forsaken all autonomy and control, and who had to, in turn, raise her own children within its confines. She tried to teach us the lessons she knew in ways a little kinder than how they had been taught to her. Mom had a lot of faith—faith in Jesus, faith in David Berg as God's Prophet, and faith in the goodness of the people with whom she shared her life.

She never knew, or never wanted to know, the worst of the things going on around her. When raised with cognitive dissonance, as she was, it became instinct to ignore uncomfortable truths. My mother was two women: she was Mom, but she was always Auntie Kristy first, the true believer, the follower of David, the unwavering and never-questioning disciple, the devout woman who would center the needs of the group above something as selfish as her children's needs, or her own. She told the story of her mother's excommunication as one in which her mother left her to God. There was no hint of resentment for growing up without a mother and with a father whose dedication to the Prophet also came before his own children.

Even though she had suffered sexual abuse since her earliest years, that's not how she thought of it. The programming had worked, and, growing up, the story of her marriage to Grandpa was one she told with reverence: It had been an honor to have been chosen for the symbolic ceremony where she married Jesus Christ. Rape didn't exist in The Family; you couldn't be raped when you were *supposed* to be sharing God's love.

When I was older, she told me the story of the one event she actually considered to be rape. Once, in the mountains of Ecuador when she was seventeen, already a mother of two, a local homeless man had tied up her male hiking partners and made them watch as he did things to her that none of them had ever imagined. When the leadership found out, they had said Mom needed to be cleansed and rededicated to God. She was tainted, dirty, and she needed to be purified before she could join the community again.

Though she was the victim, it was still her fault.

But when she told the story, she had no bitterness toward the Children of God or its leadership. She described this period of retraining as the time when she came to understand the difference between the violence and evil of the outside world and the warmth of God's love and affection that she'd been shown since her youngest years.

What that man on the mountain did was rape, the leaders had told her. What the men in the Children of God had been doing since she was a child—that was love. And so went my mother's generation, the elder Second Generation, where her experience of being sent from bed to bed, becoming pregnant, giving birth, nursing, and weaning constantly from her youngest years to the age of thirty-seven was the norm rather than the exception. They were as they were programmed: disciples first, parents second. And, as the Third Generation, the children of the children of the Children of God, we bore the brunt of the split personalities of those who, in another life, might have loved and protected us above all.

3

ACCORDING TO THE WILL OF GOD

■

Petropolis, Brazil, 1993

"Everybody get dressed! Grab your flee-bag! Line up by the door!"

I forced my eyes open and saw the blackness outside the window, that kind of darkness where I could tell that it was after midnight, but I had no clue how many hours might be left until the sun would begin to rise.

Ugh, I thought. *Another persecution drill.* These had been happening more and more frequently lately, at all hours of the day and night. Usually, the Uncles would pretend to be the police raiding our compounds and the Aunties would try to perfect their act of being scared while also flirting, our particular brand of bearing witness to win men over for Jesus, just like our heroine Heaven's Girl did in the illustrated comics. The kids would stand along the walls until we got the all clear, then we'd return our emergency bags to their neat rows and go back to bed. If we did as we were told, we could avoid adult attention and another round of middle-of-the-night discipline.

But the room felt different this time. Quieter. More on edge. My heart thumped fast in my chest as we scurried from the tops of our double- and triple-decker bunks, throwing on the clothes we always laid out before bed in case of just such an emergency. The older kids were tense and silent as they squatted under the lowest bunks to pull out the flee-bags stashed alphabetically. Mine was thrust into my arms and I ran to join everyone already standing against the wall. I took a deep breath, trying to keep myself calm. This time felt real. There was no room for panic.

I clutched the flee-bag to me, mentally checking off the contents it contained: toothbrush, extra T-shirt, underwear and socks, a flashlight, a small bag of peanuts and raisins, a book of baby and family photos. I needed my American passport. They told us the precious document would shield us above all else, though those were always held by the leaders, nowhere in sight. My stomach flipped as I thought about the kids in Waco, who we knew had been raided months earlier. Their compound seemed so much like ours, though the Aunties and Uncles insisted those Branch Davidians were nothing like us. Waco was a cult, led by a crazy man who thought he was Jesus. *We* were God's special soldiers.

Twenty-five children died in that raid. Their American passports hadn't helped them at all.

At six, I was becoming an expert at reading body language. It was a necessary skill to be able to gauge the moods of the adults, to know who to stay away from and when. As I held my bag in front of me, I studied Auntie Love, who normally stood still but now paced the length of the far wall, shoulders tensed up to her ears. She kept glancing around the room, counting us, fidgeting with the strands of her waist-length red hair, tucking it behind her ears that were as freckled as the rest of her body.

"Hurry up," she said again and again, her South African accent even more pronounced than usual. "Get in line!"

I clutched Merry's hand in my own sweaty palm. At almost four years old, my little sister was already nearly as tall as me, with bright green eyes shaped like big almonds, and a warmer, sun-kissed tone to her skin, so different from my own translucent-white complexion. We held on to each other tight as we stood ramrod straight against the wall, waiting to be counted. Persecution drills were one of the few times we were encouraged to stand next to our actual siblings; at almost any other part of the day, Merry would be separated with the younger kids. Grandpa said that being with your own siblings was a distraction. Just like we weren't supposed to get too close to our parents, being overly bonded with our siblings meant we couldn't be devoted enough to the whole Family, to Grandpa, and to God.

But the Systemites would never understand that. In a real raid, we needed to stay together in family groups so that we looked more normal to the police. We practiced all of the battle drills to Grandpa's precise orders:

> *During a raid, hold the hands of the youngest children.*
> *Six- and seven-year-olds carry the infants.*
> *Look toward the cameras. Young, sad faces make the most sympathetic pictures on the news.*

I was six, therefore in charge of Merry. I imagined a camera in front of me and positioned my body so it could see me while I said my lines. "I'll keep us together," I told my sister. "I'll protect you." It was what we were instructed to say, but I meant every word.

Auntie Love led us as we marched in a line from the dorm, our bare feet matching the silent rhythm of the children ahead of and behind us. We quietly chanted the hymn "Onward Christian Soldiers" as a cadence to keep ourselves in perfect step. I had a hundred questions. Did Jesus reveal to Grandpa that persecution was upon us again? Or was it worse? Were the End Times starting? Was the Antichrist here? Were we all going to be martyrs soon? But I knew, for once, to keep my questions to myself.

When we reached the main living room, I searched among the crowd of a hundred adults, most in various degrees of dress, and squeezed Merry's hand in relief when I spotted Mom. But seeing Mom protecting her belly, swollen in the last weeks of pregnancy with Uncle Zephaniah's baby, made the cloud of doom I felt hanging over the room even heavier.

I heard snippets and whispers floating through the growing crowd: raids, police, children taken. Just like Grandpa had said. I looked around the room, trying to spot if anyone was missing, to see who among us had been taken. I tried to make sense of it all, tried to process what was happening around me, but my mind raced with more questions: Will Mom have to give birth in prison? Will the evil authorities force her to submit to a Systemite doctor? Will they take our new baby? What will happen to us?

Finally, the crowd parted like Moses and the Red Sea as Auntie Dora entered the room. The small, slight, and prematurely white-haired German woman made her way to the front. Everyone hushed without being asked. All eyes turned to her as she settled into her natural place at the head of the circle. Even though Auntie Dora was a woman, she was our commune leader and the unquestioned head of everything. She had lived with Grandpa, and she was even written about in the children's liturgy.

"The persecution is here, like we've always known," she said, and I felt the whole room take in a deep breath. "Praise be to Jesus for always fulfilling his promises, and thanks to Grandpa and all of our preparations, we know what to do."

A murmur of disciples praising God echoed through the room: "Praise you, Jesus. Thank you, Lord. You've told us this was coming. Help us to be prepared. Help us to stand up for our faith during these hardest times." I heard fear in the voices but also something that sounded like excitement.

After pausing for effect, Auntie Dora raised her voice. "A brother in Argentina called. One of our homes was raided by the police. All of the children were taken away, screaming and crying and carrying the babies in their arms, and the littlest ones on their backs. The adults were arrested. It's just like we've known would happen. The Lord showed our Prophet and he has prepared us. Persecution is promised in the Bible to all of God's true followers. Our children will get the opportunity to speak with the enemy at the gates, and they will defend us. They will be our deceivers, yet true. But we must always be on our guard."

Merry squeezed my hand, and I felt the stickiness from the sweat building between our clasped palms. I wondered how much of the doctrines she understood, if she could tell this drill was different from the others.

"Most of the American or foreign adults are going to be released, because the Systemite police don't want an international incident, but twenty-one Argentinian disciples will have to stay in jail. We don't know when we'll get the children back. We don't know what will happen next. But we *do* know that Jesus will help us. We have faith in him."

Mom bowed her head, nodding. Was she crying? Was she praying? Was she imagining what would happen when they took me and Merry? Or was she thanking Grandpa and Jesus for guiding us? For this opportunity to be tested, to prove our mettle in fire?

"We've received many prophecies from Jesus already, and he promises that the children will be fine. They might have to stay away from their parents for a while. They might be exposed to Systemite music and white sugar, or go to a Systemite school or an orphanage, but we won't lose faith. Jesus promises that those who believe in him can walk through fire and not get burned. The news is saying the same vile lies about us they've said before. Accusing our brethren in Argentina of child abuse. Calling us a cult. . . ." Gasps and sobs reverberated from all around the room. "But we don't watch Satan's news, and we know the truth. Let's all pray for our brethren in Argentina."

On cue, we took to our knees and bowed our heads and I screwed my eyes shut, wondering what an orphanage would be like. Did they have books there? How did the kids get punished? Did they get to go to school? Were they allowed to sleep with panties at night?

Auntie Dora's voice droned on, "Thank you, Jesus, we love you, Jesus, we claim your name and the Holy Spirit, Jesus. Please protect us against these wicked Systemites who want to stop us from spreading Your word. Sweet Jesus, please guard our children who are in the lion's den right now and bring them through without being harmed, like you did with Daniel in the Bible. Please blind the eyes of the evil police officers, the wicked judge, and of all of our enemies. Help our children to stand strong, like we've taught them, and to love their enemies. We know that the Devil can't win and his lies will never hold. Jesus, take these false accusations of abuse against your servants and drown them in a fiery pit, Jesus."

As she prayed, I released Merry's hand and settled from my knees down onto the backs of my heels, the most comfortable position to rest during long prayer sessions. It felt like this one was going to last for a while.

"Burn down these claims of the wicked judge and police who swear false oaths that our children are abused, touched by our brethren's own hands. Our children, our precious children, who are a heritage of you, Lord."

I opened my eyes to narrow slits, even though I knew I would be in big trouble if anyone caught me peeking. I focused on Auntie Dora's husband, our commune's First Man, sitting to her right. Uncle Jerry held her hand in his big, hairy one, his own eyes closed. I felt the anger in me rise, felt rage burn through my fear. How could they act so peaceful and reverent as she told such big lies? If the police knew about Uncle Jerry's punishment sessions, they'd take us away too.

But I was equally convinced that in the hands of the Systemites, we'd end up worse, and I was almost as afraid that I'd have to go as I was that I'd have to stay.

■

DESPITE THE FACT that we practiced persecution drills all the time, were constantly quizzed on what we'd say to suspicious Systemites, it never felt routine. The leaders always managed to add a new detail or twist to keep our fear fresh. They picked apart every mistake we made, perfected our word choice, and coached us on our behavior. They needed us to defend their reputation. There was no doubt: We, the youngest of children, were responsible for what happened to the whole Family.

Our actions could save or damn us all. We were taught to smile and say we were happy. Nobody ever hit us. Nobody ever touched us. We could see our parents whenever we wanted. The adults loved us and wanted what was best for us.

Even when we knew we were lying, we were taught that it was what God wanted. We had a whole doctrine called *Deceivers Yet*

True. We dedicated hours of "schooling" each day to practice what we would say when the dreaded persecution inevitably arrived:

"Has anyone ever hit you?"

"No, of course not. The Children of God is my true Family! Everybody loves me and would never hurt me."

"Has anyone ever touched you sexually?"

"Of course not! We have a very strict policy that prohibits adults from any sexual contact with minors."

Deceivers Yet True had been distributed throughout the world for every Family child to read, memorize, and repeat. It was a fun read, illustrated by Uncle Zephaniah, Uncle Jerry, and others, and helped show, especially to us youngest children, the duality of living under a system in which lying could get us into the worst trouble, but was also a technique necessary against police and evil authority figures. I loved the dramatized Bible stories and tales of famous Christians who had to lie to continue God's work—every narrative centered our superheroes evading the bad people. There was Rahab, the prostitute in Jericho, who hid the two Israelites and lied to authorities to help them escape—that was an example of lying for God, and also of "good prostitutes," like in the old days when my friends' moms had done Flirty Fishing, going out to sleep with the Systemite men to bring money and disciples to The Family. That practice ended before I was born, but it had brought a lot of good men to the cause. Then there was Brother Andrew, a Bible smuggler who brought the word of God behind the Iron Curtain, misleading border guards to evade arrest and execution as he spread the Gospel through the godless Soviet Union. I especially loved the story of the Prophet Samuel, who deceived King Saul to anoint David as king. God himself was the one who showed Samuel how to lie by pretending to sacrifice a heifer.

On and on it went, with example after example of the good guys lying to the bad guys. We understood that, under persecution, anything was justified if it got us home again. Lying to the good guys was forbidden, but lying to the bad guys was our sacred right and responsibility. If heroes, and even God, could lie, we could too. It was us versus them.

I also understood that Brazil and Argentina were neighbors. We'd visited that exact commune earlier in the year during one of our bi-annual faith trips, where we'd leave the country and reenter at a different place to maintain our tourist visas, which Auntie Dora reminded us was another example of how the Children of God needed to lie to evil Systemites to do God's will. I tried to remember the faces of the kids I had met at that commune. I wondered if they were scared, if they were remembering how to lie right. I pictured the little girls with whom I played, like eleven-year-old Abigail, with her long straight black hair, beautiful dark eyes behind donated glasses a lot like mine, and her nondescript flowery dress from the donation pile. In my mind, I saw her huddled together with the other kids, afraid, enduring hour after hour of questioning.

What would I do when I was tried and tested, like my heroes in *Deceivers Yet True*? How would I act when the enemy was at our gates? Could I be a good girl who would defend our life for Jesus? I hoped so.

But then I imagined the kids doing worldly things like eating ice cream, drinking Coca-Cola, and watching television. We had been warned the Systemite authorities might use those tactics to bribe us into talking. My stomach growled. Maybe I wanted to be bribed, too.

I was supposed to be scared of being captured, of being stolen away, but the fear intertwined with a secret yearning I could never name out loud: I wanted to experience the freedom of the outside world. I wanted to be brave and good, but I also wanted to be far away from Uncle Jerry and all the other leering Uncles.

Over the next few weeks, the sensational news penetrated our closed world as Auntie Dora filtered each outrage of our persecution. The Systemites attempted to brainwash the children to think they had been sexually abused, even though everyone knew that all our sex was from God and done in love. An Auntie described rigorous medical examinations in detail, how children were stripped naked and held down on tables, then poked and prodded with cold, metal tools until they cried. Her descriptions did their job of terrifying me, and I decided never to let a man in a white coat touch me. I believed the adults when they told us doctors were evil.

Again and again, Auntie Dora called everyone into the great room and we spent hours, days, weeks going over the explanations:

We were not a cult.

"Cult" was an evil, horrible name that Systemites used to describe any group they couldn't understand.

Cults committed suicide, like in Jonestown. They told their followers that their leader was Jesus and spread false doctrines, like David Koresh did in Waco.

We were different. We were the only ones living the true word of God. That meant persecution.

The governments of evil countries like America and Argentina demonized religious groups so that they could slaughter them— slaughter *children*—with impunity. Like what had just happened in Waco.

We were not like Waco. We were like Waco. It was so hard to keep track.

Waco embedded itself in my nightmares and scared me enough to stop wishing for the police to raid our commune: Systemites killed children. As much as I loved to fantasize that I had different parents, a family with money and real jobs who sent their kids to normal school, who weren't punished for their spontaneous moments of joy, I spent my days equally terrified of being taken away from my family and the Children of God.

I couldn't survive in this world. But it was the only world I knew. At age six, these two truths were already at war inside me.

Finally, after almost two months had passed, we learned that all of the children and jailed adults had been released and reunited. The Systemites dismissed every charge, and the evil judge fell from his high perch, sanctioned by the courts for religious persecution. The kids had done their job and protected the adults. They had convinced the law that we were good, that we were God's children. Here was proof that God would protect us, like Grandpa promised.

It was proof, too, that nobody was coming to save me from this life. Not the police. Not the big, bad System. No one.

The story of "The Raid" became larger than life, the center of our make-believe games. Grandpa even had Uncle Zephaniah and some of the other artists make a new comic book, *Victory in Babylon,* telling a fictionalized version. We loved reading about the excitement of the police raids, imagining the taste of the white sugar and soda pop the children had been given. We were awed by the depictions of the court cases where young children, like the fictional character Gabriella, valiantly defended the Children of God on the witness stand. She became a superhero to us. We read her words over and over until they became our script. I imagined that Abigail, who'd come to live with us now, had been like her, eleven years old and called on to testify for her faith.

There is something comforting about wanting what other people want, to be united in the fervor of shared desire. I hoped and prayed that, one day, I'd be one of the chosen ones asked by God to defend against the enemy at the gates. I wanted to be a hero like Gabriella, like Abigail. I took the drills as seriously as every child in the commune. No one wanted to be "tried and found wanting" when our turns inevitably arrived.

But still, there was that nagging desire to escape the fear, hunger, and what I knew must be abuse even as we were drilled tirelessly to deny it. What I couldn't understand was how no one else saw what I did. In the adults' minds, they told the truth when they denied the abuse. Their lives revolved around the Prophet's teachings and they believed him: If you spare the rod, you spoil the child. In pictures of us, we seem like happy children, dressed in matching outfits, photographed singing and dancing on the streets. The mind can believe whatever it wants, can handpick the evidence, and can throw away the rest.

But behind those happy Family photos, behind the singing and praying and praising Jesus, there was a little girl who had already started fantasizing about her own death. Who, from the age of four, developed a nail-biting habit so severe that blood constantly dripped from her nail beds and cuticles, who couldn't stop ripping and tearing her skin, despite the adults praying over her, despite the burning hot sauce they poured on her wounds.

After The Raid, I began making a low, guttural humming noise in the back of my throat. The scratching feeling soothed me. I couldn't stop, even though it constantly got me in more trouble. My ability to control this nervous tic at some times, but not at others, was seen as proof of my willfulness and often earned me more beatings, after which it would become even harder to control.

When I began to wet my bed again after years without accidents, nobody connected it to harsh punishments, or to the sexual abuse we would never name, that we never talked about. The Aunties only spanked me more, telling me it was my rebelliousness, telling me it was my sin. All I knew how to do was believe them.

4

ANOINTING THEM WITH OIL
IN THE NAME OF THE LORD

■

Petropolis, Brazil, 1993

There were times when my nervous tics would subside, when I was able to escape—for a few brief, beautiful moments—the near-constant fear and confusion of my childhood. On Friday nights, we sometimes got to watch Systemite movies, as part of a complicated reward and punishment structure to ensure our good behavior during the week. Though there was a strict ban on Systemite music, and almost any kind of outside influences, the Prophet liked movies, and so they were another thing to be controlled, doled out, their lessons distilled and pontificated on. We mostly kept to ancient "classics" like Charlton Heston's *The Ten Commandments* or *Ben-Hur*; musicals like *The Sound of Music*, *Brigadoon*, and *My Fair Lady*; or any movie that could be used to reinforce the idea that the outside world was evil, like *Escape to Witch Mountain* or, later on, most surprisingly, *The Matrix*, which was supposed to be an allegory for the Systemite world being slaves to delusion while the Children of God were the only ones free, but which we really just liked for the special effects and action scenes. My favorite was *The Sound of Music*. On weekends, I imagined we were a real family like the von Trapps.

Saturday nights were the best: Parent Night, when we got to leave the dorms and sleep on the floors of our parents' rooms, which would lead into Sundays, when we had permission to spend the day with them and our immediate siblings. Other than a few hours of devotions in the morning, and a few more hours of studying the Bible during midday nap time, we had no agenda. We even got to skip the hours of Bible reading if we were out on adventures. Sometimes we went to state parks. Sometimes we even took trips to the beautiful Brazilian beaches, where I would spy on the other children, copying how they played in the surf and built sandcastles, imagining I could understand their words, that I was a normal child just like them.

On family outings, we didn't have to stand in long lines and Mom hardly ever yelled at us. She wasn't an Auntie in those moments, telling other adults if we did something wrong. With no one else watching, she was just Mom. We got to be her kids, not Family kids. Even Uncle Zephaniah relaxed when it was only our family, away from everyone else, nobody judging his level of spiritual devotion based on the behavior of his stepchildren.

My favorite days were picnic days. We had food, just for us, and those were the few times from my childhood when I can remember feeling full. Often, our picnic food was bread with butter and a slice of cheese, but sometimes we would have canned sardines or tuna— usually saved for pregnant or nursing women—to eat with our sandwiches. Because Mom was pregnant or nursing almost all the time, she had access to those precious cans, and on picnic days, outside of scores of watchful eyes, she could share with us, too.

When I was six, on a gorgeous summer day, we went out for a picnic on the hills overlooking the commune—Mom, Uncle Zephaniah, Merry, baby Timmy, just a few months old, and me. Hibiscus flowers as big as my head flourished in all colors, their petals wide open, decorating the landscape like a rainbow, the smell of gardenias sweetening the air. We climbed to the top of the largest hill and spread out a blanket under a wax apple tree, the special tropical fruit normal Americans never got to eat. Mom laid baby Timmy on the blanket, his peach skin standing out against the patchwork quilt we had crocheted a little each night from random scraps of yarn. Life was suddenly in color on the hills—the bold white of the frangipani flowers, with their sunset insides against dark green foliage, and bougainvillea flowers in every color from pale yellow to the deepest violet, the different shades of blue from the blanket, the red apple clusters above, the bright green grass all around.

The bread was only a little stale, surely donated by one of our "contacts" in town once it was unsellable, but the tangy, salty sardines covered up most of the bad taste, and we got butter, too. I climbed the tree and threw wax apples down to Merry, who gathered them in a small pile on the corner of the blanket, and then we ate and ate until we felt satisfied. Alongside the safety of the trees, away from the Uncles and Aunties, we played tag and screamed at the tops of our lungs. It was exhilarating to hear my own voice so loud, unrestrained by the big open sky. Uncle Zephaniah played the guitar, and we all sang along. The baby fell asleep and, for a while, everything felt perfect, like we really were the von Trapps.

These moments of happiness were always shadowed by the knowledge they would soon end, and I would have to go back to my group after dinner, to that dorm room, to a whole new week of waiting to spend time with my real family again. A week of getting punished at night because I cried for my mommy.

As it always did, time slipped away and we had to return. Mom carried the baby and held Merry's hand, while I helped Uncle Zephaniah stack the dishes and picnic things into his arms. I followed him as he started to navigate his way. The hill looked much steeper than I remembered from our climb up. My feet slipped back and forth in my donated rubber flip-flops, always a bit too big. I had to catch myself several times to keep from tripping.

Halfway down, I spotted a large metal sheet lying on the grass. Uncle Zephaniah explained it was a water tank, sunk into the ground, and it was the source of our commune's water. I walked over to investigate. "Daniella!" Mom called, and I turned quickly. I don't remember losing my balance, only how beautiful everything looked, the hill and the sky and the grass, all suddenly turned upside down. I put my hands out to catch myself and felt the cold, rusty metal as my hand struck the ground, my body following behind it.

I leapt up, brushed the dirt off my scraped knees. Why was Uncle

Zephaniah running toward me? Why did he have that look on his face? Why was he throwing the dishes from his arms? An empty sardine tin tumbled down the hill, and I wondered why he would litter as I pictured the posters hanging on the walls of our dorms with quotes like "Cleanliness IS Godliness." Grandpa would be so mad, I thought.

My palm burned slightly, where it had touched the edge of the water tank. I looked down and, for a moment, could not connect what I saw with my own body. Blood was pouring onto the bright green grass, drenching the pink flip-flops on my feet, and gushing around bone that stayed, somehow, miraculously white. My hand looked like it had been carved open, the wound pulling apart like the letter "O" that was so easy to write in cursive.

I screamed, and nobody stopped me, nobody shushed me, nobody slapped me. My mouth opened and everything came out, a sound from the very depths of me, a sound I didn't even know I had. I didn't care what happened to my hand. I wanted to keep screaming.

I don't remember how we got down the steep hill, but I learned later Uncle Zephaniah carried me. By the time we got to the big house, I was delirious from the pain, my head fuzzy from the loss of blood and my yelling. The grown-ups poured cold water and alcohol over my hand. It felt like fire, shoved directly inside my palm. They called one of Uncle Zephaniah's musician friends, Uncle Micah, because he had had medical training as a dental assistant during the Systemite war between America and Vietnam. Uncle Micah pushed the skin and prodded it together, winding meters of gauze around my hand and a small wooden plank as a splint.

Nobody dared suggest we ask for outside help. Nobody used the words "doctor" or "hospital." We did what we always did when someone got hurt or fell sick. We cleaned and disinfected the injury, we called whoever passed as an expert from the commune to help out, and then we prayed. And prayed. And prayed. If we prayed hard enough, asked God to forgive our sins, and truly believed, then, eventually, we would be healed. I knew that Uncle Zephaniah and Mom would be required to pray too, would have to share with the leadership why they thought God had punished their child. They'd have to write about it in their "open heart reports" for the home shepherds to review. What lesson was God trying to teach them by hurting me?

After my hand was bandaged, I rested on my bunk, alone, my whole arm throbbing under the layers of bloodied gauze. I tried not to move, not to make any sound as I cried. I begged God to forgive me, to forgive my parents. God knew my thoughts, knew how bad I was. He knew I had fantasized too much about life outside the compound. He knew I had been too happy on Parent Day, had been enjoying the fruits of this world, and not the fruits of the Spirit, and not thinking about him at all. So he punished me. He made me bleed and ended Parent Day, and it was all my fault.

The adults said napping would help the wound close. But sleep felt impossible, with the nausea and throbbing fire in my hand. Somehow I eventually managed to drift off, but pain jolted me awake. It was almost night, but still light enough that I could see the entire bandage had turned light red. My sheets were sticky with blood. I wanted to pull the gauze off and see how much Jesus had healed my hand, but I knew I'd get in trouble for it. So I got out of bed, thinking of Humpty Dumpty and wondering how long it took Jesus to put him back together again.

I could hear dishes clinking when I approached the big dining room, the sound of hundreds of people eating together. I found my parents and, seeing my bloody hand, they called Uncle Micah, and also Uncle Pethuel, to examine me. When they opened the bandage, a smell like something rotten filled my nose. The wound's edges were bright red, looked angry, and were filled with yellow pus. They argued about what to do with me. Someone said "time is of the essence." Someone said "hospital."

The forbidden word. The evil place. That's where they were taking me.

As they packed me into the car, I wondered if I was such a bad sinner that Jesus didn't want to heal me.

I sat up front between the driver and passenger seat, motion sick the way I always was in a vehicle, as we drove through the mountain high above the sprawling city of Rio de Janeiro, along Petropolis's cobblestone roads to the nearest public hospital. Uncle Zephaniah held my hand in his lap, his fingers clenched against the makeshift splint. Mom stayed behind with Merry and the baby.

Nobody reprimanded me even though I couldn't stop crying. They were taking me to a Systemite doctor who would examine and hurt me like he did Gabriella and the kids from The Raid. I knew Mom and Uncle Zephaniah would get into trouble, and I knew I was responsible.

When we got there, we were seen right away. As soon as the doctor unwrapped my hand, she started yelling in Portuguese. I couldn't understand her but I caught snippets of what Uncle Pethuel translated to Uncle Zephaniah. She was mad at them, blaming them for not bringing me in sooner. They argued with her over how many hours had passed since I fell. The doctor yelled strange new words—"negligência, anestesia"—and Uncle Zephaniah yelled back: "No. Nó." I lay on the hospital bed, being yelled over, like I wasn't even there.

Nurses prodded me, and even though it was different from the Aunties' slaps, it still felt like I was being punished. I was already dizzy, so it was easy to do my trick of going away, of floating above myself and watching. I couldn't feel anything as I stared at the metal instruments, all devices I knew were designed for torture. Auntie Dora had been right. She told the truth about the hospital.

Finally, Uncle Zephaniah explained they needed to give me something called shots. Then I would need to stay still while the doctor sewed my hand back together. He said it would hurt.

It was so cold in that room. There was fear in Uncle Zephaniah's eyes. I imagined myself as our blanket of granny squares crocheted out of tiny scraps of waste yarn, being stitched together piece by piece. I tried to stay floating, but I couldn't.

The liquid from the tetanus shot burned as it ran through my veins, the Devil's work thrusting through my body. I would be forever tainted, impure. I tried not to cry, fearing it would add to my eventual punishment. The nurses moved me to a big table covered with a paper sheet. The doctor hid her face behind a white mask as she stretched my hand away from my body, her fingers clasped around her sharp sewing needle.

The whole scene looked exactly like a music video we'd filmed, where the Antichrist's soldiers held down a true believer while an evil doctor implanted the Mark of the Beast in her right hand. I sucked in my breath and told myself this was different. Since it was my left hand, I'd be okay.

Six people pinned me to the hospital table. The doctor pushed the needle through my skin, with no more effort than stitching cloth. I screamed as the pain shot through my body, as the Systemite doctor with her horrible needle sliced black thread directly through me, in and out, over and over. I was trapped. I was being tortured, just like Auntie Dora said. I screamed like hell and fought with all the strength I had in my skinny arms and legs, like we'd been taught in the comics. But my powers from Jesus didn't come through.

Uncle Zephaniah covered my mouth with his big hand, the freckles and red hair on his arms oversized and up close. But I kept screaming, kept writhing and kicking, even as Uncle Pethuel held my other arm, even as the masked Systemite nurses held down my feet. I tried to bite Uncle Zephaniah's hands, and he looked at me with tears in his eyes, and I thought maybe something hurt him too.

It seemed like it took hours for the stitching to end, but pain and memory are terrible companions. On the drive home, Uncle Zephaniah hugged me tightly and told me how much he'd wanted to punch the lady doctor in her face. He told me he was so sorry that he hadn't left the dishes on the hill and held my hand instead. But he also declined the painkillers and evil drugs we'd been offered, because we had the power of prayer.

I didn't understand why he was apologizing. Adults didn't apologize to kids. But he said he had received a "check from the Holy Spirit to hold my hand" when we were walking down the hill, and had ignored it. Despite my pain, a nice warmth came over me. Maybe it wasn't my fault after all. Maybe Jesus wasn't punishing me. Sometimes God punished children for their parents' sins, as a way to teach them a lesson by watching their kids suffer. That meant Uncle Zephaniah was my real dad, not just an Uncle. I fell asleep in the car with my head on his shoulder, comforted by this thought, thinking maybe all that pain had been worth something.

■

WHILE I RECOVERED, the Aunties made me read a lot of *Life with Grandpa* stories about healing. The comics taught us everything from how much toilet paper to use to how we were supposed to pray when we got sick. Grandpa taught us that all illnesses and injuries were messages from God. If I had a fever, I knew I needed to spend time in quarantine praying, getting right with God, and asking him to show me why he made me sick. I would only be released when I explained the specific sin that caused the illness satisfactorily to the Aunties. In serious cases, the whole commune would gather, pouring olive oil on the patient as the Bible instructed. Everyone would lay their hands on her, praying over and over until she got better.

Sometimes people got better but sometimes they didn't.

Miriam was one of the children God took to Heaven. There was a measles outbreak at another commune in Brazil that left many kids sick. Miriam recovered, but then died suddenly after a cold, the new infection too much for her weakened young body to handle. Grandpa received prophecies from her, and from Jesus, reassuring us that it had been his will, that little Miriam was too special for this world—so he had taken her home. It was the same thing we always heard when little kids died.

Any kind of illness, especially chronic ones, were proof of a person's moral failing. Despite all the work Dad did for the Children of God, Grandpa wrote a blasting letter declaring that Dad's asthma attacks were caused by his lack of faith. He didn't need an inhaler; he needed Jesus and good exercise. We watched him struggle for years, taking to his bed for days at a time, with no energy to do anything but sit cross-legged, concentrating on every single breath. We prayed a lot, asking God to grant him the faith to trust in him and not succumb to using medicine.

Dad seemed to be cursed with more than his share of tragedy, which confused me. He seemed like one of the "good Uncles," but God seemed to punish him a lot. Before he married my mom, he had seven daughters, but also a son, Andrew, who died of pneumonia before he was two. By the time the Uncles realized how sick Andrew was, nobody could save him, so God took him to Heaven. But Dad's first wife, Auntie Hope, would not get over her son's death the way God, and the home shepherds, demanded.

Robin had been the prom queen of her Minneapolis high school back in the System, and then she'd married the goofy class clown, followed him into the Children of God, and stood beside him as he changed his name to Zephaniah and rechristened her Hope. My stepsisters later told me how much Auntie Hope loved all her children, taking care of them as much as the home shepherds allowed, sometimes sneaking Systemite movies that weren't permitted into her room on Parent Night, showing them to her daughters on a borrowed television. She grieved hard when Andrew died. She began questioning the ban on doctors and whether her baby's death had been the true will of God.

After fifteen years and eight children together, even though some of them were from the mandatory sexual sharing with other Uncles, cult leaders separated Auntie Hope and Uncle Zephaniah. They did that with couples who had been together for too long, had too many children from the same father, or who caused trouble. Shortly thereafter, Uncle Zephaniah met my mom and fell hard. He was forty, she was twenty, and the home shepherds heard from Jesus that they should be together.

Meanwhile, Auntie Hope continued to grieve. Shipped to a home on the farthest edge of Brazil, she developed severe headaches. The leadership said it was a sign from God to quit her rebellious ways. Auntie Hope did as asked. She prayed, confessed all her sins, repented, asked the Holy Spirit to speak to her, and prayed some more, but the headaches intensified. The commune prayed, laid hands, anointed her with holy water and oils. But after years of getting worse, she became too weak to work and was forced to her bedroom while the home shepherds tried to decide what to do. She began having seizures, a sure sign of demonic possession, and the Children of God rallied to exorcise her, tying her down, as all the adults in the home prayed over her, anointing her with oil over and over again to cast out the demons in possession of her deficient body and weak soul.

On the day her pain became so intense she couldn't leave her bed, her oldest daughters took her to the hospital, consequences be damned. The doctor told them Auntie Hope had an advanced-looking mass behind her eyes. Auntie Hope realized how sick she was and why her memory was disappearing. She snuck a collect call to her mother in the System, in the United States, and told her about the exorcisms, about how the home shepherds had put her on silence restriction to stop her from infecting the others when her words made no sense. Her mother wired her money for a plane ticket home, where she was diagnosed with a tumor the size of an orange, with spaghettilike tendrils that wrapped all around her brain. Her best chance at survival was chemotherapy and surgery, both forbidden. Auntie Hope left the Children of God, her children, and her adopted name to receive care from the family she hadn't seen in almost twenty-five years.

When the Children of God excommunicated her, the leadership told us she deserved brain cancer and the drawn-out, painful death that would occur. God would punish her, not once, but twice, first by taking her son, then by taking her life.

Auntie Hope passed away two years later, abandoned by the faith she had dedicated her life to serving. My own mother, by then a twenty-two-year-old mother of three, became the stepmother to seven additional children, including one who was only two years younger than herself. A revolving cast of "older sisters" would come to live with us, and we would adjust, our family expanding and contracting as they came and went. The older girls weren't resentful of Mom for her youth, or for being with their dad; they were just sad, like something inside them had been broken and would never be healed, no matter how much love Auntie Kristy gave them, or how many times they called her "Mom."

5

HEAVEN'S GIRL

■

Petropolis, Brazil, 1993

Grandpa had told us that jade was one of the stones used to build
The Heavenly City, the magical place inside the moon where we'd all
live after we died as martyrs in the End Times. Auntie Jade was only
sixteen, born in The Family like me, and I understood why she was
named after something so precious. I loved her: She taught us how to
braid our hair, sew our own dresses, and take dictation with the tiniest
letters as she read to us from the King James Bible. She had a special book for learning about cultures around the world—the Family's
mission for Jesus was *international,* after all—and she always had fun
projects for us to do when it was her turn to teach, like making butter
out of cream when we learned about Norway, or folding Chinese lan-
terns and paper birds when we studied the far east. Every Auntie had
to hit us sometimes, of course, but her smacks were never very hard.
She had so much patience that we had to be really bad to get sent off
to an Uncle—it almost seemed as if she didn't like seeing us punished.

The morning was sunny but slightly chilly, normal weather for
Petropolis. We were in a second-story classroom, with plate glass windows poor little birds always flew into, and beautiful Brazilian wood
flooring. I sat with my legs crossed neatly, right next to Auntie Jade. I
smiled warmly at all my friends as I reveled in the certainty that I was
Auntie's favorite. She told us the rules of the day's game: repeat what
we heard one time in our friend's ear, no questions, no hesitation, and

we'd see how the telephone could break as we passed it along. She whispered a phrase in my ear, a well-known Bible verse that we had all memorized. "All things work together for good to them that love God. Romans 8:28." *Easy,* I thought, *how could this get messed up? Everyone knows this verse by heart.* I leaned over and whispered the verse to Virginia as fast as I could, but my six-year-old tongue got caught on the "s" the way it sometimes did, and my lisp and excitement changed what she heard. "All sings and to ever for the love of God robbing aid-to-aid."

She giggled because it sounded so funny, but there were no questions allowed, so she leaned over to whisper it into the next ear, and around the circle it went. Johnny was the last one in the circle, sitting on Auntie Jade's other side, and when he blurted out the phrase, "Asians forever love God and Robby is aged," everyone burst out laughing, even Auntie Jade, rolling onto the floor, tears spilling out of her eyes.

We quickly got control of ourselves, not wanting to get in trouble for foolishness. While I was laughing, a question popped into my mind that confused me. Grandpa taught us that the stories of Genesis and Exodus, the rules of Leviticus, and the dreadfully boring books of Numbers and Deuteronomy had been handed down by word of mouth for five hundred years, starting with Adam and then his sons and so on, until Moses had written down the whole history of mankind. I blurted out my thought before I could catch myself: "How can the Bible possibly be true if it was passed down by broken telephone for five hundred years?"

When I heard the sharp intake of Auntie Jade's breath, I knew I'd made a serious mistake. A familiar cold fear crept over me. I looked around the circle and saw that Virginia, Johnny, and all the other kids stared at me like I'd climbed into the lap of the Antichrist himself to enjoy some Coca-Cola and white sugar. Auntie Jade stood up and left the room, telling us all to stay seated and no talking. I knew this was going to be a bad one.

"You got us all in trouble," Virginia hissed, anger in her eyes.

"No, it'll just be me," I said with a shaky voice, as I silently wondered who was on punishment duty.

I knew I couldn't pray for mercy this time, because Jesus would be too mad to listen. Minutes stretched out, leaving me with time and space to imagine how the story was spreading. I pictured the adults with their own version of telephone, "Do you know what Daniella said!?!" going from ear to ear throughout the commune, my words becoming more monstrous with each retelling. My parents would know by dinnertime, and then I would probably get a second punishment too. That didn't scare me as much as the thought of my Mom getting in trouble, of being branded as the mother of a kid who said such doubting things. Though I thought of Dad as one of the good Uncles, I knew the worst thing I could do was embarrass him in front of the leaders. I was going to get it.

There was no question that Jesus was punishing me when the door flew open, banging against the wall, and the balding head of Uncle Jerry came into view. In a society that had no rank, no class, and no money, Uncle Jerry wielded the power of a general, a duke, and a billionaire. Before he found Jesus and joined the Children of God, he'd been one of the founding members of an evil rock band, which had made him a very famous, and very rich, Systemite. He was one of the few people in our world who still had a regular income from outside because he received royalty checks. He gave all his money to The Family, and the money bought him security and impunity. We all knew the leaders would never side against Uncle Jerry. He was married to Auntie Dora and so famous, the only one who could touch him would be Grandpa himself.

He marched over and grabbed me by the hand, and I forced my feet to run to keep up with his pace as we left the room. My heart pounded hard as I frantically searched for Auntie Jade, a hopeless instinct since I knew she couldn't help me. She stood by the door, where she'd stayed frozen after following Uncle Jerry into the room. She cast her head down, and I knew that she never would have wanted *this* to happen. I also knew that she didn't have a choice—if she hadn't told on me, one of the other kids would have given testimony to their parents. By the time it had made its way up the chain of command to the leaders, both of us would have been in even more trouble. As I passed her, I tried to catch her eyes, to let her know that I'd be okay, that I knew it wasn't her fault, but her gaze stayed fixed on the polished wooden slats of the floor.

My head jerked as the meaty, sweaty hand holding mine yanked me down the hall. Uncle Jerry's arms were muscular and covered in graying hair, his grip crushing. He was short compared to the other Uncles, but he looked like a giant to me. We exited the building, the bright morning sun shining so cheerfully at us, starting to burn off the mist that gathered on the mountaintops almost every night. We walked across the stone path, past the huge swimming pool, and I wished I could jump in, stay under the water, and not have to come out ever again. We entered the second building, a pool house converted to the recording studio and art rooms where the talented adults, like Dad, created the shows and comics spreading the Prophet's words. It was what made our commune special. The door banged open as we entered, and I saw Dad and some of the other artists working at their tables, but nobody paid any attention. We moved quickly toward the stairs leading to the soundproofed basement that housed several small rooms with recording equipment and spare beds.

When we got to his punishment room, Uncle Jerry told me to take off my dress and underwear and stand next to the bed. He left me there to find a wooden hairbrush from the bathroom down the hall. I thought briefly about making a run for it, but I knew God would make Uncle Jerry punish me even harder for thinking it. My forty-pound body shivered while I waited, even though it wasn't cold in the room.

Uncle Jerry opened the door, the light from the hallway shining behind him for a moment, making the hairbrush look like a bat in his hand. He entered the cubicle of a room and swung the door closed behind him, clicking its lock.

"Okay," he said. "This is going to be a warm-up."

He sat down on the bed and I knew he wanted me to bend over his lap. As he started the first swats with the hairbrush, I tried to focus on not crying. I tried to go limp and numb because that always seemed to make these punishments go faster, but Jesus wouldn't let me have that relief. Jesus was so angry with me, it hurt even worse than usual. The pain was sharper, the sound of wood against my flesh louder. The fear of what would come next set everything on fire.

I had to hug him afterward, like we were trained to do following each punishment, to thank the adults for the lesson. He started touching me gently, those hairy hands rubbing my bottom. "To help make the stinging stop," he said. After being hit so hard, it felt nice to be touched this way. If he had to touch me, I'd rather it be like that.

But I wanted him to stop. I wanted to kick and punch and bite him. I wanted to draw blood. I hated every single thing I was feeling in my body, everything nice and everything painful. It was all wrong. But as he started touching other places, I knew there was absolutely nothing I could do to stop him. My body was a tool given for the glorification of God—and Uncle Jerry would be quick to remind me of that if I dared to resist.

He pulled away and took down his pants. He didn't bother to tell me not to move. He knew I wasn't going anywhere. As hard as I tried not to, I still cried a little. I put all my energy toward trying to get my tears under control. If I focused on that, I wouldn't have to think about the other things.

I knew not to fight it. The best thing I could do was accept what was happening and wait for it to be over; that's what we were taught in the story of Heaven's Girl. That made it easier to leave, easier to separate from my body and not feel a thing.

When he finally finished, I let myself hope that I would be able to go back to my group. I didn't care if I had to wear a sign around my neck for the rest of the day, the rest of the week—I wanted to get out of that tiny room and away from him. But instead of cleaning me up and telling me to get dressed, Uncle Jerry said, "I'm going to spank you again. I need to make sure that the Devil isn't still in you."

That made sense to me. What I had done to earn my punishment was inexcusable—of course the Devil had possessed me. I knew I deserved what was happening. Everyone was mad at me. Jesus was so mad at me He sent Uncle Jerry to deliver this punishment.

Uncle Jerry put one leg into his pants, then the other, and pulled them over his waist. He grabbed his belt from the pants and bent me over the bed, my knees on the ground. I couldn't control myself and I cried out each time the leather belt bit my bottom and thighs. Every sound I made added another strike. Seconds turned into minutes until time was meaningless, until the only thing that existed was pain and fear as he hit me again and again, grunting a satisfied little "mmm" with each swing.

Then, finally, there was a moment when the swatting paused. I tried to swallow my whimpers but they were so loud in the silent room.

"Get on the bed," he said, and I scrambled onto the dirty mattress. He stared me down. "Don't even think of moving."

I nodded my agreement and he turned toward the door. I squinted at the harsh overhead light that poured in from the hallway when he opened it. How long had I been here? He paused in the doorway, holding on to the doorknob with his giant hands. "If anyone comes in, you're forbidden to speak with them at all." I nodded my head yes again, afraid to disobey him by speaking. He looked even bigger and more menacing backlit in the doorway as he stared at me until I cast my eyes down. After the door banged shut, I heard him put a sign on the door, one of the "do not disturb" ones they used when recording live music.

I had no way to tell how much time had passed. At first it wasn't so bad. The pain dulled the longer I was in there. I reminded myself none of this was new. I told myself I was going to be fine, like I always ended up fine.

But soon I needed to pee. I squirmed in place, sat up and crossed my legs, and tried to think about other things. I sang some Bible verses under my breath, and I prayed for Jesus to make the pee go away. But when the discomfort of my bladder turned to pain, I got desperate. I listened for footsteps down the hall for someone to let me out. Nobody came. I scanned the room five, ten, a hundred times, but my searching did not make a toilet appear. Then I realized that I was already in the worst trouble possible—I had let the Devil in. I had doubted the Word of God. How could I possibly get in any more trouble for peeing the bed?

So I buried my head in the pillow and prayed to Jesus to forgive me as I unclenched my muscles. There was something comforting about the warmth spreading under me, though the pee burned coming out. I had been so cold. As I drifted off to sleep, I wondered if I would have to wash the sheets myself.

I woke up when Uncle Jerry opened the door. It must have been hours later. The bed was cold and wet under me.

"You wet the bed!" he yelled before he was even fully over the threshold. I could smell what he smelled. The tiny room stank of pee. It stank of his own fluids.

Out came the brush again, and he bent me over his lap to repeat it all over.

I wondered if this would be my life now, if I would be stuck in this room forever as Uncle Jerry came and went, as I moved from his lap to my knees to the bed, again and again, until I died. I thought of the Mo Letter Grandpa had written called "The Final State," where he'd had to drive the Devil out of his own granddaughter for refusing to submit to him. She had been tied to a bed for weeks, and many different adults had taken turns beating the Devil out of her. We all read about it for devotions. I was so happy that nobody was here to witness my shame, to write about it for the whole Family. I agreed with Uncle Jerry that it was so much better to keep these things private.

But finally, he was done. For the moment, anyway. Maybe he grew bored of me. "Get dressed," he said. "Now I have to take these to the laundry." He gathered up the dirty sheets and left the room, closing the door behind him again.

More time passed as I sat isolated in that cold, dark basement room. I knew it was dinnertime when I got hungry, but nobody came back for me. Would Mom notice I was gone, would she ask about me? But I knew she wouldn't ask. Everyone knew that anyone who complained about discipline got disciplined. She would have heard about what I'd done and agreed I deserved to be punished, so I was in isolation. I doubted God, I doubted Grandpa's teaching, and I had let the Devil possess me. I was weak and unworthy. If Jesus was mad at me, then Mom and Dad and all of the leaders, maybe even Grandpa,

had to be furious. I prayed they wouldn't take it out on Mom, that she wouldn't be punished for my sins. She was so good. She deserved a better daughter than me.

With no one around to hear me, I let myself cry. I wished it was Parent Night. I imagined climbing into my mom's bed, her arms around me, listening to her say "shh" as she caressed my hair. There was nothing confusing about those touches. My body tingled painfully in all the places where Uncle Jerry had laid his hands on me.

Finally, when it was very dark, the door creaked open and Uncle Jerry poked his head around the corner, silhouetted once more by the hallway light. It was past my bedtime, and I was sure he would beat me again for being awake so late. But he didn't seem mad. He sat down on the bed and he pulled me onto his lap. He ran his finger over the scar on my cheek that I got from oil popping off a pancake cooking in a skillet on my sixth birthday. Uncle Jerry always told me how much he loved that scar, how it made me special. He held me close and said that again. He smiled and talked softly, gently petting my head. He told me that enough time had probably passed for the evil spirits to have left me, but still he laid his hands on me and prayed. "Dear God," he said. "Cast the Devil out of this child once and for all." I wanted to feel something, maybe a whoosh or a shiver of the Devil leaving me, a promise that I would stop sinning, but I only felt the pressure of his big hands on my face and on my chest.

God wasn't here. God wasn't anywhere.

"I've got to wash your mouth with soap," he said. "Then you can go back to your group and we can forget this ever happened. It's our secret. I promise you wouldn't want to tell anyone."

Afterward, I ran back to my dorm alone. Even after everything that happened, that is what scared me the most—being alone in the dark. The boogeyman could swoop me up in the night and no one would even notice until it was too late. I ran as fast as I could, calling on Jesus and all the spirits I knew to let me get back to the other building safely. As if I didn't live with the worst boogeymen possible, as if I didn't have to call them Uncle.

When I got back to our dorm, Auntie Jade was still awake, her

face blotchy and red like she'd been crying. Seeing her brought fresh tears to my eyes—even though she had to be up early in the morning for devotions and prayer meetings, she had waited for me. I did not deserve this kindness. She knew how bad I was.

"I wanted to make sure someone tucked you in," she said softly. She held me in a deep hug and whispered, "You won't be in trouble forever." Her words made me choke on my sobs. I wanted to believe her, but it felt impossible.

"I know how to put a smile on your face, baby," she said. She motioned for me to follow her to the adjoining bathroom and held my hand as we tiptoed past bunk after bunk of sleeping children. In the bathroom, she dug into the back of the vanity drawer and picked up a red lipstick she had hidden.

"Promise not to tell?"

That promise felt like a real promise, a good promise, not a threat.

Auntie Jade drew two smiley faces, one on each of my cheeks. I looked in the mirror and laughed, a sound I was surprised I could still make.

"I promise I'll come for your pillowcase in the morning. You're not going to get in trouble for getting lipstick on the sheets."

Maybe I was delirious from everything that had happened, from not eating, from being awake in the middle of the night, but right then, in that bathroom with Auntie Jade, far removed from what everyone else was doing, I felt brave. Or maybe foolish. They so often felt the same.

I leaned into her and asked, "Auntie Jade, does everyone who grows up and leaves the Children of God go to Hell? No matter what?"

She didn't answer, only hugged me tightly, looking over her shoulder, to the closed bathroom door, as if worried someone might be standing outside it. She squeezed my arms hard, but it didn't hurt. As she looked deep into my eyes, she said, "Never, ever, say anything like that again. Not where anybody else could ever hear you." Then she kissed my forehead, opened the door, and escorted me to bed.

In the dark, lying on my bunk, I made myself a promise. I didn't care if I had to go to Hell: I would not grow up to be in The Family. I

had prayed so much. I had tried so hard. I had begged Jesus to help me accept the paradoxes I saw. But I didn't believe. I couldn't. I was done praying. I didn't love God. I didn't want to serve him. Not like this.

I didn't want to be a Child of God anymore. I didn't want this Family. I was a sinner—dirty, broken—and I would never be anything else. I *wanted* to be a backslider. One day, I knew I would become a Systemite. I was already evil, after all.

I imagined a jeweled box, something more beautiful than anything I could ever hope to be allowed to own. In my mind, I crafted every tiny detail of that box, along with the golden key that fit perfectly into the ornate keyhole on the front. No one would ever have access to that key. No one but me would ever be able to touch it. I locked my thoughts away, hid the box deep inside my mind, where no one could find it.

That night I wet my bed again, but in the morning, Auntie Jade came and quietly got my sheets. She hid the lipstick-stained pillowcase deep inside the bundle as she carried away the evidence of my sin, like she'd promised.

6

A HANDMAID'S TALE

■

Rio de Janeiro, Brazil, 1994

I ran my hand over the maroon leather cover of my brand-new Bible, traced the grooves made by the etched gold letters, felt the weight of it heavy in my lap. I opened it to the center, the pages seemingly untouched by human hands. The off-white paper was impossibly thin, as though it was made by God's breath itself. I turned to the second half, the Gospels, Christ's words scored against the paper in deep red, as if the blood he spilled for us had leapt onto the pages. I closed the back cover with the care a Bible deserved, and with my eyes closed, I turned the book around in my hands, trying to feel the weight of its holiness, a glow or shiver that would prove its truth. But what it felt like was a brick, covered and disguised by something soft.

I opened the inside cover again and reread the inscription in Mom's perfect handwriting:

> Daniella,
> Happy 7th Birthday! This will be your companion as you learn and grow in the Lord. I'm so proud of you and who you are becoming, my smart girl.
>
> Love,
Mom and Dad

I traced my name, letters bigger than my fingertips, my mother's marks pressed deep into the first page—permanent, fixed. Mom had gotten permission to buy it new, and I'd never owned anything so pristine, nothing that was a hundred percent mine. Because it was the Word of God, none of the Uncles could take it from me or say that I was spending too much time reading it. It was the only thing the Aunties couldn't force me to share with the other kids. In this small way, it almost felt like God was protecting me.

I always felt unsure when the grown-ups talked about God, but I loved escaping into these stories written for Him. Stories of adventure, war, miracles, and love. Stories of family, connection, and people who knew their lineage in a way I never would. I especially loved the stories of women who stood up to bad men by driving giant spikes through their temples while they slept, women who brought them to their knees by cutting off their magical hair.

But there were other stories, the ones that felt too close, that were anything but escape. King David taking what he wanted from naked Bathsheba after sending her husband away to die in battle. Lot having sex with his own daughters after God destroyed his town in a rage. Rachel sending her slave Bilhah to have sex with the man her father had tricked into marrying both her and her sister. Queen Esther appearing naked before a king—the same one who'd killed his first wife for her unwillingness to undress in public. I wondered why this God we worshipped seemed to love sex and violence so much. I did not understand how these words could be part of the same book I loved, how the violence was supposed to be as true as the beauty of Jesus's teachings. But I was just a child. I would learn to understand. I had to trust the adults who claimed they already did.

"Thank you, Mommy," I said after she handed the Bible to me. "I'm excited to read every word."

"Just not the Book of Samuel, okay?" said Uncle Zephaniah. "That's our bedtime story series. Can't have you blowing through it, honey."

"I won't, Dad," I whispered, the word still new and strange in my mouth. Ever since I'd cut my hand open—the scar now pale and pink on my palm—I'd taken to calling Uncle Zephaniah "Dad." The word alongside Mom's written in my new Bible made it official. He had become a permanent fixture in our lives.

Mom must have sensed something in my quiet promise, so she used her perkiest voice when she said, "This weekend is your birthday party!"

We had monthly parties, organized around sun signs, because Grandpa had met and liked an astrologer named Linda Goodman and told us that she practiced true science. "It's the Gemini party, Mom, not 'my party.' There are twenty-three Geminis, you know," I said. I had seen people using air quotes and I decided to try it, bending my fingers around "my party." Maybe this would be a good substitute for rolling my eyes, which always landed me in hot water.

That week, all forty of us kids buzzed with excitement. I took the crown for my Queen Esther costume seriously, gluing together scraps of cardstock with bits of flowers that I'd collected and pressed between the pages of my new Bible. Mom found me beads and a plastic emerald I prized as the center stone. I saw the other girls creating their crowns—there were many beautiful queens throughout the Bible—but none looked as real as mine did to me.

On the day of the party, I took my turn in front of the mirror one of the Aunties had set up for us. For the first time in my life, I really did feel beautiful. My hair fell loose to my shoulders, formed into soft waves from the braids I'd plaited the night before. The cardboard crown tamed my hair and kept it from springing all around. Glitter twinkled and the emerald sparkled, bringing out flecks of gold and green in my hazel eyes. I took off my oversized glasses, even though Dad said being able to see was more important than how I looked. But obviously nobody in Heaven, especially none of the holy people in the Bible, needed vision correction. With everything a little blurry, it was so much easier to imagine I was someone else.

I had asked Auntie Love if I could borrow her special scarf, the one she'd brought with her from her home in South Africa. I knew she would share because she couldn't say no without being accused of selfishness. I didn't know Auntie Love well, but she was Auntie Jade's mom. I was sad Auntie Jade wasn't there for my birthday because she was sent to another home in Europe, but I believed she could somehow protect me if I wore her mother's scarf, as if we could connect through a single piece of fabric. Auntie Love helped me tie the fabric, transforming it into a regal cape fit for a queen. For a moment, my costume felt perfect.

But then Auntie Love reminded me that I probably shouldn't wear panties—everybody knew Grandpa said there were no panties in Heaven. The lace teddy I'd borrowed from another Auntie to wear as a gown was nearly translucent and everyone would be able to see through it. But I did as she said and slid them off.

I had to keep reminding myself that shyness was the sin of pride. Grandpa told us that we were supposed to glorify God with our naked bodies. Systemites were the ones who hung on to covering themselves all the time. We needed to obey Grandpa. I understood that girls were supposed to sleep without underwear because we had to "air out" the smelly and disgusting parts of ourselves, but I still burned with rage every night when the Uncles, especially Uncle Jerry, came into our dorms to do panty-checks.

I looked in the mirror and fixed my eyes on the emerald in the center of my crown. It was my birthstone, and this was my birthday party, after all. I would have fun. Tonight, I would be a queen.

As we approached the big living room, I heard the familiar sounds of all one hundred plus members of our home gathered in one place. Uncle Jerry pumped his professionally produced worship music through the speakers, and his amplified voice echoed off every corner of the room. As usual, it was the Uncle Jerry show.

Nobody noticed as Merry and I slipped into the room. I immediately scanned the crowd for my parents. In one corner I saw big Uncle Jebediah, who I was convinced was the tallest man in the world, dressed in robes and a crown, surrounded by five or six scantily dressed Aunties and teenage girls—David and his Bathshebas. My five-year-old sister, also dressed as Bathsheba, would be one of them. Merry would be called over to pose for a picture with everyone, Uncle Jebediah's long arms draped over their bare shoulders, pulling the girls close, making them his. Auntie Dora, Uncle Jerry's wife, led a bunch of Aunties as the Fruits of the Spirit, from the Book of Acts in the New Testament, all of them naked except for little bikinis made of string with strategically placed cutout hearts printed with virtues: Love, Joy, Peace, Longsuffering, Gentleness, Goodness, Faith, Meekness, and Temperance.

Several Uncles had formed a circle, talking loudly, near a buffet table. One was dressed as Rasputin, one of Grandpa's spirit helpers. Another was Fidel Castro, who wasn't dead yet, but who I assumed would be in Heaven one day, since he was a friend of Grandpa's. Lots of Uncles were clothed in sheets to look like prophets, while Aunties bared their skin, breasts peeking through sheer fabric, if they wore any clothes at all. There were so many pairs of Adams and Eves, all at ease in their nudity because their first sin had not yet been committed. As always, there was an older teen girl dressed as Salome, who was famous for belly dancing nearly naked for her father; her payment, the papier-mâché head of John the Baptist, lay on a silver tray beside her.

I wondered, briefly, if other people had parties like this and if people from the Bible actually dressed anything like these getups.

Finally, I spotted my parents and pulled Merry through the crowd of sweaty bodies to reach them. They were dressed as Grandpa and Mama Maria. Mom wore a severe top bun, oversized glasses, and a see-through negligee. Dad wore a big snowy white beard and a bathrobe, the way he drew Grandpa in all our cartoons. Almost nobody in the Children of God knew what Grandpa really looked like, ever since God had warned him to go into permanent hiding. I had a quick feeling of pride as I remembered that Mom did know Grandpa's and Mama Maria's faces; she still wore the wedding ring Grandpa gave her when she was thirteen.

I hugged Mom and deposited Merry with them, hoping my sister wouldn't follow me around all night, then I dashed through the crowd to catch up with my friends. None of the adults paid too much attention to the kids during parties, and we could run about with a level of freedom that I loved. An Auntie dressed as the Prophet Deborah served the cheap sparkling wine that the adults were allowed on special occasions, and I stood in line to get the half glass that kids were sometimes allowed to drink during a party.

I loved champagne, which was nothing like the sharp, cheap, vinegar-like wine that we had every Sunday for Communion when I had to screw up my face and swallow as fast as I could without making a sound. Champagne was sweet and cold and bubbly and instantly made me feel almost calm around the adults, like I could finally breathe, like I didn't want to crawl out of my own skin. I chugged my glass, knowing that when I saw Merry again, I could convince her to give me her share too. I knew Dorothea and some of the other younger girls didn't like champagne and, if I promised to take some of their future spankings, they'd fork theirs over as well. After enough of those little half glasses, I knew I wouldn't feel so scared. I traveled about the party, ignoring grown-ups, blissfully ignored, downing sips from plastic glasses, swaying to the music and waiting for the magic of those bubbles to kick in.

Soon it was time for the party games. Several of the more harmless Aunties arranged musical chairs in a circle, and I breathed a sigh of relief. Even though we mimicked the dance moves from classic musicals and the 1950s and '60s "wholesome family films" we watched during our Friday movie nights, our party games were always different, depending on the Uncle or Auntie in charge. The Aunties thankfully gave out normal rules: The last one standing at musical chairs was out of the game. But then someone suggested another rule: When the music stopped, the one caught had to shed an article of clothing. I wasn't wearing enough clothes to lose.

Then I heard the unmistakable sound of Uncle Jerry on the slide guitar, signaling it was time for cake instead. He came into view dressed in his usual costume of fat Elvis in the white jumper, who'd joined the lexicon of "good people" in Heaven, even though we still couldn't listen to his "Devil music."

Everyone started clapping and I scuttled over to the table where a few Aunties set up a giant sheet cake covered in homemade frosting. The musician Uncles, including Dad, warmed up their guitars to accompany Uncle Jerry. Crowded around the table with the couple dozen other Family members also born in May and June, I wondered what it would be like to have a party for myself, with only my family and friends in attendance, the way Systemite kids did. What would it feel like to be celebrated by myself? I knew I was being selfish, as bad as a Systemite. I looked around, saw myself surrounded and watched, and I knew if I showed any sign of being upset, there'd be hell to pay. I squared my shoulders, painted on a smile that would let Jesus's love shine through my eyes, and told myself to look like the queen I pretended to be.

Uncle Jerry led a long riff into the happy birthday song, and everyone started bopping along and praising Jesus. I edged closer toward them, trying to escape the Uncles who kept squishing their bodies against mine.

And then it was time for the honors, the Family tradition in which everyone would share what they liked about each Gemini. To start, Uncle Jerry called out Peace, his nineteen-year-old daughter-in-law, whose belly swelled with her first child. The room filled with the excited voices spouting off her attributes.

"Her eyes are always smiling and welcoming."

"She's so sweet and humble."

"She's so beautiful and sexy for Jesus!"

It went around the circle this way, first the popular teens, then the Uncles, then the rest of the Aunties, and then the kids, each praised for what made them admirable and good Children of God.

Uncle Jerry always seemed to get bigger over the course of the parties he hosted, as if he fed on our attention. His roar seemed louder as he bellowed across the room, "Last and least, what do we have to say about *her*? Little Daniella, always a firecracker." His laughter pierced me through the crowd.

"She's always got a smart response."

I couldn't place who said it, but it didn't matter. The nods and quiet *oohs* from the crowd let me know it was what everyone thought. I cast my eyes down. In a world where we put humility above all, that wasn't a compliment.

"She's got so much energy, and she always likes to have the last word," Dad said. I raised my eyes enough to see his were twinkling. I tried to smile back, but the crowd's hearty laughter shamed me. My behavior was always out of line, they told me, and I caused myself much harsher punishments by talking back, by trying to "justify" the way I acted.

I wanted Mom. I scanned the crowd until I met her eyes. She held my gaze as she patted baby Timmy's head, attached to her breast. At the Pisces party two months earlier, the room had only said good things about how beautiful, full of God's spirit, and perfect she was among David's Handmaids, a woman willing to do anything for God, her Prophet, and the Uncles around her.

Why did I turn out so different?

"That hair of hers is always praising the Lord!" called out Auntie Lydia, who'd struggled to tame my curls in the past. All the women, the older teens, and even little Dorothea could glorify God with long, beautiful hair that fell past their waists. Not mine.

"She's as smart as a whip and can even keep up with the teens in my dictation class." It was Auntie Patty's voice, tinged with her warm, faint honeyed Jamaican notes. A rush of gratitude overpowered me, and I swallowed hard to keep any tears from falling. In that moment, I felt worth something, and it didn't matter that my intelligence—or anyone's—was valued by so few in this community. Auntie Patty saw it. Auntie Patty thought it mattered, thought *I* mattered. She said, "Daniella has it in her to be one of the arrows in our quiver. She will confront the enemies at our gates." And, to my surprise, many of the adults echoed calls of "Amen," "Praise, Jesus," and "Thank you, Lord."

Maybe I wasn't so broken after all. Maybe I did belong.

Auntie Patty smiled as she handed me my slice of cake, the whole wheat flour and honey mixture falling apart under the heavy frosting. "One day," she whispered, amid the din of plates and forks scraping, "you'll be a star." Then, placing what I'm sure she assumed was my night's first half glass of champagne into my right hand, she turned to the next person in line.

Balancing my plate and glass of champagne, I pushed my way

through the crowd to stand in front of where Mom sat on the couch reserved for nursing mothers. Merry had squeezed in next to her, frosting already smeared all over her face. She was safely nestled beside Mom, and I felt myself relax. I had lost count of the tiny glasses of sparkling wine by then and, for a moment, as I ate cake next to my own mother and two siblings, everything felt all right.

But the feeling was short-lived. Dad walked over with Uncle Jerry in tow, their hands gripping plates of cake, their guitars slung behind their backs, a few Aunties following in their wake like good little groupies. Dad took the open seat next to Mom, patted the baby, and grinned. Uncle Jerry stood a few feet away, staring at me. The air felt different. Parties always changed after the cake had been eaten. That was when the adults *really* started playing their party games.

"Time to go, Merry," I said, hopping up quickly, grabbing my sister by the hand and yanking her from the sofa.

I wasn't fast enough. Uncle Jerry's hand stopped me. Surely, he wouldn't dare here, in front of everyone? He looked me up and down with his eyes, lifting my hand in his to spin me in a slow circle. My cape flew upward and one strap of the oversized nightgown slipped off my shoulder. "You know," he said, a sneer across his lips, "little girls are always supposed to glorify God in the dance. You are wearing the perfect outfit." I was supposed to parade, I think, drop my sister's hand, twirl and take the compliment. But I was paralyzed in the place between fear and embarrassment, fury and despair. I said nothing as I looked at the floor, as I willed it to swallow me whole.

His thick, hairy finger forced my chin upward until my gaze fell into his watery eyes, eyes that always looked a little too excited. I tried hard to see what everyone loved so much about him. They called him playful, handsome, and funny, but to me he was short, old, and bald, his goofy British accent and unfunny jokes a cover-up for how dangerous he really was.

"You know," he said again, his breath on my face, "the real Queen Esther was totally naked when she presented herself to the king. That's what saved her life."

The fifteen or so adults within his booming earshot—groupie Aunties and Uncles alike—laughed. I could feel my cheeks burn hot, but I refused to cry, refused to give him the satisfaction of knowing how much power he had over me. I saw through the side of my vision that Mom watched me with a laser focus. But what could she do if he insisted that I strip naked in front of everyone? I stood very still, reminding myself to be careful of the direction of my gaze. Heaven forbid he decided I had rolled my eyes at *him*. That would be all the excuse he needed to carry me off for another punishment, and no one would be able to stop him. I heard the low baritone of Dad's voice, chatting nearby with someone, oblivious. I stared at Uncle Jerry's nose as his eyes bored into me, waiting for whatever came next, knowing I had absolutely no power to change any of it.

After seconds that seemed like hours, he released me from his gaze and dropped his hand, allowing my chin to return to a normal level. He turned to Dad and resumed whatever conversation I'd interrupted by trying to leave. Merry's whimper brought me back to reality, and I realized how tightly I'd been gripping her hand, even though she hadn't made a sound. I called "Goodnight, Mom" over my shoulder as we ran from the room. I pushed Merry up the stairs so she wouldn't see the adult game we passed, five Uncles sitting blindfolded and tied into chairs, with a row of Aunties atop them. The winner would be whoever could pick out his wife by the feel of her hand and mouth.

On party nights, we slept upstairs in my parents' room, directly above the communal living room where the celebration would go into the wee hours of the night. I took off my cape-scarf and folded it carefully to return to Auntie Love later. I felt safe in this room, usually, but I didn't feel beautiful anymore. I didn't want to. I wanted to be invisible. I wanted to disappear.

But that wasn't a choice. The older boys next door were our babysitters. "Panty check," I heard Abel say as he came into the room to put us to bed. I didn't understand what I was feeling—a mixture of relief, fear, and rage. Embarrassment. Something like yearning. Abel and Titus were in the role of the adults, and I felt like such a little girl.

I didn't want Abel to look at me that way. Even as I hated him, I still wanted him to think I was beautiful.

In the silence, alone, after the boys had done what they came to do and left, I could close my eyes and think about anything I wanted. I thought about Heaven. Not the cheap imitation of that party downstairs, but a place where I could finally be safe, where no one would watch me, where I wouldn't have to serve anyone, where I wouldn't have to do anything I didn't want to do. Not for the first time, I wished I didn't have to wake up in the morning, that I could go to Heaven right away. Maybe I'd die in the night and wake up far away, finally free. But I remembered that Jesus only took the "good kids" to Heaven early.

I thought about a game we loved to play called The Heavenly City. All the kids would design our mansions in Heaven, the ultimate reward we were told we'd be granted in exchange for all the deprivations and pain during our lives on Earth. Different kids had different dreams: Many wanted a house all to themselves, all the food they could imagine. And typical kid desires too: pets, toys, candy. All the things we never had.

But not me. I didn't care about streets of gold or all the clothes in the world, or the real jewelry that Dorothea and the other girls fancied. I wanted books. I had a secret dream that my mansion in Heaven would be a giant library, beautiful, with tall shelves in every room, filled with every book that had ever been written. I pictured myself like the cartoon Belle, a sparkling girl with a worldly name that didn't come from anywhere in the Bible and meant *beautiful,* who'd been gifted the most precious thing I could imagine—the freedom to read, the ability to teach herself anything she wanted. Even though she was a prisoner in the Beast's castle, Belle had the freedom of her own mind.

That night, when I finally fell asleep, I dreamed I was curled up on the plush rug in front of my very own fireplace with a big, leather-bound book that didn't use the words "Grandpa," "Uncle," or "Heaven" even once. I knew that even wanting these things meant

I was going to Hell. Still, I imagined myself far away, alone with all those books, protected by strong doors that locked, the lockbox in my head wide open, my thoughts finally allowed to roam free, in a room all my own where no one could touch me.

7

BOOKWORM

■

Rio de Janeiro, Brazil, 1995

It was finally testing day.

Leadership communes, like the one I lived in, were where the Children of God tried all of the experimental policies before they were rolled out to the rest of God's Army. Normally, they were jarring and disappointing, but this time, I was excited. This time, everything would change. Despite all the lessons I had learned that proved I shouldn't get my hopes up, I still did.

My commune would be experimenting with a new homeschooling program from a real school developed by some Mennonites up in the States—another type of Christian who were righter than most worldly Christians, but still not as close to God as The Family. After a year, if the curriculum met our standards, the rest of The Family around the world would get to start using the program, too.

Since we were all of different ages and levels of "no-schooling," we needed to do a day of diagnostic tests to figure out where each child should be placed. This was a good sign, Auntie Patty explained, and proof of the virtues of homeschooling—we learned at our own pace. Not like at Systemite schools, with the students packed into a big classroom where everyone studied the same thing, with no consideration of actual abilities. Because we were free of the bureaucracy that bogged down the Systemites, we could do things our own way.

At eight years old, I knew one thing already: I loved school. The dedicated time for learning. Books and pencils. The structure. Having a place where asking questions was usually allowed, a place where my thoughts sometimes mattered. I wanted more. And I wanted to be smarter than all of them.

My schooling up to this point had been sporadic and basic. Our classes were taught by a rotating cast of Aunties, most of whom only had high school diplomas, and teenagers who had no more "schooling" than I did. We learned how to write by taking dictation from Grandpa's teachings. I loved art class with Auntie Patty, an artist who could do anything with scraps of random colored pencils. But I lived for the times when I was left alone to crack open a history book or look at the pages of a science experiment, imagining what dissecting a frog might be like, in a real classroom surrounded by things like microscopes and test tubes, a pair of big plastic goggles on my face.

Hiding inside my locked golden box of private thoughts was the wish that I would go to school myself one day. Real school, one with actual teachers who knew things, who could show me all the secrets of the world outside, who believed in science, and who knew all the information I suspected was being kept from me, and were willing to share it. It was a dream I knew I could never tell anyone, not my closest friends, not even Mom or Merry. We could never tell when someone would be "convicted by the Spirit" and tattle.

Our giant living room had been converted to a testing room for the day, with long tables from the dining room brought in to create orderly rows. All the curtains had been drawn shut, so we wouldn't be distracted by the tropical foliage or the trees we loved to climb full of colorful birds and chattering monkeys. There were new pencil cases filled with different writing utensils for each child, which must have been specifically purchased for this exam. I could feel my excitement rising as Auntie Patty set out the giant test booklets in front of each kid, moving from the laid-back confidence of the fourteen-to-fifteen-year-old "Junior Teens," to the eager twelve-to-thirteen-year-old JETTs—the "Junior End Time Teens"—where my friends Mary Dear and Abigail were. By the time she got to the wide-eyed older children (Dorothea, Virginia, me, and the others) and the middle children (Merry's group), my blood thrummed with anticipation. There were no younger children, toddlers, or baby groups around, so we'd be able to focus on this exam without anyone bothering us.

The diagnostic test went from grades 1–8. Even though some of the kids were high school age, there was no use for our schooling to go any further. Grandpa had decreed anything over an eighth-grade education was useless since Jesus would be coming back any day now. Each kid could work in the test booklet until it got too hard. I was giddy with this gift—*we* got to make the choice; *we* got to show how smart we were. It was better than Christmas and my birthday combined.

One of the reasons I loved school so much was because of Auntie Patty, who always talked to us kids like we were real people, with desires and thoughts worth hearing. She never, ever hit us. She was unique in our commune for having skin that was much darker than almost anyone else who lived with us, with a big halo of black, frizzy hair that never laid flat, either. She wore colorful clothes and had even been to college for a little bit, and she knew a lot about what she called "child psychology."

When everyone thought my one-year-old brother, Timmy, was stupid because his mouth always hung open after he'd fallen from a triple-decker bunk bed as a tiny baby, she had him hook together a series of teeny-tiny paper clips, and he was the only baby in the whole group that could do it. She told the adults that Timmy had a different kind of intelligence than what they were used to seeing. She said things like that about me, too, like how the fact that I was always restless and fidgeting during lectures and schooltime was because I was bored and it was all too easy, not because I wanted to be bad.

Right before the test, she leaned over and told me that this was my chance to show all the adults what I could do. I thought maybe if they knew how smart I was, maybe if I was good at something, I wouldn't get in so much trouble. Maybe I'd get to learn whatever I wanted, and everything would change. Maybe they'd believe, like Auntie Patty did, that I could be the one defending our life to the Systemites in the End Times. I was sure we'd need smart kids then.

Once the books had been laid down in front of all the kids, Auntie Patty explained the rules. *No talking, no peeking. This is not a test that you can fail, so don't worry. Write your name on the front cover and then start working through what you can. If it gets too hard, you can move to another section. When you don't feel like you can do more, you can leave the room and go play outside.*

That meant I was allowed to spend all day "doing school." I couldn't stop smiling.

The crisp white pages were nicer than any of the used or donated workbooks we usually had. I printed my name in my nicest cursive letters, the way Auntie Jade had spent so much time teaching me. Normally, my handwriting was atrocious, but only Auntie Patty seemed to notice that I could write as quickly as the fastest girl in the twelve-year-old group, Uncle Jerry's oldest stepdaughter, Mary Dear. I decided to be extra careful and take my time, like I was always advised, so that my handwriting was perfectly legible.

I imagined myself making it all the way through the whole booklet, all eight grades, and being praised for what a beacon I was to The Family. I would prove them all wrong, all those adults who said I was mouthy and disobedient and bad. They would finally know I was special. I was worth something.

After only about ten minutes, I saw Dorothea lay her pencil down, swish her waist-length hair around, close her book, and raise her hand. Was she done already? She hadn't had time to do much more than write her name.

Auntie Patty came over to see what was wrong.

"I'm done," Dorothea said. "Can I go outside now?"

"Are you sure you don't want to try a little bit more? It's okay if that's all you can do, everyone will start out in first grade if that's where they are."

Dorothea nodded that it was okay, and she slipped quietly off the bench and left the room. Her little sister quickly followed her, as did Merry and several of the other girls in my age group. How could they throw away this opportunity? How could they not want something *more*? I tried not to shake my head. I didn't want Auntie Patty to think

I was making fun of the kids who didn't like school. I would probably be punished for vanity, for disrespect, and for the sin of pride.

I put my head back down and kept working, fascinated by the various kinds of math problems, history questions, and reading comprehension. I had never seen anything like it before. Even when I didn't know the answers, I felt like I was learning something by simply being asked the question. I saw a world of possibility on those blank lines and inside those empty boxes waiting to be filled. There was something thrilling about selecting my answer on multiple-choice questions. With each one, it felt like I was saying "this one is mine." I noticed that sometimes I could tell from the way they phrased the answers which one I was supposed to choose, and I wondered if that meant I was cheating.

I don't know exactly how long I stayed in the room, but it was after they brought around sandwiches for lunch—bread with slices of cheese and tomatoes, with lemonade to drink, because it was a "special occasion." I loved our version of lemonade, a dark brown liquid of fresh squeezed limes off a tree in our backyard, stirred with thick raw sugar so brown it was almost molasses. The sugar was a rare treat and helped me stay focused and feel less sleepy after lunch. Only about a dozen of us were left by then; one by one, kids left the room when the questions got too difficult or they got too bored. The further along I got, the more I struggled, but I was determined to keep going, even after the questions had gotten much too hard for me to answer, especially the history and science ones. I knew a little bit about photosynthesis and the Mayflower, but mostly we had always focused on math and English, since Systemite books that taught science and history were usually filled with the Devil's lies. We had to cut out so many pages with dinosaurs, evolution, or stuff about the Holocaust that our books always ended up with more pages ripped out than not.

Grandpa had written a book called *Seven Thousand Years of World History,* which he said included everything that happened from when God created Adam and Eve until the present day. I knew this was all the history there was, but most of the questions on the test were not stuff from that book, even though this was supposed to be a Christian curriculum. I guessed the Mennonites didn't know Grandpa's version of history, either. That just proved they weren't truly God's people, some Uncle would explain to me if I ever bothered to question the disparity, before punishing me for it. Long after I couldn't answer any more questions, I sat and read through them, imagining one day learning the answers.

But I couldn't stay there forever. When it was only me, Mary Dear, Abigail, and the two oldest teens, it was time to get ready for dinner. I wondered if any of the bigger teens had made it all the way through the eighth-grade material. I made a bet with myself that I had earned a spot in fourth grade, which I thought would have been one or two grades higher than I would be in Systemite school. I ran off to wash my hands, imagining the smile on my mom's face at dinner when I told her how I'd lasted the whole day on the diagnostic test.

Decisions in The Family were complex. It seemed like this decision should be easy—just look at the test scores. But nothing was ever as simple as looking at data. Adults had to pray over everything, asking God to tell them what to do. There was always hidden meaning somewhere, regardless of the facts.

Still, I felt hopeful. I wasn't the coolest kid and would never be the prettiest, but I could carve out a place for myself as the smartest. It was what I held on to, even when it turned against me, even when smart became a slur.

A few days later, Auntie Patty, looking stern, approached me at the breakfast table. "I want you to know that you tested between the third and fourth grade levels," she said.

I could feel my face drop; I was sure I'd done better than that. But I was concerned about more than her words. Why did she need to tell me in advance, privately, if I would find out in a short time anyway?

A few minutes later, we marched into our classroom. Auntie Lydia called out, "Everyone take a seat wherever you want." There was a stack of books at each table, with our new pencil cases, still full of brand-new school supplies. Dread crept over me as I looked at the stacks.

Language Arts: First Grade.
Science: First Grade.
Social Studies: First Grade.
Math: First Grade.

I thought I would be sick.

I looked around the classroom full of other kids smiling about their new supplies, holding books that were much too easy for me. My most difficult task that day would be shoving down my bitterness. What a cruel joke it had all been, getting my hopes up like that. I should have known we would never be allowed to be individuals.

The adults had no reason to differentiate our schooling. It would be too hard on the rotating teachers. Too hard to supervise different levels of workbooks. And what was the point? We weren't supposed to be smart. We weren't supposed to think too much. God forbid we have our own opinions or start questioning things.

I wondered if Auntie Patty fought for us, if she tried to argue with the leadership to let us start at the levels where we were tested. I thought she probably had, and that's why she'd looked so serious. I wondered if she'd been punished for asking for change.

As I settled into my seat, staring at the unopened book sitting lifeless in front of me, my little remaining hope of freedom evaporated. I would never belong in The Family. I could read all the books we had and still never truly escape this world. I was trapped.

8

THE END OF THE WORLD AS WE KNOW IT

∎

Rio de Janeiro, Brazil, 1995

It was February 18, time for The Fast. Again.

Grandpa's birthday, the official birthday of The Family.

Over three long days, we would pray for the old man's health, rededicate ourselves to God, and read new Mo Letters to discover the updated revelations he had sent to his Prophet. While the grown-ups were fasting and talking to God, the kids had lots of free time to color and play, and we got to eat special-occasion food like soups and sandwiches made from donated bread, homemade mayo and some cheese and tomatoes—and, if we were lucky, even lunch meat. It was safest if we were quiet and stayed away from the adults during The Fast. Sometimes their hunger led to crankiness, which could mean extra discipline.

The day started differently than in previous years. At our dawn wake-up, we were instructed to put on our best street dresses, the single nice outfit every kid had for accompanying adults outside the commune to raise money or beg for food from shops and grocery stores. But The Fast wasn't usually a dress-up event.

We were to head to the schoolroom on the third floor of the main house, a large multipurpose space where Auntie Patty also lived. As I climbed the stairs to wait in the line of younger kids, I couldn't figure out the vibe. It almost felt like a party with adults milling outside the room, but many of them were crying. Something was very different.

Auntie Dora opened the door. Behind her, I saw more important adults already inside. There was Mom sitting with the secretary pool, all the women who would take notes today. I didn't even have to turn my head to know that Dad would be over in the musicians' corner tuning his guitar and getting warmed up for "inspiration time" before the praying began. It was nice that I didn't have to look, since I knew Uncle Jerry would be right next to him.

"Welcome to Grandpa's graduation party," Auntie Dora said, her slight German accent coming through, a big smile plastered on her tearstained face. She welcomed all of us inside and, as I entered, I saw streamers hanging from the ceiling and balloons bouncing around the floor. In the center of the room was a big easel, upon which sat a full-color, glossy, absolutely giant picture of an old man with a creepy smile.

I was so confused. What did Grandpa graduate from? Was he in school? I thought school was evil. Why would an adult go to school? Did this mean we'd get to start going to school too?

Uncles played their guitars, and the adults sang through their tears. *"We've got a lot, we've got a lot, we've got a lot to be thankful for."*

As we took our seats, I saw that each place had an oversized black-and-white picture book that read "Now It Can Be Shown," the front printed with the same photo that was on the easel—the old man with the oily forehead, big white beard, gold chain, deep-set eyes, and eerie smile that would haunt my dreams. The ultimate creepy Uncle.

I'd never known what Grandpa looked like, never even dared to imagine it. Everything about Grandpa was *selah*—our word for top secret, information we guarded with our lives. Everyone knew the Systemites had been hunting Grandpa since he first started preaching about God, and especially after he had started Flirty Fishing in the '70s, back when Mom was a little girl. Mama Maria and all the other Aunties had been sent out to become "fishers of men," like the Bible said, luring men and their money into the Children of God using sex, the best tool we had to witness for the Lord and show God's love to others. Even though there were several Mo Letters that provided precise instructions on how best to be one of "God's Hookers," we had to stop after an evil German magazine published a picture of him sitting on a bench with thirteen scantily clad Aunties around him— making them out to be religious prostitutes. It was clear they didn't understand.

Then the evil Americans twisted Grandpa's teachings when they reprinted the photo in something called *Time* magazine, and that's when Grandpa had to start living in hiding, moving all around the world. After that, all pictures of him had been cut out of any Family publications, and if they couldn't be cut out, Dad had to draw a big cartoon lion's head over his face.

But now we gazed upon a *real* face, the empty space between the black lines of the comics filled in. Our Prophet, in the flesh. A real man.

Auntie Dora explained that Grandpa had gone to The Heavenly City to be with Jesus. I knew something really big was happening, but I felt like I was missing it. Our Prophet was dead. I knew I was supposed to feel upset, but I didn't. He impacted all of our lives every single day, but I had never met the guy. I didn't love him. I glanced around, wondering if anyone could hear my blasphemous thoughts.

February 18 would no longer be called The Fast. With Grandpa's death, the day became The Feast—a time to consume God's word and rejoice that we had a new spirit helper in Heaven to guide us. I sat there, wondering if they'd ever tell us how he died, or if that would remain a secret like so much else. I wondered why all the Aunties kept hugging the picture and talking about how beautiful and sexy he was. What was I not seeing? Why was I failing to understand?

Everyone around me was crying, thanking Jesus, speaking in tongues, and generally carrying on: Auntie Gentleness, on her knees, arms lifted to the sky, tears streaming down her face; Uncle Jebediah, eyes closed, unintelligible sounds coming out of his mouth; Auntie Mary Magdalene on the floor, having apparently fainted; Auntie Temperance and Auntie Lydia gathered around her. Everyone had their parts and their scripts, and they all played them so well. They all really thought Grandpa was in Heaven, inside the moon, watching us, judging us on how well we were mourning.

It felt like a performance, like when I got picked up late at night to go spend a month at one of The Family's video production communes where we did all kinds of acting, singing, and dancing for the educational videos we watched as part of "school" and sold on the streets. I would be given a person to pretend to be that day and we'd dramatize the scene, just the way the director told us to. Once I had to play the beggar on the streets that Grandpa saw in one of his dreams. I understood that we were all acting in this scene too: The Aunties were supposed to get hysterical, the Uncles were supposed to find revelations, and we kids were supposed to not get in the way. I had to play my part the same way I did when the cameras were rolling—that was the only way to stay out of trouble. So, I did what I rarely had the self-control to do: I sat really, really still. My body stayed tucked beneath me as my brain ran its way around thousands of questions: *What does this mean? Is The Family going to go away? Are we going to have to move to America? Will I get to go to school? What will happen now that our leader is dead?*

And most importantly: *What role will I need to play to survive?*

WE LEARNED THAT Grandpa had died six months earlier, but Mama Maria, who would be The Family's new unquestioned leader, had decided to wait until The Fast to reveal it. Someone in Mama Maria's home received a revelation from God, a vision of Grandpa being taken up to Heaven in a chariot and passing his mantle down to Mama Maria. The message was clear: We had a new leader, and she had the full backing—and total power—of the Prophet. The vision had also explained that all Family members had, with Grandpa's passing, received a piece of his "gift of prophecy." All adults, and even the children, could begin receiving messages and instructions directly from Jesus. We were all "prophets" now, I guessed.

Starting at that year's Feast, Mama Maria revealed the new governing Charter of The Family. It was the first time in our history that rules had ever been written down. Never before had there been a clearly defined process for membership, expectations, or guaranteed rights and responsibilities in quite this way. On the surface, the new rules seemed so clear that nobody could argue with their details.

Several big things impacted us kids. Sitting cross-legged on the floor later that day, after everyone had calmed down, I tried to focus on what Auntie Dora was saying and not fiddle with the dusty pink carpet fibers. She started by outlining the discipline protocols, naming sections and numbers that made all the adults nod carefully. I couldn't figure out what she was talking about and examined the faces of Dorothea, Abigail, and little Merry, but they didn't seem to know either. Then she said the words that got my full attention: "If you are older than six, you can't receive any more than six swats as a punishment. It will be even less for the younger children and toddlers." I snuck a glance at the musician corner, where all the most popular punishment Uncles were, but they all sat there calmly, as if they'd already heard this before.

Clearing her throat, Auntie Dora said, "Your parents have the right to be involved in any discipline you receive, and nobody can deny that." She smiled at us, almost warmly. "Isn't Mama Maria so radical?"

The room nodded. I tried to imagine my meek mother, always "in the Spirit," marching up and intervening on an Uncle or Auntie who was dragging me off to a beating somewhere. It was a nice idea, but I knew it would never happen.

"We will no longer be using silence restrictions on the very young children," Auntie Dora continued. "And nobody should be hanging signs around your neck anymore." I thought of all the times I'd been placed on silence restriction, usually for talking too much out of turn.

"We won't be using long periods of isolation." Auntie Dora's voice broke through my reverie. "And children under twelve will always have a right to ask to see their parents, at any time." She seemed to look me in the eyes as she said this, in a way that made me wonder if she knew about Uncle Jerry, about the things he did when he got me alone. I wondered how many other kids he did it to. I wondered how many Uncle Jerrys there were in our communes around the world.

"Time-outs will cease at three hours, for older children, ten years old on down." I wouldn't be gone for days anymore, but three hours was still a lot of time. Three hours felt like ten when I was alone in a room with nothing but walls and my own skin to pick at.

Auntie Dora explained the new official Family position: Children had a right to an education. Any kind of traditional learning had always been secondary to physical labor in the communes, but now regular schooling would become an official requirement and classroom time would replace previously scheduled work hours. Our homeschooling experiment would become the standard education for every child. I did the math and realized Grandpa had already been dead when we did our testing months earlier—so that had been the plan all along, with our commune serving as guinea pigs.

As Auntie Dora explained the new labor rules, I thought of all the work we did: from physical labor, to childcare, to acting and performing on videos and in the streets, to pounding the pavement selling those same videos and literature to raise money for the adults who didn't work jobs. I didn't know how our way of life could survive without that, and I didn't believe for a second that any of it would change. They'd find a way around the regulations. They'd have to.

"Some of the youngest children are going to start going to the doctor," Auntie Dora continued. "Because Jesus has told Mama Maria that it's important babies and toddlers be treated by Systemite doctors." At this, I heard audible gasps from my friends around the room. But when I looked around, the adults had all mostly painted the usual reverent looks back on their faces. "All of you will have at least one visit to a doctor and a dentist in the next year. That way, if the police do come here, we'll be able to show them your medical records. But we'll still know that Jesus is the one who does our real healing, right?"

"Thank you, Jesus. Praise you, Lord." We all parroted the expected response. Auntie Dora's explanation made sense. Systemite doctors were still wrong, but sometimes we had to do a little evil in order to do the greater good of protecting The Family.

My mind floated back to my visit to the hospital years ago as I ran my fingers over the scar on my palm. I shivered as I remembered the feeling of the needle pulling the thick black thread through my skin. I never wanted to see another Systemite "medical professional" again.

Auntie Dora paused and scanned the room slowly, as if she was trying to take a moment to look each and every one of us in the eye. Finally,
she cleared her throat and said, "It's important for us to remember that
Mama Maria is not saying Grandpa was wrong. The Lord told Grandpa
one thing a long time ago, and he's given Mama a different vision for
our current world. We don't question the teaching from when Grandpa
was our Prophet. He still talks to Mama, and to us if we want, every day
from Heaven."

But I wasn't so sure. The fact that Auntie Dora had to point this
out struck me as suspect. I looked around the room and saw everyone
nodding. Did no one else see how strange this was? That Grandpa
died and all of a sudden a bunch of his teachings were deemed wrong?
If we weren't following his teachings—if we weren't following *him*—
exactly who and what were we following?

When Auntie Dora continued, she told us about the biggest
changes of all: the rules about sex.

"Mama Maria feels that some of our ideas about sex have been
taken out of context and have been poorly applied by some bad apples
in our homes." My heart seemed to stop beating. Was she going to
name him? I knew better than to look at Uncle Jerry directly, but I
could see him out of the corner of my eye. The look on his face didn't
change a bit. He sat there, unconcerned, as if he had no clue he was
one of the bad apples Auntie Dora was talking about.

"Anyone caught having sex with a minor will be excommunicated
from The Family. Nobody under the age of sixteen is to be engaging
in full sex—though the Junior End Time Teens and Junior Teens will
be allowed some sexual touching." She looked straight at our group.
"That means we don't play games about making love anymore, okay,
kids?" We all nodded obediently.

I didn't understand what I was feeling. In the short time it took
Auntie Dora to explain the rules of the new Charter, it felt like everything in my life was about to change. And yet there I was—in the same
place, surrounded by the same people. I felt weightless, floating, like
someone had lifted a fifty-pound bag of rice off my shoulders I hadn't
even known was there. But there was something else, a fear that I'd

be caught, that hands would reach up and grab me and drag me back down to where I belonged. I heard only good news, but I knew that most of the time, good news turned out to be too good to be true.

But still, for the first time in my life, someone had said and put down in writing what I had always felt but never had the words to express: It was wrong for grown men to have sex with little girls. There were so many different kinds of punishments, and so many people who did them, but there was a clear line in my head that placed them into categories, even if I couldn't articulate at the time exactly what these categories were. I knew that I liked Dad and hated Uncle Jerry. Even though they both punished me a lot, they were different. Dad was "one of the good ones," as we called them. I locked away in my imaginary jeweled box what I knew I could never speak: Uncle Jerry was a bad man, one whose wife stood before us spelling out the punishments he'd never face.

I felt a cautious hope that it would be harder for people to hurt me quite so badly as before. If Uncle Jerry needed witnesses, he couldn't drag me down into the basement for punishment. If Abel or Titus tried to make me play another game, I could threaten to tell on them for "sexual touching," the same way they used to threaten to tell on me for not being a "Bible woman willing to serve the men" if I didn't touch them like they wanted. I had the words for it, and that was a power in itself.

Sitting there on the floor, listening to all the ways my life was about to change, I looked at my sister, Merry, six and a half at the time. I didn't know if anyone had gotten to her yet. No one, not even sisters, ever talked about that kind of thing. But I wanted to believe she had been spared so far, and that the new Charter meant no one would ever get the chance to hurt her the way they'd hurt me.

I wanted to run out of there. It was all too much. I didn't want to keep seeing Uncle Jerry out of the corner of my eye as he sat there with a serene look on his face, as if he was innocent, as if none of this troubled him a bit. I felt a huge relief, but I also felt like I needed to be alone with all this information, like it needed time to settle. What else could Auntie Dora possibly say?

The room stayed quiet and still and serious. Somewhere behind me, a chair creaked.

Auntie Dora smiled and looked at us kids, with something like a twinkle in her eye. "I told Mama Maria about the library my girls have been running with classic novels, and how much you kids enjoy reading them. She thinks that's a good lesson for other homes, and it will be especially powerful if the police raid any of us again. It'll be in a Mama Letter soon. We'll be adding more books to our library. Isn't that exciting?" I tried not to smile too hard at this news. If they knew we wanted something too much, they'd take it away.

"We're going to have more movies too, with a new ministry who will decide which ones are healthy for us to watch." I forced myself to remain calm, grabbing my ankles so I wouldn't accidentally uncross my legs and jump up. I missed more Friday movies than I saw because of punishments—I didn't expect that to change—but my mind soared as I imagined a time when I wouldn't have to hide my love of reading. I glanced over at Mom, hoping we'd get to do some reading together soon like we usually did on weekends, of good books, not just Mo Letters and Dad's comics.

When Auntie Dora was done, we prayed, thanking God for Grandpa and now for Mama Maria as his new mouthpiece. Usually my mind wandered during prayer time, but this was different. I was not faking my gratitude. That day, as I stretched my arms toward the sky in worship, I felt every bit of those hallelujahs.

As life inside the commune adjusted to the new Charter, a dark side emerged that I don't think any Family members would have, or could have, been capable of foreseeing. I celebrated that six would become the maximum number of swats a child my age could receive with a paddle because it meant that I wouldn't be hit ten, or even twenty, times with long, hard pieces of wood or, even worse, stinging wire flyswatters. But it quickly became evident that I would *always* get hit six times, for any infraction, large or small, where in the past some punishments might have just been a swat or two. Now, nobody would ever question whether hitting a small child six times was too much—because it said so in *the Charter*. For better or for worse, the rules and regulations that it contained became our gospel truth.

The same sentences and rules that codified certain freedoms also gave up others. We were given the right to ask "clarifying questions" of any part of our religious doctrines, which seemed to mean that no other child would be punished like I had been from that game of telephone gone wrong, and so many other times. But we were also responsible for doing it in a way that didn't spread doubt or schism among the members of the group—which meant any leader could still decide that your method, question, or tone was "out of the Spirit." Embedded in almost every "guaranteed right" was sneaky, coded language that still made it harder for a group member to think on their own, act in their own defense, or make decisions in their own best interests. The Charter was the "Truth," just like the Bible, but that also meant someone in power could always interpret things differently, and their word would always matter more.

9

ALL IN THE FAMILY

■

Merry and I were in the schoolroom with the other kids when Mom appeared at the door. My body immediately tensed; my instinct for the unexpected was always fear.

Granted permission, we followed her out. I tried to read her mood, tried to understand the emotion she was hiding behind her practiced, serene face. But her posture betrayed her. She almost bounced down the hallway, and it struck me, as it sometimes did, how young she was, how she was really only a few years removed from being a teenager.

Once she shut the door to her room, a huge grin burst across her face as she exclaimed, "Your grandpa is coming to live with us!"

I was completely confused. Grandpa had been dead for nearly two years. *Had he been resurrected?*

Then Mom started talking about how great it would be to have *her* dad in the same house as us, like a "real" family. Even in the privacy of her bedroom, she dropped her volume as she said it. We could never be too careful. There was always someone around a corner who could question our commitment to The Family.

It carried weight within The Family that Merry and I were Third Generation, with a grandfather who was important to the leadership, but it also meant we didn't know him. He was too *selah*. My understanding of grandparents was that they gave lots of presents and sometimes Family kids got to travel to America and vacation

with them in places called hotels. I'd only seen hotels when we witnessed in their lobbies and patio restaurants, performing our song and
dance and telling them about Jesus, before requesting cash in support. But the Family kids with grandparents would actually sleep in
hotels sometimes. They'd return from their trips with toys and clothes
they got to keep, in case the same relatives visited in the future. I had
to work hard to hide my envy. My grandpa being in the leadership
gave me status and inspired some awe in my classmates, but mostly I
wanted regular grandparents who wanted to buy me things and take
me on vacations far away.

"Will he bring us presents?" I asked, but Mom didn't know. She
explained instead that he would bring our aunt Charity, who was
nine, right between Merry and me—generational overlap was common in The Family.

Grandpa Tom showed up early one morning, with his third wife,
Auntie Annie, and little Charity in tow. They were so *selah* that I had
never even seen photos of them, so I was amazed that the face of a
man could look so much like Mom's. Charity looked like Mom too,
beautiful in a way I knew I would never be, and I was immediately
jealous of her looks and her clout. Charity arrived with an aura of
importance, straight from Mama Maria's house. She'd even known
Grandpa when he was alive. I expected to hate her, but when she
taught us tricks for stealing money and food from the adults, pretending to find it in legitimate places as "gifts from God," my jealousy
quickly turned to love. She was one of us.

Gramps was bubbly and friendly with a wonderful smile, a worldly
T-shirt with a cheeky i'm not 50, i'm 18 with 35 years of experience
written on the front, and he *had* brought gifts: dangly earrings made
out of colored crystal in our birthstone colors, deep blue for Merry
and emerald green for me. I'd never seen anything so beautiful in my
whole life. The brilliant color reminded me of the jewel in my Queen
Esther crown and the gems I always imagined adorned the box in
my mind that housed my secret thoughts—but these jewels sparkled
in the sunlight and looked real. My earrings matched the green foliage on the jungle-patterned jumpsuit he brought me, with tigers and

butterflies peeking out from the leaves. I wanted to wear it every day, but I controlled myself, knowing it would be taken from me if I was accused of being "too cool."

For my tenth birthday a few weeks later, Gramps gave me a brand-new copy of *The Wind in the Willows,* the classic children's book that I proceeded to read over and over until the cover nearly fell off. Because he was so important and the rules had somewhat changed, nobody would dare suggest that I couldn't keep the book he gave me. Most of the other kids didn't care about reading, so it was a present that I didn't even have to share.

I knew better than to get used to it, but with the new protections of the Charter, and with my grandfather in my life, I began to feel less afraid. Gramps and Auntie Annie had been given the big, special room upstairs, and we started to spend almost all of our family time together. I loved how his face looked like a reflection of Mom's, and how he seemed to love us from the first day, like we didn't have to earn it at all. And he was more important than even Uncle Jerry. That mattered too. I almost started to believe I could be happy. That I could be safe.

But the pendulum swung again. The Charter's new rules required only six adults aged sixteen or older to make an official commune, so our compounds started shrinking to branch off all over the world. World Services, the guys at the top, decided to downsize our home to fifty people. With the exception of Charity and Uncle Jerry's step-daughters Mary Dear, Dorothea, and their other sisters, the commune in Rio would not include families with small children any longer.

Since the invention of the internet, Dad could work remotely, so our family, with five young children—me, Merry, Timmy, Darius, and Justin—was forced from World Services, the only group we kids had ever known. Gramps was part of the decision to send us away, and I knew he was acting in what he thought were the best interests of The Family, but that didn't make it hurt any less. Despite Mom's beauty, her connections, and her exemplary work, the cruel irony was that it was her very devotion to the Prophet's teachings—"going for the gold" and averaging a baby every two years since she was fifteen—that ended her advanced secretarial career. But, like always, Mom was a true believer—she smiled sweetly when she explained the move to us, praising God and our leaders, never showing her sadness.

I was devastated and furious at the thought of losing my friends, who I thought of like sisters, but like so many Family moves, there wasn't time to process, and I certainly didn't have any say in the matter. As we said goodbye to our friends, we were introduced to two of our new older sisters—Dad's youngest daughters from Auntie Hope, thirteen-year-old twins Reyna and Jamie, who would join us in our new life. All seven of Auntie Hope's daughters had been bouncing between communes ever since their mom had been excommunicated for her cancer. Sometimes all the sisters were together, sometimes they were split up. The leadership eventually decided Dad should take over the two youngest. Reyna was tall and skinny, with brown hair and big glasses, while Jamie was much shorter and curvier, with platinum blond hair and bright blue eyes. They looked nothing alike, and nothing like their dad—which I would soon learn was because they were the biological children of a different Uncle, part of the "sexual sharing" all the Aunties had to do. The girls didn't seem apprehensive or upset, simply eager to settle into their new lives and see what cards the fates would deal this time. It was scary. And intimidating. Our genetically mismatched crew, with two new older sisters and a family who had always been The Family first, and our family part-time, expected to start over a few hundred miles away together. We may have lived alongside each other but, even when it came to Mom and Dad and Merry and my three younger brothers, we didn't really know each other, either. How would we function when it was just our unit?

We packed up two Volkswagen vans with our new family of nine, our flee-bags stuffed with our few possessions, and Uncle Jebediah and Auntie Lydia to help us make the seven-hour drive west and inland to the new commune that would be our home.

With my Bible and my photo album at my feet, I clutched my precious *Wind in the Willows* in my arms, even though I knew I'd be way too motion sick to read on the drive. Gramps waved cheerfully the way any good leader would, as if we were any other members leaving on their new mission. I tearfully said a silent goodbye to my family within The Family.

And then a realization hit me, a sudden ray of light breaking through my sorrow and grief: We were going so far away that I would probably never, ever, have to deal with Uncle Jerry again.

I had no idea what my life would look like, but I had just enough faith to believe the new Charter would protect me no matter what awaited me on the other side of the drive. No horrible Uncle would ever touch me again.

10

THE PROMISE OF PARADISE

■

Belo Horizonte, Brazil, 1997

After seven hours of driving and one of our vehicles getting hopelessly lost, I hopped out of the van in Belo Horizonte, the sixth largest city in Brazil, and the site of our new home. I'd learn that the name meant "Beautiful Horizon" in Portuguese, and it really was gorgeous. Surrounded by mountains on all sides, I breathed in air that was crisp in that mountain way, with no weight of sea salt and waves around the edges. Tropical trees created a thick foliage everywhere I looked. I saw the familiar ten-foot cement walls encasing the new commune, topped with the ubiquitous shards of broken glass bottles that surrounded the houses of those with means throughout Brazil. For the first time, I wondered about this feature of every place I had ever lived. *Are the walls supposed to keep others out? Or keep us in?*

I noticed the customary heavy wooden gate, the large brass bell out front for visitors to announce their presence and wait for admittance. But this commune was tiny. When the door opened, I could see the back gate from the front. As I entered, I spotted a pool and a combination basketball/soccer court where two girls were kicking a ball. There was an orchard in the back, which I would later discover only had four types of fruit trees, unlike the dozens we'd always had before. Instinctively, I looked for places to hide, but I did not see many options. The place was too small. What would we do with nowhere to escape the punishing gaze of Aunties and Uncles?

But there weren't that many Aunties and Uncles, either. This commune had just eighteen people, including us, which seemed unbelievably small to me. We would live with only one other family, led by Uncle Jonatas, who was just slightly older than Mom. Auntie Hepzibah, his wife, was one of the most senior translators in The Family, responsible for translating every document they produced into Brazilian Portuguese, either for distribution on the streets, or for the increasing number of Brazilian Children of God disciples who didn't speak English. There was one older teen boy who lived there, and Jonatas and Hepzibah's youngest kids—Michaela, who was thirteen, RoseAnna, eleven and closest to my age, and two younger kids. They'd be in a group with my three brothers, Timmy, Darius, and Justin, ages five, three, and one.

I bonded quickly with Michaela. She was friendly and lively, but also even-tempered, unlike her sister RoseAnna, who was prone to fits of meanness and mood swings. Michaela and RoseAnna looked very different than most of the girls I had known until then, with their darker skin, thick manes of black, wavy hair, and hips already starting to show on their preteen bodies. To my dismay, I still looked like a little boy, a head and a half shorter than the others. I immediately knew I would be nowhere near the top in the hierarchy of teenage girls, but I was glad to be aligning myself as Michaela's friend.

I quickly grew to appreciate Auntie Hepzibah and the smaller commune life. Though she was a stickler for cleanliness—Reyna, Jamie, Michaela, RoseAnna, Merry, and I spent a lot of time scrubbing walls with toothbrushes and sweeping the tile floors until they were spotless enough to meet her demanding standards—she also seemed fair with discipline and open-minded to the world outside. Brazilian culture defined her at least as much as Family culture, and she shared that with our commune, over which she was the undisputed matriarch. She quickly saw my shame that I couldn't speak Portuguese—despite the six years I'd lived in Brazil already—and began to teach me, repeating everything she said in Portuguese, English, then Portuguese again. It only took a few months for me to start understanding the words, and a little more of the world, around me.

Outside our commune's walls, Brazil was colorful and noisy, the downtown streets covered with cameloas—street vendors—hawking their wares, piles of intricately patterned artisanal dishes and beautifully crafted handmade jewelry, full of the semiprecious stones and agates this state was known for, all stacked on top of colorful blankets. We mingled in the streets and listened to the music of voices in Portuguese around us, with lilting sounds and round vowels, everything rolling and flowing together. I loved passing the stands showcasing dozens of different kinds of grapes in various little piles, every color and shape under the sun, with flavors that would burst into my mouth every time I was lucky enough to try one. Tropical flowers in every color lined the streets and decorated the high cement walls that rich people lived behind; they spilled from flower boxes in apartment windows and were braided and pinned up into women's hair. Colors were everywhere; even the buildings were painted green, bright pink, lavender, and gold.

The Brazilian flag was flown with pride—I could look up anywhere and see the bright gold diamond atop the bold blue circle against the emerald-green background, symbolizing the rain forest, the precious metals, the Amazon river, and the nature that surrounds you everywhere you go. Even though I had lived in this country for six years, this was the first time I really started feeling like I was a part of it. We had been so much more isolated at the commune in Rio, but here, in Belo, we were not as cloistered behind our concrete walls.

We left the commune a lot more often, needing to raise money to support our life in "the mission field" more than when we lived in the leadership compounds. Those ran on tithes from the communes in the mission fields, and as a commune tasked with doing the work of witnessing, our tithe was expected for World Services. Walking up and down the streets, surrounded by a language I didn't understand, the sun beating down on us, I'd recite memorized phrases to passersby on the street, people in their cars at stoplights, and store clerks. "Oi, posso falar com você sobre Jesus?" *Can I talk to you about Jesus?* "Somos missionarios," we told them, missionaries here to help, needing money to keep doing God's work. It always felt like a lie, a trick we were playing on those unsuspecting people. They smiled always, friendly and sympathetic to the little poor blond children out raising money for God.

Everywhere I looked outside our commune, I saw people whose skin was darker than mine that never tanned, an ever-present symbol of my Slovakian heritage, a world I had no connection to at all. The diversity of Brazil is incredible— there were so many varieties of brown and black skin tones, white people with blond hair and sun-kissed bodies, brown people with glossy black hair that fell in waves down to their waists around the rolling curves of their bodies, and Japanese Brazilians everywhere too—all speaking Portuguese. It was shocking to me at first, having lived alongside almost all White people for as long as I could remember. I didn't realize that was partially due to Grandpa and the First Generation's racism. Grandpa had always told us that Black people were the descendants of Ham, one of Noah's sons punished for the sin of homosexuality, and they were destined to be unlucky forever. From what I saw, there did seem to be a hierarchy based on skin tone, with nearly all the poor people to whom we donated food for our missionary work in the slums of the favelas having darker skin. But Grandpa's explanation didn't sit right with me. People didn't deserve to be punished. They were just hungry, even hungrier than me.

As a half-starved child with a perpetually empty stomach, I thought Brazil always smelled good. Somebody somewhere was always cooking something delicious even if they only had a few ingredients, and my mouth started to water every time I left the commune walls. The food was different, and we started to eat better in Belo— with fewer mouths to feed, we could afford better meals: brown beans flavored with bacon and sausage over rice and collard greens; farofa, a dish of tapioca flour fried in butter, bacon, onions, garlic, and spices, which looked like sand but paired deliciously with the thin slices of salted, barbecued meats we grilled on the churrasqueira.

Uncle Jonatas and Auntie Hepzibah had a good ministry going in Belo, and plenty of contacts who donated food of all kinds—including meat and chicken. But even in Belo, food was still heavily controlled, and there never seemed to be enough to get full.

We got almost all of our food from donations, traveling to the open-air markets and telling people the story of who we were—God's special missionaries who needed large food donations to support our cause. With fewer adults, the older children, like me at ten, often accompanied an Uncle or Auntie to the markets for our food runs as the assigned battle buddy even the most senior leaders had to have. The market vendors would share snacks and pastries from their stalls with me, eager to reward the tiny blond American girl for struggling to speak a few words of Portuguese. With a benefactor standing there observing, the Auntie or Uncle couldn't deny me the treat and I gobbled down what would have ordinarily been extremely forbidden deep-fried or sugary delicacies that helped sustain me between our meager meals.

I loved that, in this home, we really did do the charity work we promised people we did when we were performing on the street or begging for donations from those inevitably struggling even more than we were. Every Friday afternoon, after working in the sun separating fruits and veggies into disposable garbage bags, we'd hand them out to families from the favelas that had lined up at dawn for vegetables so old or donated in such large quantities that even we didn't want them. I had thought I'd known what hunger meant, but seeing those skinny little kids waiting so calmly for a few carrots and some greens taught me the difference between having at least something for dinner versus having nothing at all. I wondered if the market vendors were so generous with me, not because of my precocious song and dance, but because of the look of hunger and longing coming from my eyes.

One day, after we'd been in Belo for a few months and I was complaining about the lack of space to escape the adults' watchful eyes, Michaela grabbed me by the hand, finger over her lips, and we tiptoed up the stairs into her mom's bedroom and translating office. Even though she was three years older than me, Michaela and I had similar personality traits—we were both Geminis, and we shared the same experience of being constantly in trouble. I suspected she might be a reader like me, and it turned out I was right.

"We don't have much outdoor space as in the big communes, but we have this," Michaela said, gesturing to the stacks of novels in Auntie Hepzibah's room. As I leaned down to read their spines, I realized they were all in Portuguese. *Is that why nobody questioned this?* I wondered, and this subject would later become a frequent topic of conversation between Michaela and me, as did other things I wouldn't have dared talk about with anyone else in The Family. We guessed Auntie Hepzibah could say the books were references for her work. Or maybe they were her rebellion. Maybe we were so out of the way, so far from any of the big leadership communes, and she was so unquestionably in charge, that she did it because she could.

"I've read them all," Michaela whispered, and I felt the joy of a partner, a fellow reader who'd been denied books as I was. I was so used to being suspicious of other kids, knowing they could tell on me at any time if they saw some benefit in it for themselves. But here was Michaela telling me a secret and trusting me to keep it. No kid had ever trusted me with anything. "Sometimes, I pretend I'm reading the Word," she said. "And then I put one of these books behind it. If you get the top bunk, nobody will ever notice."

Because of my access to Auntie Hepzibah's stash, turning eleven became an experience full of stories and other worlds. As soon as I finished my chores and school each day, I would slip to the balcony of her room with a book and the heavy Portuguese dictionary. Sometimes I would actually read the dictionary or even an encyclopedia, fascinated by the various definitions of words and how each encyclopedia entry was a mini-story in itself. Nobody had damaged these books, or ripped out sections about science or history that went against Grandpa's teachings. They still had all their pages: Classics like *Ali Baba and the Forty Thieves,* and *Alice's Adventures in Wonderland,* mixed in with Brazilian folklore, came to life before me. My favorite was the story of the god Tupa transforming sinners into fantastic jungle animals and vicious monsters because they'd harmed nature. I wondered if somewhere there was a god who punished the monsters who harmed children.

I wasn't just reading in secret, I was reading for school, too: It really had become a daily scheduled routine, several hours each morning, like the Charter had promised. Mom was our teacher, by default more than anything else, but she was a good one—she studied and taught herself lessons the night before she taught them to us, learning along with her own children the first time she'd been given the opportunity. Dad still drew full-time and Auntie Hepzibah translated. Uncle Jonatas hardly spoke English and spent his days being the missionary of our bunch, witnessing to lost souls on the streets and collecting donations from rich "sheep" for our charity projects. In the schoolroom it was the six of us girls—the teenagers Reyna, Jamie, and Michaela; and RoseAnna, Merry, and me; plus baby Justin, who crawled around on the floor while we took turns entertaining him. Finally, Mom, already big with the next baby, could focus on us and our education, teaching us the lessons she'd taught herself only the night before.

And it was glorious. We switched over to a Mormon homeschooling program from what I learned was a state in America called Utah. But even though they came from the States, the textbooks were the opposite of evil—big and beautiful, with hard covers and glossy photos on every page, like a real school. With no higher supervision, Mom ordered the books she wanted, including English Literature, which would have been impossible if we still lived in the big commune in Rio.

"I want you to have a better English education than I did," Mom said to me during one of our walks. We'd begun nightly strolls through the grounds of the commune at dusk, far enough away from everyone that I could speak my mind as myself. Even though I knew Mom was a true believer, I also always knew that she'd never betray me. Mom spoke her mind to me, too, and I felt like I was getting to really know her for the first time in my life. She'd even recently stood up to an Auntie who was savagely beating nine-year-old Merry, as the Charter had given her the right to do, to my surprise and delight.

Over the next few months, in our small commune in Belo, things felt the closest to safe I had ever experienced, and I wondered if Mom felt the same way. It was so hard to tell with her; she had fifteen years more practice than me to perfect the blank smile of a devout Family member, and her faith remained so strong. But every now and then, she expressed some doubts, or told me things I knew she wouldn't be saying if anyone else was around, like how she sometimes wished she could stop having babies, or that we could live with just our family. We were growing closer, and Mom spent her days planning lessons and protecting our mornings, giving us the full attention previously devoted to transcribing for the Prophet. For the first time ever, I felt challenged, engaged, and encouraged; expected to think deeply instead of being punished for it.

Even though I was eleven, I made it my goal to keep up with Michaela and the other fourteen-year-olds, which seemed about the right pace for me. Reading was our work. We diagrammed sentences; we memorized poems from Robert Frost, Emma Lazarus, and other American writers. More importantly, we talked about what they meant, and I felt alive, like the way the Aunties described the Spirit moving through them when they read Scripture.

We talked for hours about the Declaration of Independence and the Constitution, and I understood how important a few written documents could be, how much potential they had in their promise of freedom, much like the Charter had changed everything for us. But, also like the Charter, its power had limits, and it saddened me to be told that America had not delivered on so many of its promises. What had once been the Land of Freedom, the City on the Hill, a refuge for the tired, poor, and downtrodden masses of the world, had become so evil. Mom emphasized how things could start off good but end up rotten.

I understood that truth completely.

The new Charter prohibited older Uncles from touching young girls, but rules and reality were very different things. For me, the best part about moving to Belo was that Uncle Jerry, and many other Uncles, were no longer a daily presence looming over me. I was convinced that there were no more "bad" Uncles in my home, and even if there were, the Charter would protect me from them. Uncle Jonatas seemed like a true missionary, a genuinely nice man who never yelled, spanked, nor touched anyone. But years later, I'd find out that he had been molesting his stepdaughters for years before we arrived and would continue raping one of them well into her adulthood. There was nothing any of us could have done, even if we'd known, and I think Michaela took to protecting me, taking on the role of my older sister, the way I'd always tried to do for Merry. The way Michaela wished she could have done for her own little sister.

I would also find out the older teen boy in our home was abusing my older sisters and Michaela, and would go on to hurt even younger girls. But at the time and through my eleven-year-old eyes, I felt lucky. Nobody was bothering me. I was happy to finally be left alone.

"Dani, I need you," Auntie Hepzibah said one afternoon, as I struggled to teach one of my little brothers to read. I followed her into the kitchen and saw piles of cooked pasta, steam lifting off the noodles in heavy layers. She started with some Portuguese words that I was beginning to recognize. "Eu vou precisar de sua ajuda hoje pra fazer jantar." I could pick out the most important ones and felt a surge of pride as I translated them to myself: "I . . . need . . . help . . . dinner . . . you." Why was she asking me for help with dinner? But the English translation quickly followed. "Dani, with your mom out with the baby, and your sisters out raising money, we'll need you to take care of making dinner today. I have a big deadline."

She showed me something about ham and cubes, informed me dinner was at seven, and said that I shouldn't worry. And then left me alone in the kitchen.

I had never been authorized to even open a cupboard by myself, let alone use the stove and knives unsupervised. What if I screwed something up and then everyone had to eat nasty food? What if I cut myself and got blood on everything? What if I turned on the stove wrong and blew up the whole house? I looked down at the pile of steaming, plain noodles and the cold block of gelatinous pink ham and couldn't help but laugh. This was one of everyone's most hated meals—no flavor besides bland, no texture besides squishy; pasta, cheap and filling, with a few pieces of processed meat. There wasn't much I could do to make it worse, so I might as well try.

Walking over to the fridge, I paused a moment and looked around.

It was me alone in this giant kitchen, tasked with doing an adult's work all by myself. I reached forward, put a hand on the big white handle of the refrigerator, and pulled it open, revealing the forbidden world of food inside. I wasn't sure what I was looking for because everything I needed had already been set out, but the freedom went to my head. I wondered if there was a way to make the meal better, something we might even be able to enjoy. There was a part of me that wanted to prove to everyone I could be great at this, maybe even the best. And plus, shoving pieces of ham into my mouth when nobody was looking was definitely a secret perk of the job.

I closed the fridge and walked in the other direction. In the dark, cool room off the kitchen we used as a pantry, my eyes found the giant industrial-sized can of margarine, basically one step up from plastic. That would do nicely. With a wooden serving spoon, I scooped up a large chunk as I noticed a hanging bag of garlic heads. I swiped one on my way past, heedless of the consequences. As I made my way back to the counter, I briefly wondered how much trouble I'd get in for using ingredients that were not allotted for this meal, but it wasn't enough to stop me. I knew that we wouldn't have enough butter for next week's baked bread that Mom or someone else made from scratch every two days, or we'd have no garlic to salvage spaghetti sauce made from excess ketchup that had been donated by the ton to our mission. But somebody else could worry about that. I wouldn't be in charge of those meals.

Back in the kitchen, I turned to the big skillet. The flame leaped up when I turned the knob that released the gas and I had a brief image of my arm going up in flames as the fiery tongues gobbled up the air around it. A slight smell of burning hair tinged the air as I put the spoon of margarine in to melt and began to peel the garlic. I fried the noodles and ham in the margarine and garlic and found produce for a salad, inspired by how Michaela got away with not eating the really gross dinners by creating a giant salad. I grabbed at things until my arms were full—cucumbers, radishes, wilted lettuce that still had some crunchy inside layers, tomatoes that wouldn't last another day. A dressing made from limes from a tree outside and some olive oil from a big metal can, all donated from somewhere, topped it off. After about an hour, dinner was ready to be served, and right on time, too. I set the two giant dining room tables, one for each family, and then I rang the dinner bell that called everyone.

I watched Dad's face as he took a bite, not expecting anything different than any other meal, but his eyes shot up quickly.

"Who made dinner today?" he asked.

"Dani," Mom said, as if it were the most natural thing in the world. She had tiny newborn Samuel at her breast and looked exhausted from the birth that had happened only days earlier.

"Our Dani? This Dani?" he repeated, eyes on me. I knew what he was seeing. I looked even younger than my eleven years, having not hit puberty yet, a fact that was mortifying to me. I was short, with bushy hair Mom cropped before each new baby, probably in hopes it would simplify her life, but it only gave the unruly curls more personality. Based on appearances, I looked as likely to be eight, and I briefly wondered if Dad would get mad about little kids in the kitchen, about my time away from school. I worried he was thinking about the extra garlic and butter I obviously added to the meal, judging me for my wastefulness and lack of foresight.

But he smiled instead. "I don't know what you did differently, but this is really quite good. Watch out, before long you'll be on cooking ministry all the time."

And so I was. Auntie Hepzibah woke me at dawn to teach me how to make bread and cook eggs, and then trained me in every other meal. She showed me how to scrub aluminum pots to a shiny finish with steel wool pads.

I thought about my beautiful books in the schoolroom, untouched, while up to my elbows in suds from the dishes of twenty people. I thought about the "school every day" promise of the Charter, a promise not being delivered to me anymore—not once I'd been needed more as labor. Occasionally Jamie or Reyna or Mom would take over a dinner or two so that I could get my weekly schoolwork pages completed, but I'd have to cram all my learning for the week into a couple of hours. Most nights, after the bread was kneaded and set to rise overnight, after the dishes washed and dried, after my nightly dose of briefly skimming the words of our Prophet that someone in Mama Maria's commune had received in prophecy from the spirit world, and after writing my required "reaction"—something I could do by reading the headlines and regurgitating whatever I knew the adults would want to read—I would curl up in my bed and work on diagramming sentences, long division, or catch up on my social studies.

Like my mother, I had made the mistake of being too good. Maybe if I had failed miserably at that first meal, they never would have wanted me to cook again, and I would have been able to return to school. Maybe if Mom hadn't had all those babies like she was supposed to, we wouldn't have been kicked out of our home in Rio.

I reminded myself it could always be worse. I missed the longer school hours, the lesson plans with Mom, but I enjoyed cooking and was less hungry most days. Besides, it was better than helping with the children for hours on end, or the embarrassment of walking up and down the streets asking for money. It was certainly better than the world I used to live in, those giant communes with barely any school at all and books totally forbidden, under the watchful eye of so many adults, under the same roof as Uncle Jerry. Even with my hands red and raw from scrubbing pots, even having to wake up before dawn to bake the bread, life was so much better in Belo. I put my head down and did my work. I knew from experience that anything this good couldn't last.

11

APOCALYPSE NOW

■

Belo Horizonte, Brazil, 1999

Throughout the last year of the millennium, our level of persecution panic and preparations increased steadily, and it seemed even the Systemites were paying attention this time. They'd given this version of the Apocalypse the name Y2K, and it was coming because of man's reliance on computers and their lack of trust in God. After our last predicted Apocalypse of 1993 hadn't occurred, many had lost faith, or been "purged" from The Family. I wondered what would happen this time.

The adults were near euphoric, as though everything they'd sacrificed in their lives—all the creature comforts, money, careers, and family connections—was finally going to pay off. They would be vindicated and proved right. All I understood was that as soon as it became the year 2000, we weren't going to have electricity or clean water anymore. I lived each day worried about whether the ensuing mass confusion would be the beginning of the End Times, something that I'd secretly begun to hope would never happen, blasphemous since preparing for the End Times was the whole point of our religion.

I guessed Mama Maria had learned from Grandpa's past predictions, because she never flat-out said that Y2K would be the end of the world. Grandpa had a few prophecies not come true, lost a bunch of followers, and then had to explain all the reasons why and assure everyone he was still the voice of God. The ones who stayed, like my parents, doubled down on their beliefs. This potential Apocalypse worked the same way as all the other times, though. Something big was coming, and we needed to be ready. Everybody had to get right with God, rededicate themselves to his will, and spend additional hours every day reading his word and praying for guidance. We all needed to recommit, to become true believers, to deepen our faith and dedication. There were endless special ceremonies and loads of disaster preparation. In the end, we—God's chosen people—would be saved, while everyone else would spend an eternity in Hell.

I wanted the date to come and pass so we could move on to the next thing. One year to the next didn't make much of a difference to me. A lifetime of disappointment and growing doubts had reached their breaking point. At age thirteen, after getting excited and then disillusioned by the Charter and how much it would really change our lives, after two years of cooking and labor instead of focusing on school, I'd decided that I was basically done. I knew I probably wouldn't be able to leave The Family until I was eighteen since I didn't have any obvious relatives or connections on the outside, but, as The Family prepared for the coming Apocalypse, I started my own preparations. My plans to leave were the secret I kept in the deepest part of the box hidden in my mind. Until I could escape, nothing would matter much, even the supposed coming Apocalypse.

In addition to my solitary time in the kitchen, I spent more time on long walks, by myself. My one-on-one time with Mom disappeared as our walks expanded to group outings with the other teen girls through the neighborhoods surrounding our commune. As much as I missed our time alone together, I knew being with the teenagers gave Mom a kind of freedom that she'd never had before. I could see how much she enjoyed planning canned food drives, going to the free zoo, and taking us to ride bikes around a nearby lake. With us kids and teens, she was out of the presence of the watchful eyes of other Family adults for the first time in her life, just like we were.

On one such walk, my whole world changed.

We were on a group outing in December, the middle of summer in Brazil, and the flowers were out in full force, rain showers coming to water them at a moment's notice and then moving on, leaving blue sky and drenched earth. Getting caught in the rain was a pleasant-enough feeling in the intense heat of an equatorial summer, but eyeglasses and the rain will never be friends, so I fell behind the others while trying to wipe the drops from my lenses, squinting hard to avoid tripping over my feet. I had to run to catch up to Mom, who looked back with a casual air and said, "Well, at least your vision isn't as bad as your sister Claire's. She's had to wear Coke-bottle glasses practically since she was born."

But I didn't have a sister Claire.

For some reason, the expression "Coke-bottle glasses" slipped around and around in my brain. I had never heard the phrase before. How could Coke bottles possibly help anyone see? And what would Mom know about the most evil of sodas?

But my head felt like it was going to explode. "What sister Claire?" I whispered hoarsely, more of a demand than a question.

A look of surprise and confusion traveled across Mom's face, but she continued as natural as ever. "You know, Claire and Cherish and Jonathan and Deborah from all The Family music videos? Their dad is your dad, too."

My head felt light and funny the way it did with champagne, the way it did with the boys playing their games back in Rio, with the Uncles and their punishments, like I wasn't really in my body anymore. By this point, I had stopped walking, but Mom and the rest of the teen girls were still moving ahead. I was frozen in place as all the puzzle pieces fell into position inside my mind. *Claire.* My middle name. I thought of my baby photo album, full of pictures of me and my fifteen-year-old mom and our family tree. In the spot for "dad" was the teenage boy my mom had been married off to when she was sixteen. They were together for two years, and he was gone before I was five, before I could really remember much about him. Everyone said Merry looked like him, but I never thought to question why I didn't. I watched Mom walking ahead, chatting casually with the older teen girls around her, as if my life, my very knowledge of myself, wasn't being completely transformed.

My mind made connection after connection, and I tried to make my legs race as fast as my brain to catch up to the rest of the group, scared I'd be left behind on that dirt road and never figure out how to get back to the compound. When I caught up to them, out of breath, they were still laughing and talking. Nobody else was surprised by this revelation. Everyone knew, and everyone thought I knew—because it hadn't been a secret, it just wasn't talked about much. I was the only one who'd been left in the dark.

When the gates of the compound finally came into view, I felt a brief reprieve from the fear I always carried that I would be left on my own after dark. But as soon as we were inside, I bolted from the group, running to where I kept my book of photos, one of my few prized possessions that made every move with me. I frantically flipped through the pages until I found what I was looking for, and then I stared and stared.

That single photo of me at not quite two, in a pink dress with an old-fashioned lace collar and a head covered in baby curls snuggled next to Mom. She's wearing a nondescript tan shirt and a hippie style long skirt, and I can tell she's probably already pregnant with Merry. Sitting next to her, previously unexplained to me, is Uncle John, the olive-skinned, curly-haired, and bespectacled lieutenant in the Prophet's inner circle who had been sent away somewhere secret after I was born. He was at least twice—if not three times—her age. There was no reason that Mom would have been allowed to keep a picture of another adult, especially one so *selah,* if what she was saying wasn't true—that man, that fifty-year-old man, was my real father.

In almost every way but my skin color, I saw that I could be his mirror image. Everything made perfect sense: my unruly curly hair that none of Mom's other kids had, exactly the same hair two of our most famous video stars wore long and unencumbered on nearly every video we watched— my sisters. The extremely poor eyesight I had but Mom and Merry and the boys didn't. Why Merry and I looked so obviously different from each other, even though I'd always believed we shared the same parents.

This was why I looked nothing like Mom, because this man's- —*my father's*—strong features overpowered all her soft ones. A moment of relief washed through me that I'd never had a crush on Jonathan from the videos—my brother—with his movie-star looks, the way all the other preteen girls did. From the way the Aunties were sent from bed to bed, and based on how important Uncle John *still* was, I wondered how many other siblings I had in our world that I didn't know existed.

But as I stared at the picture, I understood what I had always known deep down but had never been able to articulate, something more significant than having my world turned upside down and the basis of my identity changed. As I studied his face over and over, seeing elements of myself so clearly reflected that I wondered how I'd never seen it before, I realized what was wrong.

She was so young.

And he was so *old*.

I'd never thought too much about having a young mother, other than the fact she was cooler than any of the other Aunties. I'd known she'd gotten pregnant with me at fourteen, which was younger than a lot of the girls, but not by too much. There were plenty of fifteen- and sixteen-year-old mothers in the Children of God. And, yes, I knew after my birth there had been a Mo Letter with Grandpa chiding older men to be more careful about getting the young teens pregnant—and from there the rules about sex with minors had gotten stricter, at least outwardly. But I realized then it had been *because* of my birth. I could picture Gramps, so young looking, with his quirky smile and that stupid I'M NOT 50 T-shirt. *Was my dad older than my grandfather?*

When the Charter came out and made sex with kids an excommunicable offense, the adults acknowledged it was wrong, though we'd still been warned to never go backward, never question what the Prophet had taught us at the time. I knew when Mom had gotten pregnant with me there hadn't been any rules, sexual contact between adults and minors had been considered God's will, and limitations we placed on it were only because of the outside world. So according to The Family, the adults in charge hadn't done anything wrong. Uncle

John having sex with a fourteen-year-old girl was allowed—so nobody questioned it. Despite the new rules, we still couldn't question what was done before.

But that was impossible. Uncle John had stayed in the senior leadership, protected. The old way and the Charter were opposites: they could not both be true. My thirteen-year-old mind reeled: The people in charge were, and always had been, full of shit.

The word rape was anathema to us. Our children's comics, like *Heaven's Girl,* taught us that it was impossible to be raped if we yielded, and we were always supposed to yield to sex, to any advance of a man. Smile. Be pretty. Show Jesus's love. If we chose to give our bodies to attackers as a sign of love, it was not rape. Neither was anything done in The Family *of Love*. Ever.

I realized then the truth I had always suspected. They were liars. They had always been liars. But even worse, they hurt kids. They hurt *us*. A series of thoughts repeated in my head over and over, lines of writing burned into my skull: *That was rape. That was wrong. Nobody should hurt young girls the way I've been hurt, the way Mom has been hurt. That should never have happened.*

I couldn't stop my head from spinning in circles, could not stop the thought I knew I would never be able to unthink:

I should not exist.

That night, I lay under my covers in the dark, the photo stashed under my pillow, with a bottle of bleach I'd pilfered from the laundry room tucked alongside my mattress. I imagined drinking it, dying a painful but hopefully quick death. This was the first time I seriously contemplated the actual logistics of suicide. I didn't know if I could make it to eighteen. Those five years felt impossible. I had been living this life for thirteen years, and I couldn't imagine doing it for one day more. Not one more lie, not one more betrayal, not one more abuse, or rape, or torture. I couldn't pretend anymore. I didn't believe in the Children of God. I didn't believe in God. I didn't believe in family. I didn't know if I even believed in myself, because in an instant, it was so easy to discover who I always thought I was had been a lie, along with everything else.

I watched the darkness fade outside the bars on the window as light threatened to dawn on yet another identical day. As the sun crested over the mountaintops, I tried to stuff everything I'd learned, everything I couldn't change, into the box within myself, but the box was too crowded. Or maybe I no longer had the key.

I remembered with relief that maybe, just maybe, the world was ending soon. It wouldn't matter anyway.

12

COMING TO AMERICA

◼

Belo Horizonte, Brazil, 2001

I couldn't believe it: We were going to America!

Of all the places to relocate, America seemed like the best possible outcome. I loved Belo Horizonte but, at nearly fourteen, I was eager to see more of the world. I had lived in eight different communes in six different countries by then, but all I could really remember were the walled compounds in Belo and the ones scattered around Rio. I was finally old enough to recognize the pattern. We moved every couple of years when someone didn't like something and *boom*! We could wind up on the other side of the world. In this case, Jesus had told Mom and Dad and the senior leaders they reported to that it was time. Of course, all the praying in the world wouldn't have changed that Auntie Hepzibah and Mom didn't get along—conveniently, Jesus agreed. Mom had arranged for us to go to a commune in Mexico, but when that fell through, we had no choice but to go to the States, where it was easier to find somewhere to land. It would be temporary, but it would be America. So we would fit whatever possessions we'd managed to scrape together into a small suitcase, leaving behind everything else. We knew we'd never see our friends again once we said goodbye.

This move was even more complicated than most. Right before Mom's twenty-ninth birthday, she discovered she was pregnant yet again, the seventh baby in fourteen years. We knew that ultrasounds were a trick of the Devil to make women get abortions, but because we were moving across the world, my parents decided that packing would be simpler if they knew the baby's gender. They only had to convince the other commune adults—always in favor of practicality when it was more convenient—to vote in agreement, which wasn't hard.

So Mom and Dad went to the hospital for what should have been a routine ultrasound. It wasn't.

Our baby had spina bifida, probably advanced, my parents told us when they got back. They explained it was a birth defect in which the spinal cord fails to develop properly, no longer a death sentence like it had been in the decades before when children would die during birth, or soon after, because of a gaping hole where the spinal cord should be. Our baby would probably live, but she might be paralyzed, brain damaged, incontinent, club-footed, and prone to other bad infections and illnesses.

I remember the placid look on my parents' faces, not horrified at all. This was all a part of God's plan, Dad reminded us. Trust and believe. Maybe this was God's way of introducing us to the medical establishment so we could witness to them. And oh, by the way, we're having a girl! Isn't that great? My head couldn't stop spinning—something was going to be very, very wrong with our new baby. How were we supposed to handle that? An image of clubbed feet stuck in my brain and wouldn't get out, like the "cripples" in old Bible movies we watched.

After the diagnosis, Mom saw a lot of Systemite doctors. The first one told her to get an abortion, and we were not surprised an evil Systemite doctor would want us to murder our baby. Another doctor told her about a new surgery she needed immediately. Doctors could prevent the condition from worsening and maybe even correct what was already damaged. The spinal cord might get the chance to heal and develop in utero. But the surgery only had a 50 percent survival rate for the baby. Choosing that surgery was almost like choosing an abortion. Jesus would never allow that, either.

Dad explained our faith was being tested. Did we really trust in Jesus and believe that he never made a mistake? This was clearly his plan, so why should we take it on ourselves to correct it? But I had read the diagnosis paperwork they sent home from the hospital, and some of the articles Mom downloaded from the internet, and had looked up the words in Auntie Hepzibah's dictionaries. Spina bifida was caused by a lack of folic acid—found in all prenatal vitamins, which I knew we didn't usually have. I concluded that my mother's body was too depleted to grow a healthy baby. I had been watching her deteriorate for years as she ballooned with each new baby, as each pregnancy got harder and harder, as she kept looking more tired, as she kept getting sicker and more nauseous, as she kept breastfeeding whenever she wasn't pregnant, as she miscarried once, and then again, late term. If I was so hungry all the time, never given enough food, how much more so was my mother, who was supposed to be eating enough to grow a life inside her? And that question led me to a bigger one: *How much damage had been caused to all of us by hunger—explained by science, explained by human neglect, and not by God?*

I decided I needed to do something special for Mom's birthday that week. She deserved it. I wanted to help her—help my baby sister—so the girls and I came up with a plan. Every day after lunch was quiet time: the two hours that had been so dangerous for me when I was younger had become my salvation as an adolescent. As soon as the adults retreated to their naps, which always lasted at least an hour, Michaela began taking care of the dishes while Merry and I snuck into Dad's office. We didn't need much money, only about ten reais. Merry was the pickpocket while I stood guard. The whole operation took less than five minutes before she appeared with the money and the key to the side door by the big wooden gate where Reyna and I waited. All we had to do was sneak out of the commune. It wasn't our first time.

We knew exactly what we wanted to get Mom—our favorite box of chocolate bonbons, a specialty in Brazil—and we could find them at the corner store a few minutes' walk down the small dirt path through the overgrown field by our home. We planned to tell her we had saved the centavos one coin at a time while fundraising, knowing she'd be too tired to ask many questions. What mattered was how happy she would be. What mattered was how happy I would make her.

We hadn't planned on the storm. The rain in Belo, always fast and ferocious, surprised us as the sky exploded, drenching every inch of our bodies. Even before the raindrops pelted us, Reyna said we needed to run. We had lost track of time and only had five minutes before Dad would expect us for Bible study. Michaela had been tasked with stalling him, but we didn't know how long that would last.

"Be careful with this mud puddle," Reyna said as she sprinted around it, Merry hopping nimbly behind her. But it was already too late. I felt my feet slip out from under me, then the jerk backward as I lost control and saw only blue sky overhead. Panic seared through me as I landed. Something was very wrong. For a moment, I flashed back to the day so many years earlier, that perfect family picnic turned into a horror when I cut my hand. In my body but somehow also above it, I looked down and saw a leg attached to me but twisted at a disturbing angle.

"My leg is broken," I said, strangely calm, the words like marshmallows in my mouth. My mind raced past the field to the house, to the study room, to the clock on the wall ticking away, to Mom's bonbons that would never be eaten, wet and muddy on the soggy ground.

"It's not broken," Reyna encouraged. "Come on, get up!"

But all at once the pain hit me. Not just from my leg but from everything else too. Everything was broken. I tried to do one nice thing for Mom who never got anything nice, and this is what happened. I screamed at the top of my lungs: "I FUCKING BROKE MY LEG!" A part of me retreated and watched, suspended, surprised at how easily that terrible and forbidden word came to my lips. Then it didn't stop. Every bad word I'd ever heard, in Portuguese and English, spewed from my lips.

Reyna went into Family adult mode. "Merry, run and get Dad. We need help." And then she picked me up, carrying me off the path and back to the main dirt road. She panted as she laid my slight thirteen-year-old frame in the middle of the road and sat beside me. Merry crested over the hill and Dad stumbled after her. His glasses were missing, and I'd find out later Merry had woken him from a dead sleep by ringing the giant gong at the front gate over and over again, a single minute before his alarm. Half-blind, he panted and wheezed with asthma as he knelt down next to me. But in that moment, my physical pain was eclipsed with a deeper concern: *He looks so angry*. He took one look at me, got up, and walked off without a word. By the time he came back a few minutes later with a car, his glasses and inhaler, and someone to drive us to the hospital, I was almost delirious from the pain.

Socialized medicine is free, but not easy. We sat in a waiting room for nearly four hours, me holding my shin in my hands, Dad pressing firmly on the break, which, unlike when I'd gashed my hand, hadn't broken skin. I swooned in and out of consciousness. When we finally got taken in for X-rays, I was ready for some anesthesia. But no such luck. Rough hands turned me this way and that to get good images while I screamed and screamed, not even words, pure pain. Then a doctor sat me on the edge of a table with my leg dangling free for a few more excruciating hours to let gravity pull the bones back to where they were supposed to be. A nurse wrapped plaster-soaked gauze from my toes to my hip, locking my leg into place. As we left the hospital, they mentioned it might not be enough, that it might need surgery and a pin. Like Mom's baby, we'd have to wait and see.

When I finally made it to a bed, I knew one thing—I'd never been in so much pain for so long. No one thought to ask for painkillers at the hospital, and nobody had any to give me. I lay there while everyone in the commune trekked through to visit, anointed me with olive oil, laid hands on me and prayed in tongues, and then the girls all signed my cast with colorful markers. Someone brought me a box of chocolates, the same kind we'd bought for Mom, which I assumed was still laying somewhere in the mud.

For three days, I couldn't leave my bed and used a bucket instead of the toilet. Sleepless and delusional, I passed the time clicking the bones of my shin back and forth across each other. I was in so much pain I couldn't pronounce words properly. By the third night, my toes were so swollen it was obvious we needed to return to the hospital. Doctors cut the cast, re-broke and reset my leg, and, as on discharge, told me not to move for at least a week while it healed. Once again, nobody mentioned anesthesia or painkillers. I kept screaming and cursing, but at least it was mostly in English so the doctors and nurses hopefully didn't know what I was saying.

It was mid-March and we were scheduled to leave for America three weeks later. Mom sat at my bedside, after she'd tried to use some crystals and something she'd read about in an online article about faith healing, or crystal healing, or energy work, I wasn't sure. She pushed her own worries aside as she listened to mine: *How could I travel internationally when I was like this? How was I supposed to help her if I couldn't help me? How . . . how . . . how?* Mom told me God would show us the way. He always took care of us.

I began to cry hard, in big sobs. The sleeplessness, the pain, and the trauma broke through any mental defenses I had, and unlocked the box where I kept all the hidden things that were too dangerous to think. The world was upside down and I was in the middle of it, a raw nerve exposed.

"I don't believe in God," I blurted in retort, the voice coming through me as if from somewhere else, without my permission.

I saw something flash behind Mom's eyes, but I couldn't place the emotion. She left the room abruptly and I grew woozy. Maybe if I were more conscious, I would have been more scared of whatever punishment was surely coming. For lying. For sneaking out. For the damning words that had escaped my lips. I knew I was crying. I knew my body was shaking from my sobs. But I was floating above it all, watching that miserable girl who looked like me, lying broken and alone on the bed. There was only room for one kind of pain.

Mom returned with a bottle of wine and two plastic cups. She filled one to the brim and poured a little into the other, then handed the full one to me. I screwed up my nose. I hated wine. She sat down on the bed next to me, careful not to disturb the pillow propping up my cast.

"I don't have any medicine to give you," she said. "And this won't take away all the pain, but it will help you sleep. I promise, baby girl."

She sipped slowly, while encouraging me to down not one, but two full glasses of the cheap red wine. It burned my throat, but my body warmed quickly and soon the fuzziness in my head began to feel less like despair and more like oblivion.

As I dreamed, I saw the visions of America I'd been given to work with, the land of white sugar and soda and toxic Systemite rock music. I imagined Amish kids riding through the streets on buggies and teenaged Mormon girls in their calf-length full skirts flitting around a beautiful school campus. I dreamed of log cabins with snow and acres of land, with giant families all living together, the way we'd seen in the old musical *Seven Brides for Seven Brothers*. I also saw the churches where Americans sat in ignorance, worshipping false ideas, unaware that God had already sent them his Prophet and, like the Jews of old, they had rejected him. I saw hopeless teenagers high on drugs and despair, searching for Christ but only finding minimum wage work at McDonald's and a life of constant struggle in the System.

Then I saw a surgeon, dressed in flawless white, surrounded by shining chrome. A surgeon in America could fix my leg, I'd heard a doctor tell my dad. Maybe in America they'd give me medicine or fix it the right way.

Maybe in America they'd do things right.

■

LANDING IN AMERICA was nothing like what I had pictured. After a long flight with a pregnant mother, five children under twelve, and a teenager with a cast up to her hip trying to fit onto a standard airplane seat, we were all exhausted and annoyed but also curious to see the evil country of our origin. The only one of us who remembered America was Dad, since Mom had left at the age of two and never returned. None of us kids had ever been to our home country before.

We stepped off the plane at LAX and the noise immediately assaulted my ears—America was so loud! The cities of Brazil weren't quiet either, but there was a warmth and friendliness there that seemed to soften the edges of the sounds, and I had been able to tune out a lot of the chatter because it was usually in Portuguese. But almost every conversation around me was in English and felt like they were going straight to my brain, all the voices bumping around at full volume inside my skull. Everyone around us seemed like they were in such a hurry. I didn't remember any of the other countries I'd been in being even close to this overwhelming. Not by a long shot.

As we moved through the terminal, someone pushing me in a thin, metal wheelchair with several bags on my lap, I caught glances of the world outside, bright and bold desert sun illuminating palm trees and large swaths of concrete. It was shocking to see English everywhere; I couldn't help but read every word of every sign and label I saw. I had only ever lived in countries where everyone else spoke a different language than us. English had only ever been *ours,* The Family's. It had never occurred to me how strange and isolating this was, to be separated from our neighbors, not only by our ten-foot-tall concrete walls, but by the very way we communicated. And here I was, in a place where I suddenly had so much in common with these strangers I had been taught my whole life to hate.

Grandpa had said America was rich, and that certainly looked true as we exited the terminal. Shiny new cars sped past, without peeling paint or rusted metal, and most still had their bumpers. Everyone I saw, even the kids, was dressed in stylish and impeccably clean clothes that fit them well.

I would eventually make my peace with the way English assaulted my ears, but it took much longer for me to get used to the huge houses, how anyone could walk right up to the door of a five-bedroom mansion and ring the bell. No giant gates, no concrete walls, no guys in camo standing outside the fanciest ones with automatic rifles. What did rich Americans do with their glass bottles if they didn't break them into jagged pieces and glue them to the tops of walls to stop thieves from climbing over?

The lack of walls, it turned out, would change everything in our lives. It was probably also one of the main reasons there weren't more Children of God communes in the US. The suburbs of America can't hide compounds filled with a hundred people, half of whom should have been in school, grown women walking around half-naked quoting "the word of God and Moses David," or Uncles doling out punishments.

We moved into a three-bedroom apartment in San Diego that we would share with another family. The new family had five sons still at home, so we were eighteen people total, crammed into a thousand square feet with an RV as overflow, and it felt even more crowded than my childhood days of sleeping in triple bunks. As a result, and out of necessity, we spent more time in public than I ever had in my life. I sat beside the swimming pool at the apartment complex, the sun on my face and leg cast while Merry played with the youngest of the teenage boys, Isaac and Angelo. I hiked about on crutches in the California mountains and explored the RV park next to our apartment building with our dusty and unsupervised group of teenagers. Despite living among the Systemites, we still weren't allowed fellowship with them, so there were a lot of Children of God gatherings with other households. We even had an organized youth group, with monthly picnics, ball games, and pool parties.

It was one of the first times in my life that I experienced adults planning something special for teens and children for the sole purpose of wanting us to enjoy ourselves—with hardly any religious programming involved. Because we had to hide that we weren't in school, they couldn't make us spend our days on the streets begging for change or passing out pamphlets about the Rapture and Apocalypse with half-naked angels on the front. From what they told us when we asked them if they wanted to ask Jesus into their hearts, Americans seemed like they were all Christians anyways, though I had been trained to expect they were sheep in wolves' clothing.

And there were boys. In Belo, there had been six teenage girls in the commune, but we hadn't lived with boys our age for years. Reyna, Jamie, and I had interacted with enough Systemite teens when we did our various missionary stuff to think *those* boys were both different from Uncles—and very intriguing. At almost seventeen, Reyna felt she was a little old to still be single, but moving into a house full of boys fixed that problem. She paired up happily with the oldest son pretty much the day we showed up. I had no such luck. Despite being in the land of the heathens, at fourteen I was still mostly undesirable, still the weird girl with frizzy hair, glasses, and a bonus giant leg cast.

Even without romance, even crowded into our tiny apartment, with the constant pain of my broken shin knitting itself slowly back together, the worry about Mom's pregnancy, and the general sensory overload and stress of yet another transition—especially with how much I missed the culture of Brazil—my life felt better in America. It was the closest thing I'd ever experienced to what I thought of as a "normal" life. I felt a knot loosen that I hadn't even known I'd been carrying inside me, even as I tried to remind myself not to get too comfortable and not to feel too safe. I knew it would only ever be temporary. And like everything in The Family, I had no idea how long this temporary would be.

13

BABYLON THE WHORE

■

San Diego, California, 2001

"Why are we watching a movie at eight in the morning?"

I didn't understand why that large building was on fire, why a reporter stood in front talking about an airplane flying into it. Mostly, I didn't understand why the television, live television, *Systemite* television, was on.

My friend Isaac, standing next to me in our living room, laughed and said, "This isn't a movie. An airplane just flew into the World Trade Center."

I didn't tell him I had no idea what a world trade center was, or where in the world it might be.

"How do you know that?" I asked.

"It's right there in front of you, on *the news*."

I'd heard of news before, usually in the context of it being fake or evil, but it took me a minute to connect the dots. Live news meant what was happening on television was happening in real life, in real time, in a real place, in a place called New York in this case—a city I'd heard of and seen in the classic movies we watched. All I knew about it was that it was another hotbed of evil, and one of the larger ones.

I looked at the screen in time to see another airplane flying low and straight behind the head of the reporter on-screen. Then, impact. Flames. The reporter, who I could tell had been trying to stay calm, was obviously shaken. "Oh my God," he cried. "Oh my *God*."

Is this it? I wondered. *Is this the beginning of the Apocalypse? Is it finally here? Will all our waiting and wondering and worrying finally be over?*

As we watched, people trickled in from all over the house, till our whole commune was there, transfixed, as the towers burned and black smoke filled the New York sky.

We had moved from the apartment complex where we landed to our new commune in San Diego, which was basically just a large four-bedroom house. Uncle Byron and Auntie Meekness had lied to the landlord, telling him they were just a family with five teenage sons, and then we all crammed into every corner possible. Reyna, Merry, and I, along with our four little brothers, shared a giant room over the garage with more space than the seven of us had ever had. I neither hated nor loved it; I knew better than to care about our living situations. Who knew how long they'd last, anyway?

Mom had given birth the month before to Grace. Grace was beautiful, with white-gold hair and bright blue eyes, alive and active, the way most of her body wasn't. Her spina bifida had been well advanced, along with the hydrocephalus, paralysis, and clubbed feet— God hadn't answered any of my prayers to heal her, it seemed.

Grace had a lot of surgeries, so I guessed we were cool with doctors and the medical establishment, though I hadn't seen Mom or Dad do a lot of witnessing. Before the C-section, the doctors asked her if they wanted her tubes tied, since she'd already had seven children. They told her that her uterus was so weak it could rupture if there were another pregnancy too soon, resulting in death. But like a good soldier, Mom shook her head, insisting she'd trust God to take care of her.

My parents also took me to a consultation with a surgeon, crossing the border into Tijuana to visit a free one a Family Uncle named Jose in Mexico had found. We said it was God's will providing, but I knew it was because we couldn't afford care in America.

When my cast came off, we learned there wasn't much to be done—it had healed the way it had healed. So I walked with a fierce limp the surgeon said would probably get better with time. My parents had also registered us for Medicaid and Social Security cards, desperate to get some kind of medical coverage before Grace was born—so all seven of us kids now had Social Security numbers, all in a row, maybe still a record. I wondered briefly if that meant we'd have to go to Systemite school, now that the Systemites were tracking us. Medicaid also bought me a new pair of glasses and asthma medication for Dad, and covered everything for Grace. We were settling into our version of life in America—and against all odds, it didn't seem bad or evil. Life was turning out to be pretty good, though I knew better than to ever say that out loud.

But, here it was, the judgment that God had promised Grandpa would be rained down on America—on Babylon the Whore. As much as my faith had waxed and waned over the years, I didn't need anyone to tell me what to think in this moment—this proved that our Prophet was right and had always been right. America was evil and it was being punished.

Then I saw the bodies dropping from the towers, as people made the impossible choice to plunge to their certain deaths rather than be burned alive or crushed by debris. I saw the people in the street covered in ash, tears streaking through the black soot on their faces, crying for the family and friends they could not find. For all the thrill we were taught to have about the Apocalypse arriving, all the fire and brimstone, laser tips we'd shoot from our fingers to kill the Antichrist's soldiers, and glory, I could see that real people were in pain, real people were dying. Not stories. Not ideas. Not faceless masses we were taught to hate or, at best, pity. Individual people. America the *country* deserved its punishment, but did *they*?

If this was the land of Sodom and Gomorrah, of everything that evil had come to represent in our world, why hadn't I met anyone evil in the previous five months? Everyone seemed so friendly, like they cared about their children, and they were so overwhelmingly Christian. There it was—the crack, the fissure in my belief system that I had felt so many times over the years and had willed myself to forget, impossible now—as I heard Auntie Meekness next to me, stunned, horrified, praying for the wounded and dead, and thanking God for his will being done, as we always did in prayer. How could we wish for people's death and pray for them at the same time?

The TV remained on for hours as we watched the towers fall, repeated over and over, united in that experience with the rest of the Americans we so reviled. Every crash, every flame shooting high, every attention-grabbing moment coming through the television prompted more praise and prayer from the adults crowded around. "Thank you, Jesus. Help us, Jesus. Thy will be done, oh Lord. Your fiery judgment is here, Lord, like Dad always warned us. Help us to walk in thy light, show us what to do."

Then the television caught our attention again and silence fell as we listened to the newscasters talk about religious extremism. The bad guys were Muslims. They were terrorists. We prayed and prayed. We praised the Lord. But all I could hear were those two words: *religious extremists*. We thanked Jesus for his judgment. We prayed some more. But something was happening in my brain, some kind of short circuit, and the prayers sounded like glass in my ears.

Religious extremists.

Around and around, the words rattled in my head.

Sometime after the second tower fell, we turned the TV off, and just like that, we returned to our normal day. Almost every afternoon, as soon as it was acceptable for children to be out of school and the Systemites wouldn't ask too many questions, we would go out singing. We'd drive around and find a nice neighborhood, then walk house to house, knocking on front doors offering to sing people a song, and then we'd apply high-pressure sales tactics to get them to buy a Family music CD from us. People were generally pretty nice, especially when we told them we were raising money for our Christian band. Of all the kinds of begging I'd had to do in my life, this was definitely the easiest and most successful. What we told them wasn't technically a lie, since we did get to keep about five or ten dollars a day to save up for new musical equipment, after sending our 20 percent tithe to the Family leadership, and the rest going to support our commune. That day, every door was opened by sobbing adults, bewildered children, or earnest teenagers who suddenly seemed to care about the world far more than usual. People stood together and hugged their families while Isaac strummed his guitar and Merry and I sang about love and a better world.

But when we moved in for the CD sale, the smiles immediately disappeared from their faces, replaced with white-hot anger. They yelled at us for trying to make a buck off their pain. America was suffering, they said. America, *our nation,* was under attack. Who the hell did we think we were?

I was confused. I didn't understand why they were so upset. Yeah, there was that thing that happened on TV, but it didn't happen to any of them. In the developing countries I'd grown up in, people died in large numbers all the time, and nobody in the world paid attention, not like this. But I hated the way these people looked at me, felt the stirrings of shame sloshing around in my stomach, so I told Isaac and Merry we should go around and sing without trying to sell anything. I liked the feeling I got when we performed then, the way people smiled and calmed while we sang, like we were helping them feel better. Usually we were so focused on making money, but maybe, for only one day, we could focus on helping. I knew we'd get in trouble, but we could handle the heat from the grown-ups when we got home.

It was the best day singing that I ever had—doing something to cheer people up, to help them cope with tragedy, without asking for anything in return. I wondered if this was what witnessing for the Lord was supposed to feel like all the time. The way people pulled us in and hugged us, I felt a true connection with perfect strangers, and I wondered why, if they were so evil, it was so comforting. I wondered why we always had to ask for money. It felt so much better when we didn't.

We ended up cutting the day short because it was also my brother Timmy's birthday and we were having a party. Ever since we'd been living in smaller communes, we'd gotten used to celebrating more individual birthdays, so different from the collective monthly sun-sign parties of before.

That evening, the TV was off and the house returned to the sound of eighteen humans negotiating over food in a kitchen built for a family of four. Mom had made a beautiful, marble cake and slathered it with homemade icing of whipped butter, sugar, and vanilla. When we bowed our heads to pray, I stood next to Merry, as Uncle Byron said, "Jesus, this has been an incredible day. We know that everything is done in your will, and according to your plan. We know you don't make mistakes, Jesus. All things work together for good to them that love the Lord. And we love you, Lord."

I cracked my eyes open, as I always did during prayers, and looked around the room. All I could think of were the bodies I'd seen falling from the sky that morning.

God's will? I thought of the apocalyptic predictions of the Book of Revelations, of the fire and brimstone always promised throughout the Bible. But how was there any possible scenario where mass death or horrible disaster was the will of a merciful God?

As we sang the birthday song in English, Spanish, and Portuguese, Timmy blew out his candles, and I found myself thinking of all the things I'd seen that day—God's fiery judgment on America; burning buildings and shrieking metal; firefighters rushing into that building, continuing to serve even as they saw that their buddies would never come back out, but doing it anyway because their help was needed. If anything felt like God's work, it was what *they* were doing. Not us.

I thought of the normal American families I'd seen that day, heartbroken by what was on the news, shaken to the core, their lives changed forever. And then I looked at our little celebration. Had we gotten it all wrong? What if we weren't God's chosen people? What if we didn't have all the right answers?

What if we were religious extremists, too?

■

MY ADOLESCENCE WAS full of vivid dreams, of towers falling, of escaping my life, and sometimes—in dreams that felt as though my rapidly changing body was betraying my mind—of boys. Sex had surrounded my life and overwhelmed my world since I was born, but it had only ever meant bad news to me. I used to spend hours wondering if I could make myself a lesbian so I would never have to deal with men ever again. But while bisexual activity was technically allowed for women in The Family—because it was enjoyable for the men—any suspicion of being exclusively gay could be big trouble. Still, I was surprised when, suddenly, in my young teenage years, I began to dream about tall, dark, and handsome boys. Like so many other unwanted encounters, I woke from those dreams feeling gross and unsettled, like something was terribly wrong. I tried to ignore what was happening in my body, but it was getting harder.

Shortly after we moved to San Diego, I experienced my first normal kiss. "Normal" meaning with someone my own age, not forced or coerced through power or threats. But I still didn't like it. It was wet and creepy and gross—not surprisingly, fourteen-year-old boys, also kissing for the first time, aren't terribly impressive. And something about the boy's desire, even at that age, felt threatening. Like something about it erased me.

David appeared at our commune a few months later, and he was very off-limits. He was one of Uncle Byron and Auntie Meekness's nine children, part of a set of twins who, at eighteen, were both backsliders from the Children of God. It had been easy for the twins to leave The Family because they'd already been living in the States, with Systemite grandparents less than an hour away. It struck me that this must be the reason Grandpa and Mama Maria had always hated it when their followers lived in the US—it was too easy to have access to the outside world, too easy to escape, to just walk away. The idea that you could leave the way David did secretly excited me. But the excitement didn't go very far—unlike him, all my grandparents were in The Family. My family was The Family; I had nobody on the outside.

David's blond hair was long, past his shoulders, shaved on both sides to create a mohawk effect when he pulled it back. He dressed in baggy clothes, worked at Subway—a sandwich shop, not an underground train station, I learned to my surprise—and spent his free time reading fantasy novels. I thought he was the coolest person I had ever met. In The Family, no one could ever look "too cool," but the rules didn't really apply to David since he technically wasn't in The Family anymore, plus things had changed a lot in the last few years, with far less supervision from higher-ups than before. America, as I learned more every day, had a way of changing everything.

Even though David had decided he was done conforming to our rules, Auntie Meekness still wanted to give her son a place to stay, and enough of us voted yes. So that was that—a backslider came to live with us.

Nobody yelled at him to cut his hair or wear clothes that fit him better. He kept his job, his Systemite music, and was allowed to keep his books, as long as he made sure they didn't "infect" the other young people in the home. He shared a room with his younger brothers but spent most of the rest of his time out or in the garage.

David tried to look cool and scowled to make everyone keep their distance, but I learned he was quiet, shy, and sweet. He'd let me, a goofy-looking kid, struggling to get her frizzy hair under control and desperate to be prettier, hang out with him. I would sit on the stoop of the garage and riddle him with questions about his job, about the world, and about his books. When he realized I loved to read, he began loaning me his fantasy novels after he finished them. I'd sit on my top bunk, a book of Mo Letters opened in my lap, and my newest prize from whatever series he was working through hidden behind it. I lapped up one after the other, never caring what topic it was, just how long it would last. Sometimes he'd give me or Merry or one of his younger brothers a couple dollars from tips he'd gotten that day, because he knew what a big deal tiny amounts of money were to kids like us. He became my friend, and began to be my escape, my benefactor, and the boy with the most beautiful hands in the world. I fell madly in love with him.

For many weeks, we just talked. I would sneak out of my bed after everyone was asleep and sit on the steps of the garage, which in my mind were still part of the house because they were connected to it. Some part of me believed that by staying on the steps I wasn't crossing a line by being in his space, not breaking the rules by being out there with him, even though we both knew there'd be hell to pay if we were caught. As I got to know him in those weeks, I learned even though he seemed to have it all together, he was still as confused and lost as I was, and I wondered if all of us children of the Children of God were destined for that future, regardless of whether we stayed or left.

One day, at about two in the morning, I tiptoed gingerly into the garage, and without even thinking about it too much, I scribbled out a note and handed it to David: "Do you want to have sex with me?"

We both looked surprised when his head snapped back up. Then he looked away, embarrassed. I don't remember the invitation being a conscious decision. It was just what we did in The Family. That's how we showed God's love. I knew I liked him, that I wanted to be close to him, and sex is what we did when we had those feelings, and often when we didn't. I didn't know if it was my love or God's love speaking, I just knew it seemed like the logical next step.

He sat a bit stunned, and didn't respond for what seemed like hours. As we sat there in silence, I wondered what took him so long to say yes. Was he thinking about what the Charter said about our age difference? Was he worried about me getting in trouble for sleeping with a Systemite? Did he think I wasn't pretty enough? People in The Family didn't say no to sex. But then again, he was no longer in The Family. Did being a backslider mean you could say no to sex?

Finally, he said, "Okay." I could tell he was nervous, which surprised me. Boys in The Family were usually so confident about sex, so entitled about taking whatever they wanted. It never occurred to me that it might have been David's first time; other boys usually lost their virginity far younger than eighteen.

We grabbed a blanket from the garage and headed out to a spot I loved, under a pine tree on the very edge of our property, overlooking a hill that looked down on the sparkling city lights of La Jolla. We spread the blanket out and sat next to each other for a long time, neither of us sure where to start or what to do. I lay my head on his shoulder, touching him for the first time, bridging the physical gap.

I started to panic. Thoughts raced through my mind as my heart pounded in my chest. I thought about making a run for it. *What have I done?* I thought. *I don't like sex. I don't want sex.*

But I loved David. I wanted him close to me. I wanted him to be a part of me; I wanted to hold on to him forever, unlike everything else in my world that was so transient. I didn't know what else there was to do.

On that hillside, on that night, I decided this time would be my "first time." Nothing that happened before existed anymore. There was only this boy, this blanket, these stars, this kiss, and these memories. All that other stuff wouldn't—couldn't—ever count. Not the men who'd forced me, the teenage boys who'd fondled me against my will, or the misguided misadventures I'd attempted with other boys in the past because it was what I was expected to do.

This time was different. It was my decision, led by me, with no pressure, no expectations. I was going to claim this as a good moment in my life. This was going to be the night I found my virginity and reclaimed it, the virginity that had never been valued, had never been considered sacred, and had never, ever been protected.

When I finally turned and kissed him, he kissed me back, gently and slowly, his hands in my hair and his eyes locked to mine. I felt a real connection. I felt the power of my decision spreading throughout my body. And I *stayed* in my body, fully present, not floating away like I had trained myself to do so many years ago. This was what it was supposed to feel like. This was what love felt like.

Afterward, looking out at those city lights, I felt warm and happy. It really had felt like the first time, like I had entered a whole new world I wanted to keep exploring with him. I decided I loved America and I knew that I always would. It was a place where I could stay forever, where I could be happy, where I could belong, where I could maybe one day be free. I was safe here—in this country, in this commune, in David's arms—and I never ever wanted to leave. We stayed there for a long time, watching the sun crest the hill with all its yellow and pink glory. I remember thinking that I'd never been truly happy before, not like this. I had only ever been trying to survive. I made up my mind then and there that I'd never let the feeling go, that I'd never let anyone take these gilded memories from me.

Then the moment was over, and we had to rush to get dressed and run back to the house. We hid the blanket in an unused suitcase in the garage, and I made it back in time to wash my face and hands, fix my hair and get my glasses on, and plop down in the living room with some overly diluted coffee, ready for morning devotions.

That was when my parents announced that, as we'd always known, our time in San Diego was never meant to be permanent, and they'd found a new place for us out in the field. It was time to be missionaries again. We needed to pack for our next commune, in Mexico.

14

NOT FIT FOR THE KINGDOM OF GOD

∎

Nuevo Leon, Mexico, 2002

"Well, fuck it!"

I wiped blood from my lower lip as I sat up on the flat roof of our commune in Mexico, then lit the cigarette I had purchased individually from the cantina around the corner during our last witnessing trip. I paid careful attention to the way the wind was blowing so I could avoid the smell seeping into the torn shirt and tattered red hand-me-down jeans I'd thrown on before I ran out of the house. Smoking was the most rebellious thing I could think to do, the biggest fuck you to everyone, and it felt somehow necessary for my survival, even though I still wasn't ready to get caught breaking such a big rule. But *I* would know I was doing it, and that's what mattered. Even though I knew it was bad for me, it was something I was choosing. And that stupid single cigarette would never hurt me as much as what had just happened.

I wondered only briefly if I should tell anyone, if I should let my parents know so maybe they would protect me in the future. But I already knew I wouldn't, like I never told about any of the other times. And like the other times, I knew it was my fault. I had told a lie so I could stay home and skip singing and performing and begging on the streets with the others. That sin had put me in his path, in an empty house, and this was my righteous punishment.

I was angry. I hadn't stopped being angry since the day they told me we were leaving the States. I was too mad to shed even a single tear as I sat on my garage step and said goodbye to David, even as I begged him to write, to promise not to forget me. I hated that just as I had finally found a life—love, friends, some semblance of an identity as an American kid—all of it got yanked away from me and I was forced back into the world of communes. Big walls, witnessing, hours of prayer, discipline, isolation. I thought about my death constantly, all the different ways it could happen; all the different ways I could make it happen.

I made up my mind that I hated Mexico and everything about it before I ever stepped foot into the country. Once there, I immediately launched my rebellion by refusing to speak Spanish anywhere the adults could hear me. I understood and picked up the differences from Portuguese easily, but I wouldn't use the language for any Family business. When nobody noticed or punished me, I found new ways to rebel. I made friends with outsiders, the neighborhood teens who I met when we took the younger kids to the park, careful never to let the adults overhear that I could speak passable Spanish. For a month, I made nothing but giant bowls of popcorn and salad for commune dinners I was still responsible for crafting. Merry and I continued regularly stealing money from the earnings we brought in from begging, too small to be noticed, but enough to buy things like candy and makeup, then cigarettes. We listened to Systemite music—Nirvana and Red Hot Chili Peppers, Alanis and Avril—hidden snugly in portable CD players underneath a disc of Family music.

Ever since San Diego, I'd developed a closer friendship with Merry, as we moved into the same age group of young teenage girls, and we continued that in Mexico, adding Tabitha and Mariana, the fifteen- and sixteen-year-old girls who lived in the home. We became an inseparable foursome, sharing all our clothes, makeup, and Systemite music in secret. The adults allowed us to go out on our own on smaller trips, to the grocery store or local gas station to sell posters, expecting our religious convictions would help us police each other because that strategy had worked for so many decades in The Family. But the exact opposite was true; our rebellions fueled one another's.

That day, I thought I had the perfect excuse not to go out with the others. It had barely been a year since my shin had snapped in half, and about six months since I'd started walking again. The adults had recently become even more afraid of being seen in public with kids who looked anything but healthy and happy, and so our "missionary" attitudes in public were controlled more than ever before. About a year earlier, some Children of God Uncles close to us in San Luis Potosi, Mexico, had been arrested for forcing their children to beg on the streets. They'd eventually been released, but it was a close call. We were still afraid of persecution, so any day I didn't feel like going out, I would play up the limp that I still had.

My legs were two different lengths, after all. The adults worried that they'd be suspected of beating their children and would happily let me stay home and run the kitchen, the job that had followed me all the way from Brazil. I didn't mind the performances we did in public—I'd been doing the singing and dancing all my life, and I liked seeing the joyful expressions it brought to people's faces, but I hated talking to them afterward, trying to sell pamphlets or CDs. Ever since the day the Twin Towers fell and we had that weird afternoon going door-to-door singing, the hustle of raising money filled me with dread, and I felt like I was doing something wrong, like we were tricking people and using God as an excuse. I hated Spanish, I hated Mexico, and I hated "witnessing" about Jesus and telling people we were missionaries. We weren't missionaries. We didn't do anything to help people. We just begged for money so we could send it back to The Family leadership, to my own grandfather who managed all the cash. They, in turn, kept us half-starved while they told us where to live and what to believe and with whom we could associate.

I stubbed out my cigarette with a long sigh. If anyone heard what was going on inside my head, I'd be in more trouble than for the smoking. They wouldn't care that I'd just been raped, only that I was doubting. I wondered how Dad would react if he knew I was sitting up there smoking and making plans to backslide. I wondered what he would do if he knew one of his "brothers" had raped me, that so many of his brothers had raped me. I'm not sure which one would have upset him more. Neither, I realized. He'd probably say: *There's Daniella, with all her drama, trying to get attention again.*

I touched my lip and flinched. It hurt. Everything hurt. But if there was one thing I knew about my body, it was its incredible ability to heal, to survive, to withstand anything. And if there was one thing I knew about myself, it was my ability to move on and not think about things I didn't want to think about. This wasn't new for me, but usually when the Uncles did sex stuff, they didn't get violent, though sometimes they threatened to hurt me, to keep me from telling. Mostly, they acted as if they didn't believe they were doing anything wrong.

But this time, I resisted. This time, I wasn't in the mood for putting up with the bullshit. Nobody had touched me sexually against my will since we'd left the mega-communes and Uncle Jerry, where everyone called themselves their brother's keeper, while they pretended they didn't know what the Uncles were doing. It had never occurred to me to resist back then. They told me it was God's love, and I believed them. What choice did I have? But as a teenager full of rage with nothing left to lose, I wasn't controlled by the fear anymore. Whatever punishment they could dole out could never be as bad as keeping things the way they were. I hated The Family. I hated "love." I hated God. I wanted out.

Let me be a Systemite and leave me the hell alone.

That day, as I'd lain facedown on my bed, sobbing into my pillow feeling sorry for myself and missing David and my American life, I felt that familiar touch on my shoulder, smelled that familiar smell of his somehow always-sweaty body. I went rigid. Quick mental math of commune members told me Uncle Jose and I were some of the only ones in the house, as Mom had packed all the young kids in the van to go to a park. Dad was probably in his office, headphones on and mind on his art, accustomed to ignoring the yells that emanated from a commune full of young children. We were alone. No one was going to come in and scare him off. I'd made a show of barely being able to walk that morning, so if I got up and dashed out of the room, I'd be in big trouble for lying and faking being sick. I was trapped.

Uncle Jose was the same "kind" Uncle who'd arranged for me to see a free surgeon in Tijuana to try to fix my leg when we'd first arrived in the US. He'd always run homes full of young teenage girls who were dedicated to the Spirit, known as a leader in Mexico. Later, he'd invited us specially to live with his family and "pioneer" a new commune in the Mexican state of Nuevo Leon.

Uncle Jose had started his advances slowly, like the Uncles always did, testing to see what they could get away with. Email was so common now that we were allowed to message Family friends from our parents' email addresses—still capable of being monitored—but Uncle Jose had the only computer available to us, which gave him power over us. On a normal day, I would be typing a message to David or my sister Reyna, or Michaela, or anyone I missed who helped me feel a connection to the old places. Uncle Jose would come in behind me. The computer faced the wall, and doors were never really closed, so I would never see or hear him until he was already touching me. He would start by rubbing my shoulders, in a way that always confused me. Was it the kind of sexual contact that was against the rules, or was it just a back rub? Was I overreacting? Did I have a right to feel so uncomfortable?

It started with back rubs, but eventually his hands would come around to the front, fondling my teenage breasts. By then, it felt too late to do anything other than finish my email and get up and leave quickly, as if the time to complain had already expired. As long as he stayed behind me, I didn't mind so much, as long as I didn't have to see his constant five-o'clock shadow, the huge droopy earlobes that seemed bigger than the entire rest of his face, and his sickly dog eyes. I could close my eyes, grit my teeth, and try to imagine it was David—someone who loved me. I tried to avoid his room, as did all the girls, especially his own daughter, Tabitha, but the pull of email eventually always won out. It was a connection to the outside world that I needed even more than I needed to be safe from Uncle Jose.

But I never thought he'd rape me. On the bed that day, I didn't know what to do when he moved from his regular touching down to my pants. Realization hit me: I knew what was going to happen, and I tried to turn over, tried to resist, but he pinned me down. Though I'd played up the pain in my leg, I hadn't been lying completely. It really did hurt, and he knew a single knee on the back of my left calf was all he'd need to effectively immobilize me. Somewhere in my mind, I was impressed that any adult had paid enough attention to me to notice that.

I tried to say no, but a strong, meaty hand pushed hard on the back of my neck, stealing my voice. I started to panic as my breath caught. He was going to suffocate me. He was going to kill me! *Just relax,* I told myself. Killing you is not what he wants. He wants you to be quiet so he can do what he came here to do. These men never last long.

When he flipped me over, knee carefully repositioned to pin my shin from the front, I knew it was going to happen. Instead of a kiss, he bit my lower lip, hard. *The sick bastard's marking me,* I thought as I tasted blood, and some part of me was almost grateful he made no pretense of romance. There was nothing left to do but go to the happy place, that place in my head I'd begun carving out when I was five or six years old, maybe even younger, the place where nobody could hurt me, because nobody could ever reach that part of my mind. It was the place where I kept my beautiful gold box and key. It was where I kept my memories of David and America and what real kisses felt like. Brazilian oceans, white sand, collecting seashells. Tropical fruit trees, birds of paradise, real friends. All the pieces of a happy life that I could imagine I had lived; the few memories that had never hurt me.

On the roof, as I tasted the remnants of the finished cigarette in my mouth, I imagined the smoke had cleansed me, curling its way through my body and neutralizing everything bad. I'd make sure that I was never alone near Uncle Jose again, I would scurry away from the room the same way I'd noticed his daughters did. I might have been confused when I was younger, but I now knew nobody could explain what had happened as love, as God's will, or appropriate for an Uncle. I briefly thought about how I was fifteen, the same age Mom had been, and I hoped I wouldn't end up pregnant. I touched my lips and looked at the red blood on my fingertips. I wondered how bad I looked, if I would bruise. He hadn't even been concerned about leaving visible marks on me, like he knew he was untouchable. I thought about what a respected leader he was, how he had run teen girl-heavy communes for years, gathering young girls from all over the world, in much the same way Grandpa had done with Mom. I remembered that he'd been the one to help with my leg, and I wondered if he'd been scouting me, even then. I wondered how many other girls he'd hurt like this.

It wouldn't be that hard to cover up the marks. Just a little bit of makeup, which the adults here were lax about. That afternoon, Tabitha and Mariana helped me—red lipstick for my split lip, a little cover-up for the fingerprint bruises that bloomed on the sides of my throat. They didn't ask any questions, and I didn't offer any explanations. At dinner, my parents told me how pretty I looked, and I smiled back. My smile never reached my eyes anymore. Nobody noticed anyway.

■

I WOULD BE turning sixteen in six months—a full adult in the eyes of The Family. To most of us teenagers, that meant two things: we could have sex and we could vote. Since the Charter, voting had become a big deal in our homes. We called a home vote to decide every aspect of our lives. At least with the ability to vote, I felt like I might have a say. And sex, well, we just wouldn't have to hide it from the world anymore.

To me, sixteen meant I could move to a different commune— away from my family. We had already left for a different commune in Leon some months before, away from Uncle Jose, but that wasn't good enough. I wanted to go back to America. I'd been begging my mom to let me move ever since I had turned fourteen, but she said I was too young. At sixteen, the prophecies said we were grown-ups, capable of making our own decisions, after hearing directly from the Lord of course. I knew I could find a commune in San Diego willing to take me back.

I also knew I needed to get away soon.

To prepare for adulthood, we spent a whole year with additional special readings and devotions, like our regular indoctrination on steroids. A boy at our new commune named Lucas would also be turning sixteen soon, and there was an entire year's worth of readings that we had to finish before we'd be qualified as voting members or be allowed to openly have sex with our peers under the age of twenty-one. Of course we were all having sex anyway—it was what we were raised to do—in mine and Lucas's case, with each other, and it would be nice to be able to do it without hiding or having to worry about being caught. I'd already been through what happened if we got caught breaking the rules—months of additional study, loss of weekly movie privileges, no fellowship with anyone my age or from other communes, plenty of additional duties, hard labor, and whatever else the adults in the home decided.

Then one day, Lucas's younger sister Faith came home from a visit to Uncle Jose's commune, only twenty minutes away. I thought I had put that whole experience behind me, determined that nobody would ever know—except for Mariana and Tabitha. They'd seen it in my eyes, like I'd seen it in Tabitha's, an unspoken understanding, the worst kind of sisterhood. But Faith told Lucas what Uncle Jose was up to at the commune in Leon, and Merry confirmed it had happened to her too, and then they'd come to me. I admitted he'd been known to give very uncomfortable massages but said I'd been confused as to his intentions, which was why I'd never spoken up. When Faith said he'd tried to forcibly kiss her, Lucas left the room in a huff, while Merry, Faith, and I began to discuss what we should do about it.

It was the first time I—or any of us—had ever talked about it, the first time I'd ever heard anyone else in The Family acknowledge out loud what I always assumed was happening to all of us, in the dark, during punishments, or anytime we were unlucky enough to find ourselves alone with one of the "creepy Uncles." We had a name for them, but we never, ever said what they did.

Then Lucas told the adults and investigations started—it was all against the Charter, after all—and this time, the adults had no choice but to respond. At first, I was angry and embarrassed. I wanted to put it all back again, back where it was a secret, back where we could pretend it didn't exist. But the girls banded together; we started sharing our stories of things we had all experienced at the hands of Uncle Jose, and other Uncles in our past. But I would never share the worst, and I suspected they didn't either. I would talk about the creepy touching but never how terrible the basement punishments really were. I didn't have the words. I never talked about that one day with Uncle Jose. I wondered what Mariana and Tabitha would say, whether they could come forward with what Tabitha's own father had done to them.

I didn't have to wonder for long. Tabitha called us all liars, claiming we were doing it for attention, like I had worried Dad would have said. Mariana stood by her. It hurt to lose them as friends, but it destroyed me to know they would lie for him.

Even so, our formal accusations forced the leadership to do something. Uncle Jose had acted outside the laws of the group, and been caught, and they had to act. For a few months, there was a constant stream of Family leadership visitors to our commune, and we were questioned at length, individually and together. Who did what, what had gone wrong, and, I suspected, how to control the damage. I answered the questions, telling the stories like Uncle Jose's back massages were the first and only thing that had ever happened to me. If only they knew half of what really happened, year after year, man after man, starting when I was little. I was so angry that this time someone had gotten past me to my little sister too, angry that the adults were pretending to care, but only because it had been made public, angry that they acted like they hadn't known what was going on the whole time—how we were being hurt our whole, broken lives. How was I the only one who saw it? There was no "where it all went wrong" or "where it started" like they kept saying they were trying to figure out. There were no such things as "bad apples," just a rotten tree they'd all come from in the first place, grown from Grandpa's toxic soil that had poisoned us all.

In the end, Uncle Jose and his whole family were excommunicated from the Children of God for his sexual misconduct with minors— one of the crimes that had been defined in the Charter. Mariana had to go live in another commune. Things with Lucas were never the same after that, confirming what I had feared—I was tainted and disgusting, and it was somehow my fault. The leadership washed their hands of the issue. Their solution was getting rid of Uncle Jose, and they had no desire to dig any deeper, to question why a predator had become such a respected leader. Their image, and their image of The Family, had been preserved.

Nobody ever asked me if I was okay.

I wasn't.

WHEN WE MOVED to our third commune in Mexico in less than a year, in Guadalajara this time, I was not only angry enough to burn it all down, I was ready. After fifteen years of being forced to worship a Prophet I never believed in, sacrifice for a God I didn't love, and live a life in a religious prison camp, where they controlled my every thought and movement, I was drowning. It didn't matter how much I loved and didn't want to disappoint my parents. If I didn't come up for breath soon, I wouldn't survive. But how could I tell the people I loved that I was rejecting their world, and everything they believed in, forever? That I was prepared to never see them again because I didn't have faith? That I was willing to go to Hell to escape them? That I was choosing me over them? I couldn't do it.

I met Noé, a tall and handsome seventeen-year-old Mexican boy who'd lived in Arizona for years and understood my English just fine. He and his twin brother, Carlos, worked at the restaurant on the corner of our street and lived across the park. I'd learned to somewhat tame my hair and wash it with lemon juice so the sun would bring out the blond highlights that had faded to brown with puberty. I only wore my glasses for reading and my body was starting to take shape—slim, tall enough, and with a few curves in the right places. I guessed I might even grow up to be pretty. When Noé noticed me first, I felt flattered. He started to come and see me every day at the park, often bringing me leftover food from his restaurant—the perfect way to my perpetually hungry heart. I still loved David and thought about him every day, but it felt nice to be pursued.

Merry and I had been given the maid's room to sleep in at this newest commune, which turned out to be the best thing that had ever happened to us. We were far away from everyone else, upstairs and outside the actual house, on the patio near the laundry lines. Our new commune friends, Melody and Vanessa, would come up and we'd talk openly about backsliding and what we wanted to do with our lives when we finally got away. We wanted freedom, and, in the hours we spent chatting in that room, we told stories of what we'd do when we could think for ourselves and have outside friends. We watched vampire movies secretly rented with money we stole from the earnings we were supposed to give back to The Family, but since we were the ones earning it, we rationalized that we had the right. We practiced Systemite makeup techniques, read forbidden books, and snuck onto the roof of our maid's quarters to smoke cigarettes. When nobody was looking, I would hold the lit cigarette to my skin, marking myself. At least it felt like something.

When Noé asked me out on a date, it was hard to explain to him why I couldn't go. More than anything, I wanted to be a normal teen, not this weird Family member. But, of course, I was a White, blond girl living in a single house with twenty other White, blond people in the middle of Mexico, so it must have been obvious that we were the furthest thing from normal. Instead of pushing, he came to our house for Bible classes. We'd spend the whole two hours staring at each other and passing notes right under Dad's nose, his in Spanish, mine in English. I was falling for him hard and it was so deliciously rebellious—he was a Systemite, an outsider, so I knew it would never be okay. But maybe if I was with him, I wouldn't need The Family. Maybe, just maybe, he was my way out.

Late one night, when the house was finally free of the noise of twenty people moving about, I lay in my bed, fully dressed under the covers, my hair and makeup prepped by Merry and Melody, trying to will myself to be brave. *I want to do it,* I kept saying to myself. *I want to sneak out. I want to meet with him.* I went over the route in my mind, picturing the obstacles and how I would surmount them—climb the window grate, vault onto the roof, cross over four houses, climb down the side of the restaurant, and run across the park to the far side where he would meet me. His parents were away and he had freedom, friends, and alcohol. I took a deep breath, threw the covers back, and silently crept out.

I returned just before 4 A.M., pushing any negative feelings out of my mind. I'd done it, I'd broken the big rule of the Charter and there was no going back now—I was basically a Systemite. Sleeping with a Systemite, someone who'd never been in The Family—and who had probably never even read the whole Bible—felt so much more dangerous than sleeping with David who, even though he was a backslider, I could still argue had come from The Family. But I didn't need those paltry half excuses anymore. I soared high on my newfound sense of freedom, the power of sex as my choice, and the amazing feeling of being wanted by someone. All day I felt like I was floating on air, two hours of sleep notwithstanding, and I knew I'd go again that very night. I knew it wasn't love. My mind kept flitting back to David, and something would tear in my chest. Maybe I was using Noé, just a little. But he was something different in a world of monotony, and someone who was solely mine.

Four days later, I woke with a start, sunlight streaming in the windows of a room I didn't recognize in daylight. I flung Noé's arm off me, noticing how beautiful his long, dark hair looked on his sleeping face while I struggled to get dressed.

"Wake up, we fell asleep," I said. "I'm so screwed! Acorda, Noé."

He rubbed his eyes, looking at me with confusion. Then his eyes widened and he leapt out of bed and began to dress with the urgency of someone who knew it was bad. Being caught in bed with the fifteen-year-old missionary kid wouldn't be good for him either.

But I knew it was too late. Mom would have come to wake us for devotions at dawn and found my bed empty. I drew one finger down Noé's cheek, and he paused with one pant-leg on, looking up at me. "Yo tengo que ir," I said. "Te marque despues." *I have to go. I'll call you later.* And then I rushed from the room, knowing that I'd never see him again.

Just before I reached his front gate, the doorbell rang. Merry and Melody stood wide-eyed on the curb.

"They know you're gone," Merry said, out of breath. "Everyone is looking for you!"

"What are you going to say?" Melody asked.

I didn't know, and I wouldn't have much time to decide. But on the short walk back to our house, I resolved that *this* was going to be my ticket out.

In the past, when I'd gotten in trouble for smaller rebellions, my parents had been understanding, even kind, while they punished me. I'd never been able to go through with telling them how I really felt about The Family, though I had countless opportunities. I was always too afraid of breaking their hearts. But now I didn't care—I wanted them angry. I wanted everyone to be as angry as I was. The rage grew as we got closer to the house, as a montage of injustices scrolled through my mind.

I opened the front door and stormed up to my room on the roof— past my blustering father and sobbing mother, past Uncle Phineas and Auntie Joy, the heads of our commune, who stood, mouths agape, sanctimoniously horrified, probably thanking Jesus it wasn't one of their kids. I slammed the door to my room and locked it, and it didn't take long for Dad to start pounding. It struck me as suddenly hilarious that the adults had forgotten to remove the lock when we moved in. We weren't entitled to privacy; they were supposed to always have access to us. We could never be alone, not really.

But I had enough of that rule. And every single other one. I was done.

Suddenly all my doubts were gone. I *wanted* this. I wanted to be free so badly I could taste it. And though she'd never been strong enough to get herself away, I imagine that looking at her daughter that day, imagining me at sixteen, just a year from now, bringing home a baby rather than a prom date, Mom wanted that for me too.

Finally, taking a deep breath, I opened the door. Dad's face was bright red, his breathing heavy with asthma and anger. He called me a slut. He asked me if I'd used a condom with "that Systemite," though we'd always been taught birth control was evil. He even had the audacity to ask me if I'd been a virgin before that night. I winced at the slur, but rolled my eyes hard at the ridiculousness of his questions, at his willful obliviousness.

Then, before I could lose my nerve, I yelled the words that had been building in me for nine years: "I want to leave The Family!"

Part II

THE SYSTEM

15

DAZED AND CONFUSED

◾

Houston, Texas, 2003

"We can't enroll you. You don't exist."

The Lamar High School secretary clicked her pen. "I'm sorry," she said, sliding my US passport and Social Security card across the reception desk.

I peered at the flimsy pieces of paper, as if they could jump out of my hands and save me, as if they were still the tickets to freedom I had foolishly imagined them to be. In my mind, I heard the laughter of the Aunties ridiculing me for all my reading, for turning my back on God to selfishly pursue my own education, for daring to think that learning mattered. Of course there was no place for me in the System.

I didn't exist.

I had stepped onto US soil a week earlier from a Greyhound bus, the last in a long series of buses starting from the compound in Mexico and ending in Houston on one of the typical mid-March days when the sun felt like a slap in the face. As with every move, everything I owned fit into a small, battered suitcase. Unlike the bag's original owner—most likely some first-generation hippie who'd left their family to follow God's earthly disciples into the Children of God thirty years before—I'd packed its contents to escape them.

As I watched Dad carry the suitcase to the beat-up elevator in the run-down apartment building, with Mom following behind him, I felt the familiar nausea. The question I'd been worrying about for weeks popped into my mind again: *Have I just made the biggest mistake of my life?* Forsaking everything I'd known—home, family, friends, and the security of being a part of a community—regardless of how dysfunctional? I didn't care about losing the privilege of being a soldier in God's End-Time Army, but I did wonder if they might be right about Hell. I wondered if freedom was really worth all this uncertainty and the *what-ifs*.

Then Heaven bounced off the couch and embraced me in a warm hug, with a friendliness that made me feel like we were more than stepsisters who'd only met a handful of times. Her red-brown hair swung around her shoulders, the dye and stylish cut announcing her as a real Systemite. Her clothes clung to her curves, clearly bought specifically for her, not just another bunch of hand-me-downs like I wore. She was ten years older than me, and looked a bit like her half sister, Reyna, and a lot like Dad. I felt so lucky that she'd agreed to Dad's request to take me after I'd been excommunicated.

"Welcome home!" she said. "I'm so excited to have a sister to live with. It's lonely out here in the real world." She cast an eyes-averted glance at her father, then stood up straight, pressed an automatic kiss to his cheek, and took the suitcase from him. With over a decade since the leadership had split up their family to "humble" them, they were practically strangers, but she still knew how to act the soldier. I recognized the same Children of God skill required of all us girls: the ability to plaster a smile on her face and talk to Uncles like they were the only important people on earth.

"It's not fancy," she said, gesturing at the one-bedroom apartment. Mismatched mirrors covered the kitchen and dining room walls in an attempt to make the space feel larger than it was. "But it's all ours!" she added with genuine glee. Like me, she had grown up without anything to call her own. But, at twenty-five, she had her own bathroom that she didn't have to share with a whole commune; her own kitchen with a fridge she could open without having to ask for permission. Even though there was little space to walk in the tiny bedroom, there were only two mattresses on the floor instead of the dozens we'd both been used to in the bunkhouses of our youth.

Heaven caught my eye for a moment, both of us trained in speaking without words, raised in a world where we would be punished for saying the wrong thing. She spoke in the silent code Children of God girls used my whole life: *You've made the right choice,* her eyes said. *This won't be easy, but you can do it.*

Mom and Dad didn't stay long, just a few days to drop me off, and to remind themselves of the evils of America. I didn't know what I was supposed to feel when they left. I had been raised to not get too attached to anyone. We always knew we could be separated at any time if the leadership demanded. Saying goodbye so young seemed almost natural—I always knew that I would have moved after my sixteenth birthday, sent to another commune as a full-fledged adult, ready for marriage, children, and sex with whomever "requested" it.

Instead of "I love you" or "See you later" or whatever it is that grown children say to their parents upon moving out, I asked, "Mom, do you think I could have twenty dollars, to tide me over until I can find a job?"

As the words left my mouth, I immediately regretted them, seeing the look of panicked disappointment on Mom's face. "I'm so sorry, honey," she said. "We barely have enough to make it home."

With no sympathetic little child to panhandle on the street for emergency cash, they needed the money more than I did to survive their commute back to the commune. I wanted to hug her and feel her cool hand on my clammy forehead, like how she sat with me after I fell down the hill when I was five, the bones of my hand punctured through my skin, or on the day I'd snapped my shin. Instead, my eyes stayed glued to the pavement. I could feel hers reading me, tears behind the stoic sadness she carried, barely thirty years old and already saying goodbye to the oldest of her seven children. I wondered if she had ever imagined a different life for herself, or for me. I wondered if there was any part of her that was proud of me.

"It's okay," I said, forcing a smile. I knew how to survive without money. I'd been doing it my whole life.

We stood next to each other for a moment, waiting for the bus, my mind returning to the word "home," how it fell from her lips, frozen in midair. I wanted it to hold power over me. I wanted to see a slideshow in my mind: images of my family and The Family flashing over me, the letters superimposed on the buildings where I'd been, like something out of the videos I'd been exploited to act in all my life. But where memories should have been, there was darkness. Where feelings should have been, I was just numb.

A small part of me felt guilty for the relief that rushed through me the moment the bus doors closed behind my parents. I would finally go to a real school. I would get a job and make my own money. I would read whatever books I wanted. There would be no Aunties around to tell me what to do or what to think, to punish me when I inevitably failed. There would be no Uncles to trap and terrorize me. Heaven had already set me up with my first email account, and I was the only person on earth who knew the password: *withoutrules*.

I was done with the Children of God.

I LEARNED QUICKLY that in the System, like in The Family, things are more likely to get done when big men with loud voices want them done. Heaven's boyfriend, Dougie, was a Texan who had been to both high school *and* college, and he knew how to "navigate the system," whatever that meant. As I sat next to him and Heaven in the school administration office, I didn't know what to think. Why was he helping me? What did he want? He seemed like an Uncle—older, confident, with a kind of natural authority that Heaven fell right into. But he didn't hurt her. Or me.

"She can't go here," the secretary said. "Buuuuut, I'm going to need y'all to bring proof that she's enrolled *somewhere* within the next five days, or I will have to send the police to your address to see what's going on."

As I tried to understand how I could be punished for needing help in the "Land of Opportunity," Dougie wouldn't take no for an answer. "Look, this girl is an *American* citizen. That's supposed to mean something," he said, his Texas drawl full of the entitlement he'd always known. "I'm sure a fifteen-year-old *child* is allowed to go to school in *America*. I'm going to need y'all to get me someone in charge."

■

THE SAME DAY I said goodbye to my parents, I walked the fifteen minutes to the nearest shopping mall and began applying for jobs. Most of the shops enforced sixteen as the minimum hiring age, but I couldn't afford to wait the two and a half months until my birthday. I needed something, anything. I filled out applications at almost all the restaurants in the food court, many of which I had never heard of, screwing up a couple of on-the-spot interviews because I had no idea what they were selling. I marveled at how many ways people could fill their stomachs with unhealthy food, and I wondered how the Aunties would talk if they saw me.

But I stopped that thought before it had a chance to get too far. The twisting in my guts was a signal to my brain that following that particular line of thinking would only bring pain.

The only place I refused to apply was McDonald's. I couldn't stop hearing Auntie Lydia or Uncle Jebediah repeating in a holier-than-thou voice, "If you forsake God and backslide, you'll never amount to anything more than a homeless drug addict, flipping burgers at McDonald's for the rest of your life." I felt the eyes of ten thousand people watching and waiting for me to fail, praying for God to judge me, hoping I'd crash and burn and come crawling back with my tail between my legs, begging God, and them, for forgiveness. I lifted my chin and walked past that big yellow "M" and got hired at the Chick-fil-A next door.

Six dollars an hour felt like a fortune. I cut chicken strips into small samples, laid nuggets onto a tray, pressed toothpicks into the white flesh, and stood in the mall, a plastic smile on my face, offering the tray to passersby, my manager constantly nagging me to smile. People walked by me saying "no thank you" and "I'm good" or, most often, they pretended I didn't exist, and I was vaguely reminded of my years as the cute little yellow-haired girl panhandling on street corners around the world.

When I got my first paycheck after only a week, I was on top of the world. Ninety-six dollars was more money than I'd ever seen in my life. Standing right there in that back room, I closed my eyes and exhaled the deep breath it felt like I'd been holding for years.

I could survive. I could support myself. I'd never have to starve again.

■

DOUGIE EVENTUALLY GOT me into school and hadn't asked me for anything in return. After several visits to the Houston School District's headquarters, he negotiated a real solution—I could enter and, instead of beginning as a nearly sixteen-year-old freshman, a state fund would cover the eight thousand dollars' worth of placement tests, which, if I could pass, would catch me up with my proper cohort.

Sitting for the makeup tests—as I tried to pass two years of classes I'd never attended—started joyfully. I finally felt like a real student. I loved the wood of the number two pencil resting against my fingers, the slightly oatmeal-like smell of the test booklets never opened nor creased before me, the newness of education being in my reach for the very first time. But testing grew tedious with the ninth and tenth and twenty-second exam placed in front of me, full of math, literature, and science concepts I had never seen. I called heavily upon my ability to write "reactions" to religious texts, giving the Aunties what they wanted to hear—in other words, my ability to bullshit—and I passed almost all of them.

But even math wasn't as hard as the real test: when I sat in front of a Systemite doctor, a clone of the ones who had hurt me before, his hands full of needles, injecting one after the other into my arm, a full course of sixteen vaccinations, the scars I'd carry as proof that I could never return to where I came from. I was forever marked, my body full of Systemite poison.

On my first official day of school, as I walked to Heaven's beat-up red car, the heat of the April morning had already descended, and I knew the humidity would only cause my hair to gradually grow more poofy, but I had more important things to think about. I'd been picturing the moment my whole life—my first day of real school, where I would learn things the Aunties couldn't and wouldn't teach me, where I'd make friends besides the kids I lived with in the commune. My first day of being a normal kid. A real kid. The day I'd start existing.

I checked myself in the car mirror. My eyes were hidden behind cheap glasses with an old prescription, but I looked pretty good in Heaven's jeans, a cute cream-colored top with colorful Native American–inspired beadwork, and sky-high heels. I had spent that first Chick-fil-A paycheck on some new clothes, the first time I could remember owning anything with a tag still on it.

"That's the bus stop across the street," Heaven said. "After today, the city bus will get you there and back."

I hadn't seen much of Heaven since I arrived. She worked nights tending bar and spent most of her off-hours crashing at Dougie's place across town. We didn't have many of the late-night heart-to-heart conversations I had imagined, sisters bonding over the shared horrors of our childhoods. Without ever really discussing it, it seemed we were both trying to shut the door on that part of our lives—and hopefully never have to look back. Even though she wasn't around, she paid the rent, the place was safe, and, when we kept up on the housework, clean enough.

As we pulled up to the parent drop-off area, she leaned over and hugged me. "Don't worry, you've got this. You're living the dream!" she said, and we laughed together.

I had barely closed the car door before she revved the engine and zoomed away. Heaven may have become my legal guardian, but I'd have to figure out life mostly on my own. She'd never made it to high school herself and my dreams of high school, college, maybe even law school, were too different from the life she created for herself out of the ashes from where we came.

Lamar High looked more like a prison than what I imagined a high school would look like, complete with a guard standing near the closed and barred doors. As I walked up, I noticed all the groups of teenagers hanging around out front, hundreds and hundreds of them. As their eyes bored into me, I wondered which group I'd belong to. I could taste my breath in my mouth, toothpasted but slightly sour, and I remembered the stories of Comstock, the high school Grandpa had attended, with all its horrible bullies, evil teachers, and school officials who took pleasure in making students suffer. Stories like these had taught me from birth to fear mainstream education, but the fear was never as strong as my yearning for it.

The officer moved toward me as I approached. Panic stabbed my heart. Did he know that I didn't belong? Would he arrest me?

"Excuse me, Miss," he said, with a friendly but firm voice. His badge said OFFICER COOLEY. "Do you have an appointment inside?"

Uh oh. Appointment? "No, I, uh, I go here now," I mumbled. "It's my first day."

I was certain I had done something wrong and deserved to be punished.

But Officer Cooley smiled broadly. "All right, well, no students in the building until the bell rings at 8:02, then you'll have seven minutes to get to class before the next bell. Do you know where you're going?"

I fumbled with the zipper of the new-to-me JanSport backpack I had picked up at Goodwill. My years of training on what to do with authorities kicked in and, without making eye contact, I silently handed him my crumpled paper.

"Okay, so this is like every other schedule," he said, as if I hadn't spent hours trying to decipher it. "These numbers tell you what building and classroom you're in and this is your locker number. You have your lock?"

I shook my head, slowly. I didn't know what a locker was, either.

He sighed, exasperated, and said, "Okay, kid, hang out here and follow me when the bell rings."

I stood near the front door of the school, feeling simultaneously invisible and like everyone was staring at me. I kept my head down but managed to sneak some looks at the other kids milling around outside. Some looked like little kids and some looked like grown adults. There were Black kids, White kids, Mexican kids speaking Spanish I could understand, groups speaking languages I couldn't, and many, many others. They walked around in pods, talking and laughing. Boyfriends and girlfriends holding hands, even kissing. Everyone dressed in different styles—their *own* styles, in clothes they chose—and everyone seemed to have a cell phone, an extravagance I could not comprehend. Did their parents really pay for that? Were they all rich? Did any of them have to work a job so they could eat?

An earsplitting ring shattered the air, and, instantly, bodies started moving toward the front door as Officer Cooley unlocked it. Four thousand students swarmed into the hallways, heading directly for the metal gray-green boxes stacked one atop the other that book-ended each corridor. I ran to keep up with Officer Cooley, wobbling on my heels. I glanced at my secondhand watch as we hustled, only three minutes until my first class. We rounded a corner, climbed more stairs than I thought possible, and located my locker. It was exactly like I'd learned: Systemite schools were designed like labyrinths to deliberately confuse and trap students, with rules designed to set kids up for failure.

"This one is yours," he said. "But I wouldn't leave anything in here without a lock."

I looked at the lockers surrounding mine, all secured with complicated-looking dials on the front. I couldn't figure out what people were storing in them; wouldn't they need their pencils for class?

"Where are your books, anyways?"

"Books?" My voice shook. How many things could I get wrong? Why hadn't anyone told me what I would need?

"Okay, look." He sighed. "Go down this hall, take a left in the center courtyard, by the library building."

I had heard about libraries but hadn't realized they could be whole buildings. As scared and frazzled as I was, my heart jumped at the thought—an entire building full of books!

"Give them your schedule and then get your butt to your home-room in building—" He stopped abruptly, then looked me up and down. "Why are you in the ESL homeroom?"

I was in trouble. I stood straighter. "ESL, Sir?" I willed away the tears pooling at the corner of my eyes. I couldn't let him see any weakness. That's when people know they can take advantage of you.

"English as a Second Language. Your English seems fine to me."

"I just moved here from Mexico . . ."

"Oh. Maybe next semester they'll fix that. I don't think you need to be in there with all them Mexicans." He smiled again as he put the schedule back in my hands and walked away, calling over his shoulder, "Good luck here. Enjoy Lamar."

Without thinking, I rolled my eyes at his back, and then automatically looked around to see if anyone had seen me. As much as I had been taught to fear authority, I couldn't help myself sometimes, which I guess is part of why I ended up there in the first place. *I'd be perfectly happy with "them Mexicans,"* I thought. At least something would be familiar. I squared my shoulders and set off to find my textbooks.

By the time I stuffed half the stack of books into my backpack while attempting to balance the rest in my arms, I had a perfectly clear understanding of why lockers existed. I finally found the door to my homeroom when the bell sounded again. All at once, every door opened and four thousand students flooded into the hallway. I stayed frozen where I stood, gripping my paper schedule like it could protect me somehow, afraid to move lest I be swept along in the tide of teenagers.

What have I done with my life? I thought to myself, again.

After minutes-that-felt-like-hours, the halls began to empty out. I stood paralyzed, my feet still stuck to the floor with a magnetic force. Two students lingered, walking at their own pace, locked in conversation.

"It's Darwinism, pure and simple," said a boy in a hoodie and a black-and-white type of tennis shoe that seemed to be popular among many of the teenagers here. "Those who evolve the fastest will survive and will have the most chance of passing their genes on to the next generation."

"And you think that's okay, even when it's human beings and not monkeys?" asked a girl with a long braid, dressed entirely in black.

My feet could suddenly move again and I found myself following them, desperate to hear two young people discussing what sounded like evolution, out in the open, with no fear of punishment, as if they believed it was real. When they said words like "social programs" and "individualism" and "state sovereignty," I felt the way I did the first day in Auntie Hepzibah's kitchen—lost, unable to understand.

I wanted to learn this language too, and have real discussions about the world. I wanted to know enough to have my own opinions rather than believing what the Uncles and Aunties told me to believe. I wanted to know real history so I could have context to comprehend the world I lived in. I wanted to understand science before rejecting it. This was what I'd been missing all my life.

Then, like a rainstorm that came out of nowhere in the Brazilian summers I missed so much, it hit me why I'd been feeling so weird. I had told myself it was different because I had moved from Brazil and Mexico. But, seeing a whole class of kids who were actually from Mexico, I realized that wasn't it at all. Listening to these students debate in ways I had never learned, about subjects that had been forbidden to me and literally ripped out of the precious few books I had read, it hit me: *I'm not from another country,* I thought, my heart sinking through the floor. *I'm from another planet.*

16

JESUS FREAKS

■

Houston, Texas, 2005

On an ordinary January morning in the uneven heat of Houston, I stood outside my apartment door with a cup of coffee and a cigarette, steeling myself for another day at Lamar High. I quickly learned I would never fit in and had mostly stopped trying. I saved my energy for classes, for homework, for work. For being an exemplary student while, outside those long hallways, I was barely scraping by.

Over the previous year and a half, I'd learned the basics: what a dress code was, where the financial aid office and the free lunch line were, and how to beat the after-school rush to catch the city bus to work at Chick-fil-A, and later on as a data-entry law firm clerk. I'd learned that number two pencils were the only tools for Scantrons, that when teachers praised my hard work catching up in front of the class it made everyone hate me more, and that walking through the cafeteria scared me to death—like everyone was watching me, waiting for me to put myself into one of the groups so they could figure out what box I fit into, but I didn't fit into any of them.

Like I had hoped, I excelled at school, top in English class and a natural teacher's pet—but only because the adults were less terrifying than the students. But I never had to pretend to love school for the teachers' benefit; while other students skipped more classes than they attended, you couldn't have paid me to stay away. I hadn't missed a single class since I started.

That day—the apartment door propped open, mid-exhale on my cigarette, while the morning news sounded from the television inside—I heard a name I'd never imagined reaching me again: *Davidito*. My mind saw images of a little brown boy, the first of the Children of God's "Jesus babies," the kids born from using sex as a tool to attract converts. He hadn't been just any little boy, he'd been Mama Maria's son, and Grandpa and Mama had raised him as the Crown Prince, the one who'd take over the Children of God and lead us into the Apocalypse. To properly prepare him, they raised him as a "sexually liberated" child, and Auntie Sara—Davidito's head nanny—had literally written the book in his name, *The Story of Davidito,* the explicit 762-page how-to text and photo album on pedophilia for God.

My feet pulled me back into the apartment with a will of their own, smoke trailing in behind me. I stared at the TV, stunned, as the face of Ricky Rodriguez, little Davidito all grown up, flashed across the screen. I heard the words "murder-suicide," "vigilante," and "Children of God." And, as the newscaster repeated it again and again: Cult. *Cult. Cult.*

The Children of God cult.

I had learned all about cults growing up. Cults were evil. Cults were cruel. Cults believed the wrong things. *Cults brainwashed people.* Cults were *other* people like those guys in Waco or Jonestown.

I put the cigarette to my lips, smoking in the apartment in clear violation of the lease. I held the smoke in my lungs as long as I could. Then, gasping for breath, I released it, enjoying the pain, reveling in the smoke searing my lungs, which hurt far less than the news story flooding into me. I flopped onto the couch, shaky, unconvinced my legs would hold me. The newscaster's voice was steady and calm as she explained that, on Saturday in Tucson, Rodriguez, twenty-nine, invited one of his former abusers to dinner in his apartment where he stabbed her multiple times before slitting her throat. He drove all night across the desert to a small border town in California and called his estranged wife, distraught. He cried to her, lamenting that he wouldn't be able to carry out his plans to find and kill his mother and the other cult leaders. He told Elixcia, the girl he'd loved since his youth, "I never realized how hard it would be to take a life." He had been planning for months, buying weapons, and releasing videos calling for survivors to join him on his quest for justice. Nevertheless, he told her how shocking it was when his childhood abuser lay on the ground in his apartment, blood from her severed carotid artery soaking into the carpet, looking up at him with complete confusion, still not understanding what she had ever done wrong. *Still truly believing that she'd raised him with love.*

He'd said goodbye to Elixcia and hung up. Then, with one shot from a handgun, he took his own life.

Davidito, dead. Davidito, the boy who grew up alongside Mom. Davidito, the son of the Prophet—the boy who was to save us all—had not even been able to save himself from the demons forced upon him. A sick kind of knowing descended upon me, a strange calm. I had dreamed of revenge on the Uncles and the Aunties who'd tortured me, but he'd done it. He'd killed her violently, slowly. I knew murder was wrong, but I was not sad for her.

The news kept calling him a vigilante, a victim avenging children like himself and his sisters. *Children like me,* I thought. Like my sisters, my friends, my mom—who also suffered her whole life, a child grown in a group that trafficked, exploited, abused, and betrayed its children in the name of God. When Davidito left The Family five years prior, the leaders talked about him like he'd been crazy, the same way I knew they'd talked about me. But standing in the mess of my apartment, I realized the truth: That poor boy never had a chance. Never allowed to grow up, stuck on the pages of what has been called one of the worst cult artifacts ever produced, a man who dominated all our lives in his child form. He tried to run, tried to hide, tried to forge a normal life, tried to forget us, and when all that failed, he tried to avenge us.

Somewhere outside I heard the whoosh of air from the city bus brakes, the one that took me to school in the normal world I'd cobbled together outside The Family. But I couldn't pry myself off the sofa, putting my cigarette out on an old napkin on the end table. There was no way I could make myself go to school, no way I could pretend to be even slightly normal. I had been pretending for the last year and a half, and I realized I was exhausted. At that moment, giving up seemed like the only real option. I would never fit in. Davidito had tried and look at what happened to him. We were too different, too broken, to ever make it in this world.

How could I even explain my absence? If I told them the truth, would they believe me? Do people realize that it's possible to become an adult without ever having been a child? How could I explain that, yes, I looked whole on the outside, but my skin was just a thin bag holding the jagged pieces together?

So I sat there frozen, my feet heavy, on a tattered couch in a Houston apartment, mind traveling fast. Back to communes in third-world countries, cold three-minute showers, leafy green mango trees laden with pink and gold fruit. Back to Bible verses and beatings, sexual punishments and preparations for the Apocalypse. Back to the cult— *the cult*—that raised Davidito, the vigilante-murderer. Back to the cult that raised *me*. Back to the people who hurt us and will never, ever have to pay. Back to the adults so busy trying to "save the lost souls for God" that they forgot to save us, the children of the Children of God.

■

THE SPEAKERS BUZZED as a Texan voice blasted through the classroom: "Daniella Mestyanek, please report to the counselor's office." The chemistry equation I struggled to balance evaporated. My heart began to beat fast.

I had been waiting for that call, fearing it for days. I knew the next steps: interrogation, expulsion. I couldn't believe I had been so weak, so gullible, so trusting. Whatever was about to happen was my fault. I had exposed my secrets to the System, something I had been trained since birth not to do. I deserved whatever was coming.

"Eu ja volto," I chirped to Dr. Bernardo, whose native European Portuguese always made me smile. I tried to act normal as I placed my books into my backpack, hoisted it over my shoulder, and walked out of the room. As soon as the door shut behind me, I couldn't breathe. What if I never saw Dr. Bernardo again? What if this was the last time I'd ever hear the way she spoke Portuguese like she had cotton in her mouth, compared to the Brazilian version that rolled from my tongue? Chatting with her was the closest to home I'd felt since leaving it.

Home. What did that word even mean? Was home Brazil? My apartment? Was home back with The Family?

I walked down the never-ending hallway, grateful that I was alone, the gray-green lockers like tombs in front of me as my mind raced through the possibilities: Where would they send me, how many police cars waited for me, could I walk out an emergency exit without setting off the alarm? Each step brought me closer to Ms. Karen Crawford, the assistant principal with all the power and none of the empathy, who I knew waited for me at the office. I imagined her standing at the door with her blond hair pulled back, her brows furrowed above her blue eyes, her arms tightly crossed, her lazy Texas drawl scathing, angry that I'd tricked her into letting me go to school, that she'd been made to look like a fool. She was the someone in power Dougie had demanded to see, and I remembered how she pushed my documents back at me with disdain, confirming what her secretary had already told me: "You don't exist, *darlin'*," she had repeated, and laughed, as if I was the best joke she'd ever heard.

As I approached the office, I reminded myself of my training—keep cool with the cops, always smile, and say as little as possible.

I peered through the glass door, but the activity inside appeared strangely normal. No cops. No sign of Ms. Crawford. I held my breath and opened the door.

"Daniella, it's so nice to see you again." The warm, Houston-tinged voice of Ms. Sharron Raibon, my guidance counselor, startled me with her calm greeting. With her soft brown hands, she opened the door to her interior office and motioned me inside.

I bowed my head as I followed her into her quiet, cool office. I still didn't know where to place my eyes around adults. Ms. Raibon lowered herself into her chair, briefly adjusting a photo of a striking young man with a close-cropped fade and dark skin that stood out in perfection against a dark blue uniform. I could see my paper sitting in the center of her desk, the reason I was in trouble now, the college entrance essay I'd been assigned to write in senior English class two days after the Davidito murder-suicide, the essay I had written without thinking, still reeling from the news, a quick decision made in class.

The essay I'd titled "I Was Raised in a Cult," as if I had no discretion whatsoever.

My clammy hands adjusted my short skirt to cover more of my thighs. I fidgeted until I could justify it no more, until the silence became ridiculous, then I glanced up, expecting to see eyes filled with coldness and finality, the look of someone about to tell me I had to go, that there was no place for someone like me in this world.

Instead, Ms. Raibon leaned back in her chair, her fingers steepled under her chin. "Daniella," she said, speaking calmly and slowly, like one might speak to a cornered animal. "We've got some time." She picked up my essay, turned it facedown, and continued, "I want you to tell me this whole story."

"I don't know where to start." Where did those words come from? I did it again, trusting the System. I should know better. "Will I get to stay in school?"

"Just take a breath, dear," she said. "I'm not in the habit of kicking children out of school for having complicated backstories. Especially not children in situations like yours." Her emphasis on the word "children" stood out. It felt foreign to me and bounced around my head until I squirmed. I hadn't thought of myself as a child for years, or maybe ever.

Seeing my hesitation, she picked up my essay from the desk, read for a moment with furrowed brows, then looked at me, her eyes serious and searing in a way I could not read.

I looked down at my lap. I *was* the cornered animal. Trapped.

She rustled through some papers, and I glanced up to see my transcript in her hand. "I see that you live here on Westheimer Road somewhere," she said, naming the same major Houston thoroughfare that housed our high school. "Is it a house or an apartment?"

If I wasn't so terrified, I might have been amused at the thought of Heaven and me being able to afford a house or anything bigger than our tiny one-bedroom apartment. "It's my sister's apartment," I said. I knew I'd misstepped when I saw her eyebrows go up. She must not have realized I had a sister; maybe it wasn't on my paperwork. I needed to explain. "It's just the two of us there. It's *such* a great location."

I realized I was talking fast, my voice an octave higher than usual. But the look of concern in Ms. Raibon's eyes meant I did something else wrong, so I tried to cover. "Heaven's great," I said. "She's ten years older than me and a bartender, so she's not home most nights." I tried to smile. I smiled too much. "It's fine because I'm never really there either, it's school, work, school, work for me. But she's a good guardian. She even took me to Schlitterbahn when I made the Honor Roll. I'm doing great!"

I knew my blabber was the reason we were trained to remain silent. I was never good at that, no matter how high the stakes. It's one of the many reasons why I got punished so much more than the other kids. I was sure Ms. Raibon would call the police.

"Okay, okay." She held her hands up, palms out, a gesture of surrender. "That's fine, dear. I always want to make sure that my students have a stable home life. It can be hard to focus on school and your future when you have to worry about what is going on at home."

I nodded my head, unsure of how to respond. She was an adult concerned about my life, my wants, my future. It was the opposite of everything I'd ever known. In our communes, kids were a workforce and school was the lowest priority. What was the point when the world was going to end before I finished twelfth grade? Gaining a worldly education that I'd never get a chance to use was selfish. Everything I was doing since I left was selfish.

"Mrs. Smithson says you're one of her best English students but you aren't planning to go to college. Can you tell me why—"

"Oh," I interrupted, "I'm planning to go to college." Then, faltering, "I just don't think I can go right away . . ." I looked at her kind face and took a deep breath. "All I've ever wanted to do is go to school. It's why I left The Family, I mean, the . . . cult." The new word burned my tongue. I expected something to happen, some Heavenly sign that I had sinned, but Ms. Raibon nodded. "It's complicated—I don't know how to even get started getting into college. I mean, I'm so different. And it's so expensive. I can barely support myself in high school, and high school is free."

She listened, like she wanted to hear what I had to say, like she *believed* me, and that kept me talking. "I talked with the Marines when they were on campus, and they told me I could sign up for a couple years of service, and then all school is paid for. I took their test and did really well, so he said I could pretty much have any job I want. I could be a linguist. I'm trilingual, you know? That's one good thing I got from my . . . upbringing. I'm fine." I smiled big for her. "I'm going to be fine."

Ms. Raibon didn't respond immediately. I tried to study her face but she was as practiced as any Auntie. After a few moments she leaned forward and swiveled the picture frame on her desk around to face me. I stared at the handsome young man in navy blue, shoulders squared, dark eyes looking right at me. "Have I told you about my son, Dominic?" she asked. "He considered the Air Force Academy, even attended their summer program, as his goal is to be a pilot. We explored a lot of different options, but in the end, he decided that he wanted the 'college experience' and received a full-ride academic scholarship to Hampton University, an HBCU in Virginia. That's really what your junior and senior year are for—figuring out what you want to be and doing the work to get you there. He worked hard to get the opportunity to attend the Air Force Academy, but it would have been a very hard path. As a Black man, he would have been in for a far different experience than many of the others."

She paused, and I saw something like sadness wash over her eyes. "So will you, as a woman," she said. "I'll support you if you really want to be a marine, like I supported my son through his journey. But I hate seeing my kids join the military because they think that's their only choice."

My kids, she had said. Something inside me shifted, unlocked.

I felt the need to defend her son and the path he'd considered. To defend us. "As far as only choices go, getting paid to see the world doesn't sound so bad."

"The travel is exciting," she said. "The military can be great, but if all you've ever wanted is to go to college, why rule that out?"

I was about to reply but she lifted her forefinger up, and I hushed. "It's what I do. It's my job to help you figure out the best path after high school. There's a way into college for kids like you, for anyone with a story like this."

"The only way that would ever happen is if money fell out of the sky," I said.

She smiled. "For a lot of kids who get scholarships, that's what they tell me it feels like. They write essays—especially ones as searing and truthful as yours—and then colleges ask them to come. They want to pay for the privilege of educating them."

"Why?"

"Because kids like you are an asset to their school." She looked me in the eye and I looked back. "It takes bravery to tell the truth. To write down what happened, to say it out loud. It's how we understand each other. You're a reader. You know how other people's stories can change you."

I nodded, but I didn't understand. People got money for being honest with their words? The only thing I'd ever seen come from the truth was punishment.

"You're a model student, Daniella," Ms. Raibon said. I had no idea what I was feeling. My heart pounded in my chest and it was hard to get in a full breath. I wanted to both run out of the room and stay with Ms. Raibon forever. "I'm sorry you've had to experience all of this. I don't know you well yet, but you seem like a young woman working hard to do well. I'm glad you decided to write this, and I thank you for trusting me to share it. I think I can help you. With your permission, I'd like to talk to some of the other counselors about your situation and see what resources and ideas they can add."

She paused, eyebrows raised in question. I swallowed hard and nodded my head.

Yes.

Maybe I wasn't on my own after all. Maybe I could trust her and let her help me, as I had let Dougie help me get into school. Maybe leaving The Family, leaving my group, didn't mean it was completely on me to live or die by my own choices.

Maybe I did exist.

"I think I'd like that," I said tentatively. Then gathering some gumption, I continued more firmly. "Let's make a plan."

"Okay," said Ms. Raibon, breaking into a grin. "Tell me, what do you know about the SATs?"

17

BRING ME TO LIFE

■

The University of Texas at Dallas, 2005

My college experience was the antithesis of life in the cult—I was encouraged to read broadly, to question every thought and phrase. No professor ever got mad at me when I asked about Plato's motivation for writing a certain line. Nobody called me out of the Spirit for suggesting that maybe Flaubert had the wrong idea in *Madame Bovary*. I wrote papers to be provocative, played devil's advocate by writing about the latent homosexuality in Dante's *Inferno* for my staunchly Catholic Intro to Humanities professor; compared two of Hemingway's works to show that the ultimate man's man held typically feminine qualities in highest esteem in my Masculinity in Literature class; and presented a paper at a conference on the ideal way to invent a god as a literary character—using *The Odyssey* and the Book of Genesis as examples. That went over like a lead balloon in a conservative, small town in Texas, but nobody punished me, prayed over me, or made me repent.

I studied and studied, read for hours and then read some more, enthralled by so much I didn't know existed. Often, sitting on the porch of my college apartment, smoking a cigarette and avoiding my roommates, I marveled at the fact that it was considered completely normal, even celebrated, to have an entire stage of life devoted to study. After so many years having to sneak around to read a small handful of books, I now wrote about books and went to class to talk about books. Like back in high school, my fellow students called me names for my study habits—my favorite was Hermione—but my professors loved my enthusiasm and supported me in my pursuit of more and more knowledge.

Money wasn't any easier in college, but my time was more flexible, so I could have as many jobs as I wanted, which was sometimes only one, but often three or four. I got a job at a daycare, an easy hire when I told them I had fourteen siblings. The kids' rich parents paid me even more for private babysitting than I made at work, and ten times more than that for my birthday party skills of balloon twisting and face painting, perfected from my years entertaining on the streets of Brazil and Mexico. One Punjabi-Canadian family took me on as a nanny and counted me as one of theirs. They were there for me in a way that was new to me, but I still kept myself mostly at a distance, determined to come off as normal as possible, panicked that I wouldn't "pass," worried what would happen if I let anyone know about my real past. As fast as paychecks came in, they seemed to go out as quickly—without any experience with money, let alone instruction in the art of making a budget, I didn't know how to deny things I couldn't afford. And after a childhood defined by denial, it was a thrill to spend my own money on whatever I wanted.

College was a weird in-between time, like a trial period before becoming a real adult. I supposed it was like that for all college students to some extent, but I doubted most of them had the same level of fear I did about what would happen afterward. Other college students didn't seem terrified about what they would do if they made it all the way through and were spit out into the real world, with no structure to support them, no professors to have their backs, no counselors to advise them on which step to take, and no family to fall back on as they figured out their next move. They didn't seem to be navigating the same tightrope that I was, nothing but the abyss beneath me if I made so much as a single misstep.

As much as I learned, I started to realize how much I didn't know. No book could teach me how the real world worked or what my place in it was supposed to be. I began to suspect that knowledge was out of reach for someone like me, no matter how hard I tried to grasp it.

I watched little groups of students walking around campus together, the cliques of people who had found each other, but I struggled to find mine. I tried to participate in campus life, even though I always felt awkward and out of place. Despite all my efforts to look the part, I feared I was too different deep down to ever really fit in anywhere. Nothing I did would ever cover up the fact that I was raised in a totally different world and that, at my core, there was something inherently *wrong with me*.

But then, one night after studying with some classmates for a science quiz—the only subject I felt completely incapable of studying for on my own, since I'd never had anything to build on—a boy with a Russian name invited me to a party. *Why not?* I thought to myself. I could use a distraction.

When we walked through the door of the dingy on-campus apartment where he lived with his three roommates, there was the requisite disgusting kitchen with bottles of vodka, Goldschlager, and mixers resting on top of a thick layer of grime. But rather than standing around aimlessly like I did at most of the parties I had attended, everyone was centered around a table where two boys played a game I recognized as chess, though I don't think I'd ever seen it played before. I was immediately intrigued, and as the night progressed and I chatted with people from all over the world, I realized I had never attended a party so interesting and enjoyable. And I learned something new about my school: We had the reigning college champion chess team in the world. The people at the party had been recruited from around the globe to play chess, and every one of them was an internationally ranked chess prodigy. The University of Texas at Dallas, with its Division III sports program, didn't give athletic scholarships, but the chess team lived on fully paid tuition, room and board, and stipends for summer travel to competitions.

It didn't take me long to realize that this was my crew, my new group—the thing I'd been searching for, without really knowing it, ever since I'd left The Family. Though I knew nothing about chess, I knew a lot about being different, and what it was like to think differently from everyone around me. But this group of people came from different countries, cultures, ages, and skill levels, all mixed together as one unit. It wasn't just that they were international—they were smart. They were curious, logical, always thinking a few steps ahead, and proud to be brainy. Quirky people who brought their whole selves to the group, and they weren't ashamed of any of it. What made them different was exactly what made them special.

In a world where there is no normal, nobody is weird. So, I could just be Dani, a translucently White American of Slovakian descent who'd grown up in Brazil with some weird missionary parents and tons of siblings—and that was fine with all of them, no further explanations needed.

By sophomore year, I had a new group of girlfriends. I'd moved in with Lilia, the only female player on the team, from Moldova, who spoke five languages, and became inseparable from Kristina, the coach's daughter who'd fled the war in the former Yugoslavia at six years old. In the world of competitive chess, rank is everything, and our school was number one, and our team was cool and engaged in the social life of the school. Apparently though, winning was old news for a team that was used to taking home trophies; the big alumni donors that funded not only the scholarships but the entire program needed more than just winning to be impressed. An all-girl team— now that would be impressive. A year later, in the fall of 2007, for the first time in the history of UT Dallas's Chess Team, there were three female teammates. But team tournament play required four bodies to win 2.5 out of 4 games, and I seemed like a great choice to meet the requirement.

"Find me a girl with a good GPA, teach her a king rook checkmate, and get her on the team before the Pan-American tournament," ordered the team's general manager. So, by proximity to the team more than anything else, I was given the opportunity to be the first, and last, walk-on member to the UT Dallas Chess Team. I was taught both chess basics and complex strategy by some of the most competitive players in the world—my friends—and I escaped the Texas winter that year and sat in a Miami ballroom, struggling for a few moves per game before tipping my king over and watching my teammate sisters skate easily to three out of four victories. Then we all went out to celebrate with mojitos on the beach. I was possibly the lowest ranked girl to ever have played in a tournament that competitive.

But even with all the trappings of friends and happiness, I still felt alone. I was scared about how my past—which I never talked about with anyone—would affect my future if anyone found out. What little grasp I had on a feeling of belonging depended on me keeping huge parts of myself a secret. I knew if I told people who I truly was, what I'd really been through, they'd realize I was too weird, even for this band of misfits. I was always too much, and I wasn't worth the drama.

So I kept my secrets, kept trying to fit into America and the somewhat nerdy version of "normal" that felt accessible to me. I worked. I studied. I played chess. When I got the opportunity to study abroad in Germany in exchange for another female chess player, I took it. I was shocked at how American I felt on German soil, and how easily I made friends, as if that extra layer of being an outsider made me more comfortable in my own skin. In Germany, there was no expectation of me fitting in or assimilating, and the people I met had no way of knowing how authentic of an American I wasn't, so I found I could relax into myself a little more.

The world opened to me in new ways while I was abroad. And when I came home, my life unfolded like a storybook. It's a compelling story, the kind people love to hear. It's the story of a survivor, working hard, overcoming adversity, and finding her place in the world: At the end of the semester, I graduated as valedictorian. I also continued to take calls from the military recruiters I'd started talking to in high school and made the decision to commission into the US Army. That could have been the feel-good ending to the emotional roller coaster of my life, with a hefty dose of patriotism to boot.

And it might have been all there was to my story. If I hadn't met Jeff.

He drew all eyes when he walked into my college biology class— tall, with a presence that demanded attention, even at twenty-one. His hawkish green eyes surveyed the room before striding over and sitting on the bench beside me. His hair was perfect, even up close, not a single strand out of place.

"I'm Jeff," he said, without hesitation.

"I'm Dani?" I said, cringing at the uncertainty in my voice as I scooted farther back on the bench.

"Is that a question? Don't you know who you are?"

Oh boy.

Pretty White American boys were not my type. This Jeff guy was barking up the wrong tree.

But Jeff was commanding from day one. He kept barking, and I didn't run, though there was a part of me that maybe knew I should have, some inner signal that knew something was wrong when guys were so confident. Biology was one of the three science classes I had to take to earn my literature degree—the classes where I felt totally out of control and hyperaware that the fragile life I was cobbling together out of spite and ideas and scholarship and hard work could all be ripped away in a heartbeat. I was terrified I would fail. I was terrified they'd realize I was an imposter all along, that I had not truly earned or deserved the seat in which I sat. I worried they could somehow send me back to wherever I was from.

Maybe that's what he'd been looking for, that day he chose me. Maybe guys like him have an inner signal too, one that alerts them to pretty girls who hate themselves. But still, he *chose* me. He was good at science and decided to help me. He said we'd study together, so we did. Again and again he picked me, and no one had ever taught me how to say no.

He'd regale me with tales of his nightly exploits chasing women before turning and asking me out, yet again. I always laughed, explaining I could never date a bigger player than me. If I was honest with myself, it made me feel better that somebody was. I was still getting used to America's strange rules about sex, how it was both bad but also something everyone was obsessed with. How men wanted girls to be sweet and pure, but also skilled and willing to put out. How someone like Jeff was manly for sleeping with a lot of people, but I could be called a slut for doing the same.

Jeff didn't seem to care about any of that. We started hanging out more and more, but it wasn't romantic. It was almost like friends, like I was one of the guys. Almost, but not quite. I couldn't put my finger on it. We spent our evenings at his place, studying and talking. He never made me feel unsafe, never did *anything*. I was so used to men looking at me like they were picturing me with my clothes off, or sucking in their breath when I stood up in an overtly sexy manner. There was always a feeling of self-consciousness, of knowing what was on a guy's mind and wondering what would happen next. I knew how to use that. But not with Jeff. For the first time, maybe in my whole life, I didn't feel objectified.

I had gotten so tired of the story I'd concocted about who I was and where I came from, the loose details I'd strung together about being the kid of "international missionaries," of never being able to go deeper than the surface. It was the story I told everyone, even my close friends, who I still found ways to hold at arm's length. But one day, I told him. Everything. The cult. All of it.

And he listened. He was interested, but not in the way other people were interested, not like the well-meaning school counselors, or the people I've met since with the gleam of voyeuristic thrill in their eyes, or the ones who ask annoying, stereotypical questions they think they already know the answers to, who tell me I'm nothing like what a cult survivor must be like even though I'm the first real one they've met. Jeff's response was different. Very different.

"This sounds like you're coming out," he said. "I've got some advice on that. I used to be gay and had a whole coming-out party and everything."

And then the conversation pivoted to him. He told me how he'd decided he was gay in high school because it was the most fabulous crowd to hang with. He didn't say it in so many words, but I could see through his tough façade how much he'd wanted to be a part of a group, to be accepted, the way he never would be by his conservative, Southern Baptist Texas world. In his words, he'd been "uber-gay" for four years, with cheetah spots dyed into his hair, glitter makeup at school, and same-sex hookups galore. Then, senior year, he fell for a girl, and that was that. End of gayness.

The story fascinated me. I was taking a Sexuality and Gender Psychology class and understood that sexuality is a spectrum. I wondered why it was so important for Jeff to be one or the other, why he couldn't allow himself the gray area of being somewhere in the middle, why he had to be so extreme. I looked at the uber-masculine man in front of me and tried to imagine him as the uber-gay teen boy he'd described, and I couldn't.

The high school version of himself seemed like a nice kid, but those guys never had power. So he changed again into the dark-haired, handsome frat boy with a chiseled jaw, sexy forearms, and large-boned hands; the guy who wore a concealed weapon like it was his identity, who was climbing the ranks of his fraternity the way he'd been taught to scale the ladder since birth, the finance and poli-sci major who was going to run the world someday. He was the guy who would ensure he had the prettiest wife, the cutest purebred dog, and the perfect little children running around. He'd made a choice to go down that path, to be the kind of man who'd be a Texas politician. That was not a path for the boy he'd been in high school.

I thought he seemed happy. He at least seemed in control. I liked the idea of being in control, of choosing my own destiny. Maybe he could have it all, or at least most of it. Maybe he gave up a part of himself, but it seemed tiny compared to the potential future in front of him. I wondered if I could choose an easier life, like he had, by choosing him.

"So," I said, exhaling smoke. He was always trying to command me to quit cigarettes, though he would begrudgingly stand beside me on the tiny apartment deck as I smoked. "What do you think your future wife will think about your history of sleeping with men?"

"I imagine I won't tell her," he said, both casual and dismissive.

I decided it didn't bother me that he'd slept with more men than he could count. So had I.

We slept together that night. And every night after that.

We got married less than two years later, in the summer after I turned twenty-one, between my junior and senior year, following his graduation from University of Texas at Dallas, our alma mater. As I prepared to study abroad in Germany for my senior year, I had tried to break things off, but his response was to convince me to marry him instead. He'd wait for me, he said. He'd support me. He told me nobody else would ever love me the way he did, and that made sense to me. So I married William Jeffrey Poole in a destination event in Puerto Vallarta, Mexico, where our parents, Merry, Heaven, and Dougie were some of the only guests in attendance, because literally everyone else in our lives had warned us not to get married. Then he headed off to US Army Basic Training, the first step in his plan to become an army officer, before getting into politics in Texas and enjoying a high-powered career. I had a new name and a husband who promised I wouldn't have to work multiple jobs while I finished school.

During my time in Germany, with time away from him to think, I saw that, without realizing it, I had been so terrified of not having any choices after graduation, or maybe of not knowing what my choices were, that I had accidentally limited them. My husband was in the army. I would need to follow him. That's what army wives did. And what was I qualified for anyway, with a B.A. in English and employment experience as a daycare teacher, fast-food worker, balloon sculptor, waitress, and cult video actor? I could be an English teacher at army bases, trailing him from posting to posting. Then I could become a quiet, well-trained political wife and mother. It sounded like death. It sounded like being controlled. Again.

Or, I thought, I could join the army and become an officer too.

To put it in chess terms, I'd been "forked"—forced into taking one of two paths, neither of them good.

I remembered my interest in the military from back in high school, the recruiters who kept calling. It seemed reasonable to me then, even exciting. Why not now? I could be anything I wanted in the army, the recruiters had told me repeatedly. I knew I was smart enough, and with a bachelor's degree I'd have even more options. Maybe it wasn't such a crazy idea to join up, do something to pay my debt to

America. Maybe this would be the thing that would finally prove I really belonged here, that I hadn't tricked everyone into letting me stay. Maybe I'd find a group, a brotherhood, like Jeff said he had. *I was at least as good as him.*

By this time, many of my childhood friends had finally left the cult. Without any education, at nineteen, Merry had gotten pregnant from the Family boy she'd been with since the age of fifteen, and they both decided to leave together to give their son a chance at normal. I was glad she was getting out, but worried that she wouldn't have the same opportunities to build her life and find her way that I had, with only one mouth to feed.

Almost all of my childhood girlfriends were in similar situations. Michaela had two children, the first when she was nineteen, from two different fathers, both of whom wouldn't release custody and were determined to keep their children in Brazil. All of my friends were stuck, trapped, in some way or another. And yet I was graduating summa cum laude—the valedictorian of the Arts and Humanities program at one of the great American universities, one that paid me for the privilege. I was lucky. Too lucky. Any day, I knew, that luck could run out.

I was lucky to simply be an American, after all. I'd won the passport lottery at birth, then pulled myself up by that Social Security card and US passport to make myself exist. My life with Jeff would make me even more secure. If I joined the army, if I *commissioned* into the army, I would always count. I would officially matter. Jeff liked the idea of *his* wife being physically fit, knowing how to handle big guns, and having a rank and a title that earned her deference. He said it was hot and showed me pictures of flawless World War II–era blond women in belted, drab-green perfection. I began to like it too, as though his desires had started to outweigh my own—until my first priority became to please him. Could I shape myself into who he wanted me to be? Besides, he'd remind me, he would always outrank me by six months.

Lieutenant Poole. It sounded good on him. Maybe it would sound good on me too.

Maybe joining the army would help me get over my guilt of using government aid to get my start. Maybe I could feel more like a real American once I'd been in the 1 percent of those who volunteer to serve. And maybe I could do some good for what seemed to me like, if not necessarily the best country in the world, at least one of them. What did I have to lose? It was only three more years of my life. And Jeff and I would be doing it together. How bad could it be?

I wrote my graduation speech, extolling my fellow graduates to follow their passion, the same advice always given to, and usually ignored by, all college graduates. I told myself I was following *my* passion, that I wanted to do this. And I believed it. I was determined once again to show the world I was right. That I knew how to choose the life and the group that was best for me. I was sure I could be a part of the army but not *owned* by it, that a person could have brains and independent, innovative thoughts and still be part of a larger group that gave their life purpose, meaning, identity, and structure, even if that culture demanded uniformity. I wouldn't be a brainwashed automaton, I'd be different. I was sure I knew what I was getting into, what I was signing my life over to, and how it would play out.

I was wrong.

Part III

THE ARMY

18

DRINK THE KOOL-AID

■

Fort Jackson, South Carolina, June 2009

I'm running down a narrow path, pushing jungle foliage out of my eyes, trying hard not to trip over my own feet. Must. Get. Out. They are coming for us. They are closing in, but I can't make myself move fast enough. I'm starving, cold. We ran out of food a long time ago. We are a blur of continual movement. They'll never stop hunting us.

Maybe it's easier to let them catch me. At least then it will be over.

I hear the heavy stomps of boots behind me. The choice has been made. I stop running. Two hands grab my arms and spin me around. I can't see my friends anywhere. I pray they got away. The cold metal barrel of a gun shoves into my ribs. I glance down and am surprised at how much it looks like a toy.

I know what comes next: isolation, beatings, torture, rape. It's time to suffer. I've prepared for this my whole life. So why do I still feel so scared?

I won't escape. They will kill me soon. I know this fact the way I know the sun rises in the east and sets in the west. I have been preparing for this moment my whole life. I only need to stay true to my faith. The Antichrist and his minions fear us. They hate our conviction, but God is on our side. It's my destiny to become a martyr for God. It is time to make my Final Stand, to take some of them with me as I show His awesome power. I will be lucky if I am murdered for my faith today. Everyone will know I am the chosen one. Maybe I am Heaven's Girl after all.

■

THROUGH PAPER-THIN EYELIDS, I see the sharp beam of a flash-light. Suddenly wide awake, I hear the voice yelling "reveille!" My mind flails around as I scramble to my feet, feeling along the edge of my hard, thin bunk to find my own flashlight, stashed where I'd staged it the night before. *Am I in the children's dorms? Where is my flee-bag? Is this a drill or the real thing?*

My hand finds my assault rifle, safely in place at the foot of my bed. No, this is a different bunkhouse. This is a different kind of waking before dawn and quick dressing in the dark, a different surge of adrenaline and fear.

Today we would run through woods so black I couldn't tell day from night, punctuated by the eerie bobbing of little red forehead flashlights. Rather than trying to evade the Antichrist's soldiers, we'd jump over logs and try to avoid capture by our own drill sergeants. In-stead of the Grecian tunics and strappy sandals of my dreams and the illustrated instructions I'd memorized from my youth, I'd march in my new tan boots, still painfully not broken in, wearing army fatigues much too big for my hungry, one-hundred-pound frame.

The smell of the recruits beside me was an acrid combination of fear and bravado. It's not that we wanted to die, but we weren't against the idea either. If it came to it, we'd die willingly enough, throwing ourselves in front of bullets for our buddies, on top of live grenades for our country, sacrificing ourselves for patriotism and honor, martyrs for our cause, for the words and ideals shouted at us each day. At least, that's what we were here to learn, I knew, as we were programmed to live and breathe army. This was my new life, for better or worse, in US Army Basic Training.

The yelling broke through the fuzz in my head: time to get in line, to march into the dark woods, to start training. If there is one thing that characterizes basic training, it's the yelling. It is a tool to teach discipline, a shock to the system, something to make you feel fear, then to harden you to that fear. *IF YOU CAN'T HANDLE A LITTLE YELLING, HOW WILL YOU HANDLE YOURSELF WHEN THE BULLETS*

COME FLYING YOUR WAY? It reminds us we are owned, 100 percent, by the drill sergeants, by the army, by the United States of America. By the commander-in-chief. Unquestioning obedience was demanded. No walking, no silence, no quiet reflection, no time to think for yourself. And always, always with a battle buddy. *It felt like home.*

For nine weeks, we ran everywhere, accompanied by yelling and orders. No books, TV, news, games, phones, or contact with the outside world. I scoffed out loud when our drill sergeant told us that Michael Jackson had died, sure that it was yet another misdirection to keep us unbalanced. With no way to verify anything for weeks at a time, all we could do was believe what they told us. My body and mind remembered the feeling and fell into the routine with a strange kind of ease.

I knew how to operate in a world like this, how to keep breathing when I was both dependent and trapped.

I was born a soldier.

Before arriving at Fort Jackson, South Carolina, I'd never had a flashback. I'd never even thought of my childhood as traumatic. Abnormal, yes. Strange, for sure, but it was all I'd known. Bad, painful stuff had happened to me, but that was just me, right, not The Family? Pretty much every cult kid I've ever met has told themselves the same story: "Sure, my childhood wasn't ordinary, but in the end we all turned out fine." I even thought I believed it.

But I started to pay the price for that denial in basic training, when the flashbacks started. The nightmares. I woke up in a cold sweat almost every morning from war dreams, abuse dreams, dreams where I was back under the total control of others. I'd zone out in line and suddenly feel six years old again, terrified and insecure in every movement, waiting for punishment. I lived in constant fear that I'd call a drill sergeant "Uncle" and never be able to explain why.

Still, basic training felt like a life I understood: standing in lines, adults yelling for no reason, prescribing my wardrobe, my actions, my words, my thoughts, *even my underwear*. Getting ready, once again, for my own death, any minute, once the fighting started. At least this time I was here for a purpose. I had chosen this path myself using reason and logic, and I was going to see it through. Sure, they could break me down physically. They could even influence my mind, but they'd never touch my soul. That was already hidden away as its own secret, in the place I had carved out when I was a young child, the shelter I could go to whenever things got too tough. After surviving this way for almost sixteen years, nine weeks was nothing.

Melting in the heat of a South Carolina summer, the first days of basic training—called reception—were designed chaos. Drill sergeants never told us what a formation was, but they expected us to stand in them for hours each day—a block of soldiers in brand-new uniforms, at the position of attention, staring straight ahead, waiting. They yelled and yelled while we fumbled over ourselves, new boots in a tangle, as we figured out commands as they were being shouted, as we were herded into one room for paperwork, the next for shots, and then to be "smoked," forced to do push-ups and other hard exercises until we reached muscle failure. We slept in bays, on orderly rows of bunk beds in concrete buildings, which I'm sure felt like prison to the other girls. To me, it was familiar, almost comforting.

The Junior ROTC kids, fresh from high school, became the natural leaders. They understood how to march and hold a weapon in the proper position during an inspection. Never knowing what actions would push each drill sergeant over the edge meant we lived in constant fear of messing up, of stepping out of line, of performing another wrong move. Fear was a constant companion, undefined and lurking on the edges, whispering in my ear that things would blow up any second, that I would lose control of everything I'd struggled to gain, that I was nothing but a six-year-old girl in a grown-up body.

Danielle Reid was a specialist, like me, a rank that meant we both had college degrees, hers in psychology, and years on the other trainees, who as a group averaged seventeen years old. She was a few years older than me—the tiniest blond, White girl with the biggest Jersey accent. We discovered we'd both go to officer school together, scheduled for the same class. We could be friends, I allowed myself to dream.

She asked me where I was from. Such a harmless little question, the one Americans always ask first. But for me, and for so many cult survivors, it's the question that makes my blood run like ice water through my veins.

It's cool, I thought. *I'm ready for this.* In my six years since leaving The Family, I had a slew of prepared answers. I had a mask to hide how shaken I was.

"I'm from Texas. Dallas." That's where I'd gone to college, which meant I'd lived there for four years. Longer than I'd ever lived any-where. I knew the city and I could answer questions about it. It would be hard to trip me up.

"Yeah? I notice there are a lot of people from Texas in the army. Did you grow up there?"

Damn. I hated lying. And Texas sounded so boring. Part of me wanted to tell her about Brazil and Mexico, the places I was really from.

"Well, I mostly grew up in Latin America. It's a bit of a crazy story."

You can't even imagine.

"Oh, yeah? How come? Did your parents work there?"

Why was this girl asking so many questions? Why wasn't she let-ting it go? Didn't she know the rules of small talk? The whole point was to keep it small.

"Well, my parents were missionaries with a really intense organi-zation, so we lived abroad my whole life. I've got a whole bunch of siblings and stuff. I moved to Texas when I was fifteen, kinda on my own, and went to school there."

I thought that would give her enough to chew on. Maybe she'd have another question or two about what church and if I was still religious, and maybe I could give her an answer that wouldn't reveal too much but would also scare her enough to make her stop asking questions.

"You're not talking about, like, the Children of God, are you?"

I felt all the ice-cold blood drain from my body.

I stood there, frozen, replaying her words over and over in my head, trying to convince myself I had heard them wrong. But she really did say it: *the Children of God*. I had only told a small handful of people the name of the "religious group" I had been raised in, but no one had ever heard of it. To them, it was some run-of-the-mill Christian missionary organization. But I gave Danielle, what? Four sentences, and she guessed. How much did she know? Could she be from The Family too?

"Huh, great guess," I said, trying to keep breathing, trying to sound calm and nonchalant. "Yeah, that's the 'group' where I was born and raised, just like my mom. How do you know about it?"

I didn't pray anymore, but I heard myself in my head begging: *Please be from there too. Please understand. Please, please be my friend.*

"I like to watch documentaries," she said. "And I travel a lot. I've heard about it before, and I saw a whole show on it recently." She finished lacing up her boots. "Seems completely fucked up."

A door in my mind slammed shut. What did she know? And what would she want to find out? No, we were not going to be friends. I hated myself for even thinking that would be possible, and I hated her. I sat half-naked on the locker room bench, a waif of a girl in big new boots I didn't know how to tie the way that soldiers did, my curly hair rebelling against an army-approved style, wearing the stupid tungsten black wedding band that Jeff insisted would be good for basic training, or because he didn't want to buy me an actual ring. His words rang in my ears: "Basic training is worse than the real army. Just keep your head down and get through it. Don't stand out."

I stood up. "Yeah, it was crazy," I mumbled as I pulled the rest of my clothes on quickly. I walked away with my boots still unlaced, my footsteps faster and heavier than I expected.

I can run and run, but I'm always still here.

■

I HAD GOTTEN used to excelling at everything I did through sheer will, but it was somehow never enough. I never felt like I would be caught up with everything I'd missed. So I clung to the belief that there was always a way to be better, that no matter how well I did, I was still failing in some essential way. As a kid who had been told from birth that I wasn't good enough, that I was nothing without Jesus, I desperately needed to prove myself, by myself, first to my teachers and professors, and now to Jeff and my drill sergeants. When I'd decided to join the army, I'd known that I needed to get in shape, and I'd gone a little overboard. I had quit my pack-a-day smoking habit, to Jeff's delight, and taken up running in the heat of the Texas summer. I wanted to not only be ready, I wanted to be army-regulation perfect. I cut off my curly, blond highlighted hair and threw away my makeup. When I showed up to basic training, I was a wiry, underweight brunette with badly chopped hair and the giant glasses they force recruits to wear for corrective vision called basic combat glasses, or BCGs, that were so ugly everyone referred to them as "birth control glasses." That was fine with me. I didn't need to be attractive; I needed to be strong.

Ugly or not, I could do sixty-plus push-ups and eighty sit-ups without stopping, and it turned out I could run. *Fast.* Six months earlier, I had never run a mile in my life, but on the first physical fitness test, I ran two miles in thirteen minutes and change. That was fast for a girl—two whole minutes faster than any other girl in basic training.

I ran so fast I ran right into notoriety. The drill sergeants knew my name, the commander wanted to meet me, and the first sergeant praised me in front of the whole company. I also ran into an angry mob in the girls' bay, where we slept. I thought they would have been excited, happy to see a woman praised, one of us running faster than most of the platoon's men. A rising tide lifts all boats. Or something.

But like in the Children of God, nothing in basic training was about being an individual. Do not stand out. Look like another pawn in the line. Up until the gun went off on race day, I fit the mold and blended into the space I carved for myself: small and ugly and quiet. Nothing to be noticed.

A six-foot-tall girl with long box-braids and broad hands balled into meaty fists threatened to punch me if I didn't keep my head down, go slower next time, and stop making her look bad. Someone with stringy blond hair, patchy skin, and brown, broken teeth asked me through the holes in her fractured smile if I'd ever been in a street fight, as if she was offering me candy.

Cross-legged on her bed, Danielle raised her head and barked out a single command, "Leave her alone, guys!" and everyone dispersed. How was she already the leader? Relief washed over me and I wondered if I had been wrong about her. Maybe we could be friends after all.

"They're right, you know," she said. "You're a bit of a stuck-up asshole."

And then the door inside me closed shut again. Her words confirmed what I'd feared three weeks earlier, on the first day of basic training. I reminded myself I was not there to make friends and that the only real friend I had, and would ever have, was myself.

So I kept running, not just on the track, but from conflict. My legs carried me out of the room, a thousand questions bouncing around my brain. Why did she have to hate me too? How could everyone tell I was so different? What was I doing wrong?

I turned a corner and then another until I found myself in the same girls' locker room where Danielle and I had first spoken. The unfairness of it all hit me and I shoved my fist—hard—into one of the metal lockers. As the pain bloomed in my hand, my hurt and anger faded. It was a relief, a kind of numbness, so I punched the locker again and again. I saw blood on one of my knuckles, but I couldn't feel a thing. *If they think I'm a bitch,* I thought, *I'll at least show them I'm not scared.* I wondered what Jeff would think of me—would he mock me for losing control? Did he have any idea how much easier his path had already been than mine? I punched and punched, my hand pounding against the metal too many times to count, until a drill sergeant appeared and ordered me downstairs.

Like the trained soldier I was becoming, I stood at parade rest while he yelled at me. What was my problem? Didn't I know they were proud of me? Did I want to throw it all away by acting out? As a woman, you'll need to be faster, and better, than the men, always. And you'll need to keep your head down. Play the game. He finished his tirade with threadbare advice: Ignore their jealousy; that means you're doing it right.

But that wasn't enough. He was missing something. Sure, I had been longing my whole life for people in power to tell me I'm special. My parents, the Aunties and Uncles, teachers, people I had dated, and drill sergeants like him. But being special had never been the thing that made me feel safe.

I stormed back into the room, my hand throbbing and bloody. "Not you," I shouted at Danielle across the room. "I can take crap from all these little girls, but not from you."

Why her? I'm not sure. Maybe if we had been allowed to read books, I could have tuned the girls out the way I had in college. But there, with nothing to distract me, I had to feel all of my fear and hurt and longing. Maybe I was scared enough to understand how much I needed someone, a real friend, to get through what seemed impossible on my own. And maybe I was smart enough to realize how special Danielle was—sharp as hell, a natural leader, driven in a way I'd only seen in myself, the smallest of the entire platoon but somehow bigger than everyone else. I felt it like a punch in my stomach: I didn't want to lose *her*.

For a moment that seemed to last forever, I wondered what she would do. I picked at my cuticles until she walked out of the bay, motioning for me to follow.

In the hallway, we lowered ourselves to the cement floor, the cold seeping through the black, plasticky shorts from the exercise uniform we wore anytime we weren't in fatigues. We were jammed into a doorway, each with our backs against one side of the frame, a place where nobody could surprise us. In the background, we could hear the noise of the other girls preparing to bunk down for the night. Soon, the lights would go out. Nobody would bother us, hidden as we were. I asked her if we could start over. I didn't know what I had done to make her hate me, but I wanted to try again.

"I don't hate you," she told me. "But I don't *know* you. I want to, but you have to let me. We're going to be together for five months, here and in officer school. So yeah, let's be friends."

Sitting in that doorway, we became friends. She told me how she'd majored in psychology while working on Wall Street to pay her way through Fordham University after dropping out of high school. She'd been to more countries than I had, traveling and volunteering, but not for any religion, just because she liked experiencing the world. She wanted to be a commander of peacekeeping operations for the United Nations, but they required women to have military experience. So she joined the army to do several years as an officer, and, hopefully, get some command experience. Everything about her was impressive.

"Now," she said. "I want you to tell me about the Children of God."

And so I did. Like Jeff, she responded without the inane questions and assumptions I'd braced myself to hear. But she was also different from him. No jockeying to have a bigger story, no competing for larger hurts. Just understanding. Just the desire to see me as I was.

We became our own little group, the two of us, still part of the larger platoon, but also separate. For the next five months, she was my teacher, my best friend, my confidante, and my protector. She understood that my strangeness came from lack of knowledge, not animosity, but she also didn't think I was all that strange. With Danielle, who was as American as they come, I learned what it meant to be an American, or at least the kind of American I wanted to be. There were little things, like "OMG, Daniella, you don't call it 'American football' when you're in America," and big things, like all human beings are worthy of our respect and dignity, even if they are extremely different from us. She showed me how to excel with a humility and grace that allowed space for everyone else to hold their heads up too. I was part of a team again, with somebody who had my back. And I realized that I'd been missing that for six long years.

It was Danielle who first broke my heart about the army. I shouldn't have been shocked, based on how much the army already felt like the Children of God, but when she explained army policy, and the female combat ban from the US Justice Department and Congress that limited which roles women could hold in the army, I was horrified. I kept thinking of my cult training, the world where women were expected to serve men, to be "handmaids of David"— useful, but never equal.

"How is it 2009 and there's an assumption that men are better at anything at all, just for being men?" I asked her again and again. "How is this even legal? What about equality?"

But there was no equality in the army. Women played support. Men led. Full stop. Every career decision would be determined, and limited, by our gender.

Army culture reinforced these values with sayings like, "As a woman, you're either a bitch, a slut, or a dyke." We heard it all the time. The drill sergeants called women "Jessica Lynch" anytime we messed up. I had previously thought she was a badass American hero in Iraq, famous for being the first successful rescue of a prisoner of war since World War II, and the first ever of a woman; I didn't realize the army blamed her as an ill-prepared woman, someone whose lack of combat-readiness, something she'd never been trained for because of the ban, had meant she was the weak link who got good men killed. They warned us again and again and again: If we weren't perfect in training, we'd repeat the same fate. We understood the underlying implication—women were the weaker sex and shouldn't be soldiers. It didn't matter how fast I could run or the individual achievements that drove me; the knowledge that I'd never be good enough in the eyes of the army weighed on me heavier than the duffel bag I'd held up to the sky on my first day.

■

BASIC TRAINING IS more of a shotgun blast of experiences than actual training in warfighting. The goal is culture shock and mental programming; soldiers learn everything else for their job in schools or at their units. Basic training also introduces all the stuff that recruiters would never tell prospective enlistees, for instance, the army's belief that every soldier should know what it's like to be punched in the face. So one day, in what they call the clinch drill, they line everyone up and punch them in the face. You pass the test by pinning the drill sergeant before they can knock you out or—as in my case—after they break your nose.

Every single day of basic training, we got up before dawn and waited on our feet, hour after hour, trying to stay awake. Physical training took place before dawn in the last bit of South Carolina's fading cool air that we wouldn't see again until after 10 P.M. Then there was all the marching—so much marching—while singing a weird sort of tune called a cadence. The one in charge creates a steady rhythm with a hard beat that makes it easier for everyone to stay in step. It seems innocent enough, like the nonsense songs children sing while jumping rope. But I remembered marching down hallways at midnight to the beat of "Onward Christian Soldiers" and saw it for what it really was—a highly effective programming tool, rhythmic, repetitive, something we soon learned by heart, something we'd parrot without thinking or questioning. Take a bunch of young adults from all over the country, throw them together in isolation but without privacy, control their food and elimination habits, add sleep deprivation, and march them for long distances, until their minds are as exhausted as their bodies, while chanting things like "when my right foot hits the ground, all I hear is that killing sound." We taunted other units, sometimes calling individuals out by name, constructing an us versus them mentality to help us bond, to feel like one team with a common enemy—the other guys. There were a lot of cadences about raping, too.

They also programmed hierarchy. The most famous cadence is "I Wanna Be an Airborne Ranger," sung in many different variations. Trainees at Fort Jackson become paper pushers, office workers, intelligence analysts, mechanics, cooks, or other support roles; none of us are set to become Airborne Rangers. But from the first day of army training, we're taught to revere Rangers as the highest among us—those whose mission is to capture or kill the bad guys. That's what we were all supposed to desire. For men, it means one of the hardest career paths in the Service; for women, impossible.

Trainees are chosen to call cadence regardless of their singing ability, which doesn't really matter as the call is more of a hoarse yell. As the only two female officer candidates in our class, Danielle and I were chosen all the time. Twelve weeks after basic training, upon completion of the officer program, we were going to outrank all the drill sergeants, so they liked to pick on us, in "preparation for leadership roles." The drill sergeants would also call us El Tee—the diminutive nickname for lieutenant used when soldiers didn't want to pay too much respect to a brand-new officer—whenever we did something wrong. Of course, we weren't officers yet, far from it, but the language was their way of making us feel singled out and alone. Different from the group. Another way to break us down even faster and make us want to do everything we could to earn the right to belong.

Five weeks in was Grenade Throwing Day. After standing in lines to file into the chow hall, shoving as much breakfast as we could down our gullets in the allotted three minutes, we changed into our uniforms, put on our bulletproof vests and heavy gear, picked up our rifles, and assembled into a line to march. That day, after a march of what seemed like several miles according to the blisters on the backs of my heels, we got to the grenade training area. Hours and hours of bonus waiting in the field's bleachers followed.

While books weren't allowed, photos were. I carried mine with me everywhere, in the leg pocket of my uniform. Whenever I got a chance, I would look at my pictures, making up stories in my head of my parents, my siblings, and my friends from college—the relationships I wished I had, open and honest, not the ones I actually had. Their absence somehow made them different people, made me love them more. The one of Dad at my wedding, dressed up in a tuxedo, in a James Bond pose, complete with finger guns and dark sunglasses, always made me smile. Looking at him preserved in that picture, two-dimensional and unmoving, I only had to think of how funny he was or how he gave great hugs. I would never think about the fact that I barely knew him even though I'd lived in the same commune as him for more than ten years. I would stare at photos of my wedding with Jeff and tell myself that I was in love with him—not just stuck. All I saw in the photos of college friends were the smiles and laughter, not the loneliness I'd felt throughout those years.

After making us wait around for what seemed like hours, the drill sergeants came back and started to give us the range safety brief. Grenade Throwing Day meant we would be playing with live grenades.

But first, practice—though not as much as I expected. It takes hours to get 160-odd people through the process of throwing even one fake grenade. After only one practice round each, it was time for the real thing.

This is it, I thought. This was my moment to prove myself as one of the strongest girls in the class, a girl about to be an officer. I had been training with imaginary explosives and warfare my whole life. *This will be easy,* I thought.

Soldier after soldier stepped to the area, a huge, sandy rectangle with a small square wall of sandbags to hide inside. To throw a grenade, we were supposed to pull the tab and toss it, releasing the spool, ten seconds max, and then duck hard down below the sandbag wall. The line proceeded with precision as each soldier performed the duty. The air filled with the satisfying smell of gunpowder. Drill Sergeant McCoy, a Black man at least six foot four, stood on the platform barking orders. He had a loud yelling voice, but also a huge smile and a mouthful of gold teeth that I don't believe ever met the army grooming standards. Mostly he was a teddy bear, unless someone made him really angry.

At my turn, I stepped up, feeling strong, maybe a bit overconfident, and picked up my grenade. I got into the position we had practiced and pulled the tab.

And that's when I froze with a live bomb in my hands. The smell of the gunpowder choked me, invading my lungs with a searing burn. I couldn't breathe. My arms felt as heavy as lead and there was no way I was ever going to be able to move them. Drill Sergeant McCoy stared at me, his eyes popping out in anger at my failure. But then it hit me—it wasn't anger. It was fear. He was standing next to an unstable soldier with an unstable live bomb.

"Poole, throw the fucking grenade! What the fuck are you fucking doing?!"

Time ticked. I couldn't hold the spoon pressed down forever. I didn't want to die, but I couldn't move my arm, no matter how much the drill sergeant yelled. My fingers seared with pain as he wrenched them open, pulling the grenade from my hand and releasing the spoon, starting the clock. Five seconds down, five seconds to go until we both lost some limbs, at the very least. With one fluid motion, he lobbed it away. Then he tackled me as the explosion shook the air around us.

I lay with my face in the dirt, struggling to breathe with at least 300 pounds on top of me, wishing I never had to get up again. As the waves of explosion passed over us, we cowered down behind the wall of sandbags.

Safe.

All those years I'd spent wondering how I would act under fire, all the fantasies of how brave I'd be when facing the forces of the Antichrist, everything came rushing back to me. I may have aced the homework, but I failed the big test. I was a coward. Weak. When it truly mattered, I'd been so scared I had a panic attack. I was going to be Jessica Lynch after all.

I was dragged to my feet and shuffled out of the grenade nest. Drill Sergeant McCoy yelled in my ear the entire walk to the bleachers: "How could you be so stupid? What the fuck happened? There is no way you'll ever be an officer. I sure as hell hope that you never go to war, you will get everyone killed. Remember Jessica damn Lynch?" I sat in stunned silence for the rest of the day, watching everyone else go through the drill. Nobody else hesitated, nobody paused. Only me. I tried looking at my photos, but they were no comfort. Suddenly, my parents' faces only showed disappointment, in my life choices, in my failure. My husband laughed at me. Even my secret lockbox remained closed.

■

SOMEHOW, I KEPT going. I made it to the capstone of basic training, a multiday event in the field. We lived outside in tents, digging foxholes and eating shelf-stable military-grade meals, the perfect survival food. Far away from the flagpole—the headquarters of the higher-ranking brass—both drill sergeants and trainees could let loose. Danielle and I made sure to always partner up together as battle buddies, and we had fun, what I imagine school camping trips must be like—plus guns and ammo. We participated in shooting matches, long runs in the woods, land navigation and capture evasion exercises, and some platoon-on-platoon competitions. One was a hand-to-hand combat tournament where I made it to the final round before getting utterly pounded into the mud, serenaded by loud chants of "Kick her ass! Kick her ass!"

The final event was a seven-mile road march back to the barracks. Seven miles isn't generally considered to be much, and I'd learn that in the "real army" twelve miles was the bare minimum, but for a group of brand-new trainees, most of whom had never exercised before enlisting, the distance was a big hurdle. It was also a requirement for graduation—failure to complete meant starting basic training all over again with the next class. Add in the crushing heat and humidity of South Carolina in late summer, and the drill sergeants had a challenge too: keep everyone alive and marching forward until we made it back to home base.

To start the road march, four platoons lined up, one behind the other, in two parallel lines. Drill sergeants scattered themselves among us. The goal: maintain a distance of five paces from the person in front of you and walk about fifteen to eighteen minutes per mile—a fairly fast clip, halfway between walking and a slow jog. Throw in the small detail that we are in full "battle-rattle" and combat load—rucksack full of gear and a rifle with seven additional magazines, each loaded with thirty rounds of ammunition, a Kevlar helmet, vest, and canteens of water—about fifty pounds of weight at a bare minimum. Anyone who couldn't keep up stepped to the side of the line, known as "falling out." The goal for those left behind was to ignore the embarrassment and ridicule from the drill sergeants and other soldiers, and to keep going at their own pace and avoid the fall-out van at the very back of the line. The van towed a towering, portable water tank, called a water buffalo, filled with five hundred gallons of water. If the van passed you, you got a free trip back to the barracks, another nine weeks of hell, and the devastation of watching the rest of your group become soldiers without you.

As good as I was at running, walking was my nemesis. When I was running, I could zone out, release my body into the pain of competition and just be. But somehow, walking, marching, all of it, felt so plodding, every step stretching out in front of me like I'd never reach the end, and humping more than 50 percent of my body weight didn't make it any easier to get through. When I was running, my mind felt clear of thoughts, and I could fly; on a march, I had to think about everything, over and over, with each hard step.

As the midday sun beat down on us, my pace began to lag. Soon, I stepped to the side of the line, falling farther and farther behind my platoon. Drill Sergeant McCoy yelled at me, and then taunted me in front of my platoon about how crazy it was that one of his "physical fitness studs" was falling behind. But the heat was something else, easily over 100 degrees and with a humidity so high it made it hard to breathe, nothing like the friendly, soft Brazilian heat where I'd grown up, or the dry heat of Texas. I was far from the only one struggling on the sidelines.

I looked to my left and saw Private Morales, who seemed to be struggling even more than I was. His head was so drooped, his chin nearly rested on his chest. He seemed nothing like the strong, jolly soldier that made us all laugh when we were killing time back in the unit communal areas. My mind flashed to Danielle, because I knew they were friends. I wondered how she was doing up ahead, her tiny legs trying to keep up with the challenging pace and the crushing heat of the afternoon sun. The final march was the one time in basic training when there weren't buddies—it was every prospective soldier for themselves.

Jonathan Morales was a big, funny Hispanic kid from Milwaukee who seemed to get along with everyone and avoided most of the personality dramas that popped up from living in such close quarters. He had graduated from high school that spring, where he wrestled competitively. He'd done an impressive show of hand-to-hand combat, taking on the commander in the field, whom he'd easily beaten, much to the glee of all four platoons watching. He was a size that the army would probably always consider fat, even though he showed an impressive amount of stamina during workouts. His strength for lifting heavy equipment or fellow soldiers was unsurpassed.

I called out, "Eres fuerte, hermano. You're strong, brother. Keep your head up. We're almost there!" He gave me a wan smile, and his head drooped lower still. I feared he'd wind up on the fall-out van. He'd have to start over. *Better keep my own head up,* I told myself. *I don't want to repeat basic training too.*

Another few miles in, the sun began to dip behind the pine trees, a welcome and glorious relief. I heard someone shout "take a knee," the command that sent our lines screeching to a halt. We faced outward and pointed our weapons into the tree lines, guarding against possible attacks, as we'd been trained to do. There wasn't anything to signal that this was anything other than a routine stop to rest, drink water, and allow the men to pee along the wood line. The women, about forty of us, would have to wait until we got back. I had the rotten luck of kneeling right next to the first sergeant, the senior sergeant in the whole unit and advisor to the commander, who must have been bringing up the rear behind me. I kept my eyes straight ahead, trying not to draw his attention.

And then we heard an ambulance racing past. Nothing alarming— could be for anyone in the main army post full of houses and training barracks. The first sergeant grabbed his radio. His voice sounded tense as he barked into it, "Someone go and check on the rider in the fall-out van." I thought of Morales, who had been the farthest back when I'd passed him, and I realized that he must be in the back of the van. *Poor guy,* I thought. *He'll have to do this whole thing again.* Then I wondered, *Who is in the van helping him?*

Drill sergeants started running up and down the line in a flurry of activity. I'd never done this before; neither had the platoon. We didn't know if it was strange or par for the course. After about twenty minutes, we started walking again. The first sergeant had disappeared.

When we arrived back at camp, tiki torches flickered in the early evening dark. Soldiers and the entire high-ranking leadership lined the path, cheering as we arrived. An American flag flew on a giant flagpole with all kinds of military flags around it—the army, the division, the brigade, the battalion, the company, each platoon. We were surrounded by the symbolism, the mythology, of the elite world we'd all fought so hard to become a part of for the previous nine weeks. We had become part of the 1 percent of Americans who'd volunteered to serve their country during a time of war. We had accomplished our rite of passage, and here was our ceremony, accompanied by barrels and barrels of a type of Kool-Aid we called "Victory Punch." We all straggled in, desperate for a drink, before pulling into a large, square formation, standing shoulder to shoulder, on the parade field.

The music of country star Lee Greenwood began to blare through the overhead loudspeakers. Soldiers continued cheering as the commander came down the rows, shaking people's hands, his expression restrained. "Congratulations, Soldier," he said, over and over again. Emotions were at an apex. Tears streamed down the face of the trainee to my right. The guy to my left belted out the lyrics with his whole chest. My lips didn't move. I could barely see Danielle's head in the front-right corner of the group, her spot as the tiniest person in the platoon. Was she feeling this way too? Almost everyone around me seemed to be singing with all their might, chanting the chorus in unison.

I'm proud to be an American,
Where at least I know I'm free.

But I looked straight ahead, my thoughts harkening back to the Prophet's "graduation" ceremony so many years before, the Uncles speaking in tongues, the Aunties chanting at God, throwing themselves on the floor in tears. The pageantry, the ceremony, the messaging. Standing straight as boards, not daring to move an inch. Singing of freedom, when we were, at this moment, anything but free.

Despite my feelings of apprehension, I also felt the stirrings of fervor, of dedication, and the sweetly sad idea of death in service of country. I saw commitment and pride overtaking fear and exhaustion in the faces of the trainees around me. I wanted to feel it with them, but my elation was tempered by the ugly familiarity of it all. *We're definitely ready to graduate,* I thought. Our programming was nearly complete; our dedication, absolute.

From the corners of my eyes, I also saw the command team scrambling. As we stood in formation, tiki torches alight, ceremony in full swing, the drill sergeants weren't participating. Rather, they huddled in a circle around the commander, first sergeant, and others in authority, talking and gesturing in a way that suggested something was wrong. I recognized the look on their faces—it was the look of people who needed to get their stories straight. It was on the face of every adult in the Children of God whenever something went wrong, whenever there was a raid on one of the communes, whenever one of us needed to go to the hospital.

The next morning, they called us to the chapel, unusual on a Thursday. There were a lot more command people than we typically saw, higher-ups on-site for some reason that didn't seem like business as usual. They broke the news fast: Private Jonathan Morales was dead.

He'd died of heatstroke at the hospital after being loaded into the fall-out van, we were told. The brass counseled us that, as trainees, we shouldn't talk to any reporters, or offer any information during any investigation that might take place; our leaders would handle it. The *Deceivers Yet True* comic flashed before my eyes, the one that instructed all the children of The Family on how to lie for God. We all sat in stunned silence, nobody moving, nobody saying a word, staring straight ahead, the silence only punctuated by sobs coming from members of our platoon scattered around the chapel. I heard Danielle's among them. Basic training is supposed to cover everything you hadn't been exposed to before. That day, we got an unplanned lesson—the casualty of a brother-in-arms.

As the day wore on, we heard bits through the rumor mill. Morales had been loaded into the back of the van alone because the drill sergeants hadn't wanted to pull anyone else out of the march to be his battle buddy. He'd been found later lying in the road, apparently having fallen out of the van, by a couple of soldiers out for a late-afternoon run, who'd called the ambulance. Morales died in the hospital of a 106-degree fever. I have no idea how much of what we heard was true or how much was gossip. But I kept replaying the moment when the first sergeant heard sirens in the distance and radioed for someone to check on the "rider." If someone fell out of the van, how could they avoid being run over by the thousand-plus-pound water buffalo that followed it? Wouldn't that have been enough to kill him? Why were they calling it heatstroke?

Get with the program! I reprimanded myself. *We aren't supposed to ask any questions.*

So, I didn't. Like I did on the march, like I'd done so often growing up, I kept my head down and continued moving. The death went down as a tragic, but inevitable, heat fatality. Much later, when I called back for some copies of paperwork I'd not managed to get before leaving, I learned that the entire company of drill sergeants and officers had been quietly relieved from duty.

◼

IN A FEW days, after nine weeks of training, we'd get to don our dress uniform for the first time, emblazoned with its gold embroidery and rank, and the few ribbons we'd earned by volunteering to serve. More drill and ceremony to initiate us into the life of a soldier.

As soon as we straggled out of the chapel, an orderly came scrambling up to me. "Specialist Poole," she said, a little out of breath. "There's been a couple calls for you. You need to call home. Please come with me."

Home, she'd said. I was so confused, my first thoughts going to Jeff, my husband, still so weird to say. Was he okay? Had something happened? What had she meant by "home"? I thought of Mom, still living in a commune in Mexico with six kids, including the eighth baby whose birth caused her to miss my college graduation, and the same people I'd left behind years before. Dad was always sickly. Merry and her fiancé were relatively close in Georgia with their new baby. What had happened? Was everyone okay?

I dialed the number to the life I had left behind and Auntie Joy picked up, running to get Mom, not even asking why a Systemite was calling. I looked at the drill sergeant supervising my phone call, wondering how I would explain this Family of mine. Then Mom was on the phone, and hearing her voice after everything I'd been through over the past nine weeks, over the past twenty-two years, broke me in a way basic training couldn't.

"Grace is sick," she said. "*My daughter* might be dying. I'm coming to the US tonight."

Mom explained that Grace, who had been relatively healthy since she'd had all her surgeries at birth nearly eight years prior, had been getting worse for weeks, but all the local doctors in Mexico told Mom that Grace was fine. But she was not fine: She had a 106-degree fever. Mom knew something was wrong, so she bought tickets for a plane to Houston that night to take Grace to the children's hospital while Dad stayed behind with the baby and the four boys. He could join them later.

My brain couldn't process the conversation. I heard fragments about Mom possibly leaving The Family, of her talking to Gramps who thought it might be time for her to find a new life. Grace dying. A fever. If Morales died of a 106-degree fever, a fever so high it damaged his brain, surely it would damage Grace's brain too. And Mom, I considered the way she said "my daughter" like I had never heard before, like she was paying attention to these kids, being there for them, in a way she had been too young, too indoctrinated, too controlled, and too afraid to ever be there for me.

"Call Heaven and Dougie," I instructed. "They'll help you. I will try to meet you there. I'll need a note from your doctor via the Red Cross to get me out of here. Mention the high fever."

Click.

After filing a Red Cross emergency request, I got permission to leave basic training two days before graduation to meet Mom and Grace, who would undergo brain surgery to remove and replace an infected brain shunt. Danielle would bring my certificates to officer school the next week. Jeff, rather than attending my graduation ceremony as we'd planned, would meet me in Houston, and after making sure my family was okay—or not—we'd drive to Fort Benning, Georgia, so I could report back five days later. But all I could think about on the plane, in my uniform because I'd come straight from training, was what the next hours would bring. One hundred six degrees, just like Morales. Would my sister die?

I thought of little Andrew who'd died of pneumonia, of Miriam who'd died of the measles, of Auntie Hope and her tragic fight with the brain cancer that hadn't been demons after all, of all the others who hadn't survived to walk away. Would the cult take my family too? Or would this be their break? What did it mean for them to think about a new life? What would *my* new life be? Who were we to each other, apart?

I grabbed my duffel bag of gear and new uniforms, and as I hailed a taxi to the hospital, I laughed, and the driver caught my eyes in the rearview mirror. Maybe my laugh was that of a madwoman, someone who had survived programming again, or maybe it was the sound of a sister, a daughter, a woman free for a few days to be in a different battle—but a fight just the same—alongside Mom again.

19

YOU'RE NOT JAMES BOND

■

Fort Benning, Georgia, 2009

Officer Candidate School, often sardonically called the "Fort Benning School for Boys," was one of the army's answers for churning out enough junior officers required for the US war machine to run smoothly, and had ramped way up for the ongoing War on Terror and troop surge in Afghanistan that had started the year I signed up. Everyone in my class knew that our first assignments could be overseas. For most of us, given the intensity of the past months of training, it was an exciting prospect—we were itching to go to war and finally do the job we'd trained for.

They told us officer school was where we would learn how to work together to lead teams of soldiers, but in reality, everything was an individual competition. Who could jump the highest, stand at attention the longest, perform the best on tests in the classroom and wherever else a cadre leader decided to question us. Perfection was the only option, and anything less was berated. *"IF YOU CAN'T RUN TO STANDARD,"* they'd bellow, *"WHY ARE YOU EVEN HERE?"* My body fell in line, primed with a kind of muscle memory from a childhood defined by constant rankings and competition, of always having to earn my place. I competed like my life depended on it. I knew my professional life did.

Danielle, in a different platoon but still my closest confidante, tried to calm me down, to convince me everything wasn't so serious. She warned me I was driving people away. I didn't have the vocabulary yet to articulate that my constant striving for perfection was primal—a drive for survival—rooted in my trauma, of always being in a world where I was wrong, in a body that had kept score. I couldn't comprehend how comfortable she was with the concept of working hard, falling in the middle-upper range of the rankings, and getting an assignment she might not love, but, hopefully, wouldn't hate. I, on the other hand, was obsessed with only one course of action: military intelligence. I *had* to be the best.

Week nine of the twelve-week course was branching week—think NFL football draft but with military uniforms. Big Army tells the cadre what branches officer candidates could select—from the highly coveted infantry (for the men only) and military intelligence, to the middle of the road branches of military, like IT, police, and human resources, jobs that could still be valuable out in the civilian world, all the way down to the branches nobody wanted, like field artillery, air defense, and chemical warfare. Then we all sit in a giant room and, one by one, they call our names and we select our future careers by picking up a little gold symbol, the branch insignia, and pinning it to the collars of our fatigues, sealing the next three to twenty years of our life.

I'd joined the army already intrigued by military intelligence. I'd read everything about it and felt I had a pretty good grasp on the role: understand the enemy and collect, analyze, and disseminate information so our guys could do their jobs with as little risk as possible. It was also the role that the cadre taunted the most: "Military intelligence is an oxymoron. Real soldiers don't get chained to computers. It's not like you're going to be James Bond or anything." Just like in the civilian world, the smart kids got teased. But I didn't care about their jabs. It wasn't the coolness of the role that attracted me, and it didn't bother me that it would be thankless and pressurized. What mattered was that I would be the expert—listened to, consulted, expected to be smart and savvy. Besides, a job where the government would pay me to change everything about the way I saw the world to understand the motives of someone else, of other groups? Learn all the rules? That was my basic survival skill. Sign me up.

But it wasn't that easy. Only six slots. Twenty-seven hopeful candidates. And an intense background vetting process for the required top-secret security clearance. I needed to outrun my past, while performing perfectly to jockey for a chance. Running, as it turned out, was my secret weapon. Once I'd figured out in basic training that I was fast, I trained like someone was chasing me. The army rated men and women on different scales, always assuming that women could not meet the same physical standards as men, based on a non-scientifically supported notion that those physical standards were necessary in the first place. But I could ace the men's standards, which made me a target for both sides of the affirmative action debate, especially given how much my career benefited from it. In a world where everything was stack-ranked and based on gender, I'd worked my way up to doing eighty push-ups, almost double the max for women, and I got thirty-five extra points for running the same six-minute mile as a male candidate, who would only receive three points. For my class, we witnessed how Officer Candidate School became a track competition, with the winners literally running their way into the army's top branches.

In hindsight, it seems obvious this type of training not only created a me-first atmosphere instead of one of cooperation and leadership, but also further alienated the men who thought women weren't good enough to belong, no matter how good we were. For me, I always felt caught in the middle, my own wins and achievements secondary to the bruised egos of the men who placed behind me.

But I made it. My name was the sixth to be called out of the more than 180 candidates who'd made it thus far, and I felt relieved more than triumphant when I picked up the gold flower pierced by a sword, the symbol of the military intelligence branch, and pinned it to my collar. That evening, the six of us new intel officers donned bow ties at the candidate watering hole as we ordered our martinis "shaken, not stirred" and laughed at the expense of our cadre, who hadn't been able to break us completely.

I'd done it. Jumped the hurdles and got the career I'd set out for when I'd started—even Jeff hadn't been able to do that, having to settle for field artillery when he'd hoped for finance, even though, in the preceding year, he had made up for his disappointment by transforming "tough combat arms guy" into a core part of his identity. Danielle graduated in the top quartile like she expected and chose signal—the IT branch—even though she'd wanted military intelligence as badly as I had. "You'll be the only signal officer incapable of operating the radios," I joked afterward, laughing away the sadness that we'd soon be separated, permanently. "You'll make a great platoon leader, wherever you go," I finished.

I thought of how Dad would probably switch to spy shows so he could continue asking me, "Is it really like this?" He'd been glued to army shows since they'd left The Family, and whenever I called, he peppered me with questions about how much the army had changed since he had been in it, back in the Vietnam War era. I knew Mom would be proud of me; she always was.

So just like that, after a mere five months of training, at twenty-two years old, and six and a half years in the "real world," looking like a deer in several very bright headlights, I found myself a second lieutenant in the United States Army. Ready, set, leadership—just add war. After our commissioning ceremony, Danielle and I took what would become our signature tongue-in-cheek photo—facing each other, palms together, each with a foot popped out sassily behind us, our carefully pressed army greens bright, our second lieutenant rank winking from our berets. Then I was on a highway with Jeff, driving cross-country in the overly fancy car he insisted I buy—the perfect officer car, according to him—and then leaving him in Fort Polk, Louisiana, his first duty station.

I stopped in Houston to see my family for Thanksgiving, which made me feel like every other American soldier on leave: something close to normal. Mom and Grace had settled close to the hospital for Grace's recovery, which was improving, and Dad had taken a bus from Mexico with the other five kids to join Mom not just for the holiday but full-time. As we said grace at the table, I bowed my head, even though I hadn't prayed once since I'd left home. I thought about all I was grateful for: surviving—flourishing even—and the new rank and title that said I was secure. Grace was alive, even if we didn't know what the long-term damage of her illness might be, and I was glad that Mom had gotten my family out. I looked at my little brothers, all young teenagers or older children, thrust into school for the first time, the way I'd been. I knew they'd have a hard road ahead. They hadn't been preparing for the change the way I had been for so long before I left The Family. I didn't even know if they wanted it. It felt like a lifetime ago when we sat at a similar table on 9/11, when the crack in my brainwashing started the painful process of light getting in.

Too soon, leave was over, and I waved to my family from the rear-view mirror. I kept driving to Sierra Vista, both a relatively small town and one of the larger cities in Arizona, right at the Mexico border. I arrived at Fort Huachuca: U.S. Army Intelligence Center of Excellence, or "spy school," as we all called it, where we would learn how to "think red"—to get inside the heads of the bad guys, the others, to play the enemy in war games and become part of a time-honored tradition of predicting where they might be hiding so that our combat forces could do their thing.

Which is how I found myself, months later, incredulous as I looked around the room, watching American officer after American officer defend the concept of torturing other human beings.

I had been sixteen in 2003, when the torture at the American-run Iraqi prisoner of war camp, Abu Ghraib, made international headlines. At the time, I had been drowning in my first year of high school and trying to figure out life outside the cult, so I had only the vaguest memories of the incident. But I took it all in as I saw those pictures for the first time on a giant screen in front of me, as the captain at the front of the room talked about the difference between what had been defined by the Bush Administration as "enhanced interrogation techniques"—things like stress positions, sleep deprivation, and the infamous waterboarding—versus what he called "real torture." Torture was what bad guys did, like cutting off fingers and pulling out teeth. We didn't do that stuff. We were the good guys. We were *always* the good guys.

But I couldn't see a difference. I looked around the room and felt

certain none of these people had ever spent any time in endless isolation. Maybe it was easy to call stress positions humane when you'd
never had to hold the King James Bible in your outstretched arms
for an unspecified period of time, before you were even old enough
to read it. Maybe they had never been subjected to days of imposed
silence where you have nothing to do but chew your own skin and
sift through your own thoughts. They didn't know that hunger, sleep
deprivation, uncertainty, and horror will get people to say anything,
do anything, to make it stop.

"Well, as one of the few of us who's already been to war," said one
of the prior-service lieutenants who had crossed over from being a
staff sergeant and already had years of experience as an interrogator,
which he reminded us of in every conversation, "I can promise you
that these are *bad guys.* If I have to torture a thousand *innocent* people
in order to save one *American* life, I'll do it, no question!"

I studied one face to the next, each nodding in agreement and
mumbling confirmation of their righteous rage at anyone who dared
to not be an American. How was it possible that nine out of the ten
most intelligent, competitive, best-of-their-class army officers were
casually—and publicly—expressing their belief that torture is justified, for any reason? Not to mention against the *innocent.*

But I knew. It was part of why I never really felt at home, never
American enough—I hadn't gotten the same indoctrination as everyone else growing up. America does what the army does, just at a
larger and more insidious scale. The programming begins at birth:
America is the greatest country on earth. We are the best, down with
all the rest, and if we have to torture a thousand innocent people to
prove it, so be it. When you believe you're the best, the chosen ones,
then the end can always be made to justify the means.

That day, I promised myself that I wouldn't hate groups of people:
I'd seen where that could lead. I knew I couldn't share that out loud.
There was no room for disagreement in that crowd. Looking over at
the prior-service lieutenant who'd spoken, I briefly wondered how he
would respond if I stood up and said, "Well, as one of the few of us
who's experienced torture here . . ." But my words stuck in my throat,

and I thought this would be a secret I'd have to keep for the time being. *I won't hate groups of people,* I repeated to myself. Not the Afghans, not the Iraqis, not those we partnered with who ended up betraying us. Not even the terrorists. Sure, a year's worth of nonstop training was starting to make its way into my brain, programming me alongside my peers, but I, at least, knew it was happening. And knowing it was happening meant I could draw some lines in the sand, lines that I'd know not to let the group pull me across.

As I made my way through spy school, embedded in studying countercultures, I realized that this was all nothing but a bet, a conviction based on blind faith at best, narcissistic delusion at worst. We weren't inherently better than anyone; I knew that for a fact. By serving in the army and going to war, we were betting our side was the right side. Looking around the room was a game of Russian roulette—I knew that some of us might die for that bet. And I found myself asking the big question in spy school that wasn't on any test: How does a scholar, a strategist, or a soldier understand a culture well enough to predict future outcomes without being willing to understand that *all* humans, from their own perspectives, are living a truth and reality as valid as ours?

■

"YOU DON'T WANT to be twenty-five and divorced, do you?"

Jeff's steely voice sliced through the phone. He knew exactly how to wound me, how to twist the knife.

But I wasn't Daniella the cult baby anymore. I had a new identity: US Army Lieutenant. I *mattered*. And the more I pictured my future, the life I was building for myself and what I wanted to do, see, and experience, the more I realized I didn't see Jeff anywhere in it.

Since we'd posed as bride and groom in our wedding portraits two years prior, we'd been apart, spending maybe a month total together in the same city. I'd had time to think about why everyone in our life said we shouldn't get married—that we'd been far too young to know what we really wanted—and our overly rushed courtship and ceremony started to make me feel like I had been tricked, somehow coerced into a life I didn't want before I could change my mind. I suspected he was more interested in sleeping with men than sleeping with me. I'd never minded that, at first. It was a relief to not be the object of desire. But I'd started to realize that anytime I felt beautiful, he'd try to take me down a peg. When I'd beat him on a timed run, he'd point out the flab near the tops of my thighs that could be improved. After my valedictorian speech, he'd said that the other guy's talk had been funnier. Something in me clicked and I no longer saw his comments as "just Jeff"—like me, always striving for perfection. I began to see that I would never be enough for him. He wanted to be married to me, even though it was clear that I wasn't what he wanted. It was almost like he wanted to collect me. To own me.

And something I'd seen in him scared me.

I finally admitted that to myself, releasing the quiet dread I had locked in my heart. I didn't want my career tied to his. The life I'd imagined with him, the one I'd glimpsed and decided to grab because I thought it would be good enough, felt like a prison. I didn't know if I could undo it, but I couldn't live with myself if I didn't try.

"No, Babe," I said, turning my voice cold and hard like I'd learned to do while briefing. "I want to be divorced at *twenty-three*."

His reply was a simple "no," one syllable across the phone line that stretched from Arizona to Louisiana. For once, I had nothing to say. We sat in a long, cold silence.

"I *want* to be married," he said flatly, not a hint of romance in his voice. "And you're my wife. My beautiful, perfect wife."

"You can't force me to stay married to you, Jeff."

"I can."

More silence. He meant it.

Our marriage was like chess, always was, without me ever realizing it. I tried to think a few moves ahead, the way I'd been trained. *What can he do to me? What does he know that I don't?* I was worried. I picked up the new smartphone I had just bought, the one I hadn't told him about yet, though I couldn't have said why, clicked record, and placed it near the Blackberry we were speaking on.

"If you try to divorce me, I'll tell your commander you're having an affair with a classmate from officer school." He named a specific one. He knew we were still friends.

I swallowed hard. "You'd lie to try to force me to stay married to you? Why?"

"My chaplain told me that it's God's will for people to stay married and try to work on it."

"Jeff," I said, "you're not any more of a Christian than I am."

Wow. I never said that out loud. Now it's recorded. It was a thought I knew I'd have to revisit. But later.

"You won't be able to prove you're *not* having an affair, and they'll kick you out. You're an *entry . . . level . . . officer.*" He spelled it out slowly. "Nobody will believe you, and nobody will want the trouble, anyway."

I knew the equation: Woman + support branch < Male + combat soldier. Everyone knew who always won the "he said, she said" game. Suddenly, I saw the parallels I had missed before, the ways Jeff resembled the cult Uncles, the ones who needed to control everything and everyone, the ones who were untouchable, no matter their crimes. I wondered if that's what my friends saw and tried to tell me. I wondered if the familiarity was what, in some sick way, drew me to him.

I shuddered.

"Jeff, I want a divorce," I said. I hung up the phone, my hands shaking as I took out the battery. I'd just committed a crime and I knew it. As an intelligence officer, even one who hadn't been certified yet, I knew enough to know that it was highly illegal for an agent of the military to surveil an American citizen or record them against their knowledge.

Adultery is also illegal in the military, and if Jeff followed through on his threat, I could have been court-martialed. At worst, jailed; at best, quietly discharged to make me go away without scandal for the group. Either way, I might be forked yet again, my military career ended because of his false accusations. It could work the way it often did, when legislative "justice" is applied selectively and with bias, especially regarding issues of sex in the army, the ultimate boys' club. But Jeff's threats were illegal too. Knowingly leveling a false accusation

20

CAMP FOLLOWERS

■

Fort Campbell, Kentucky, 2011

The contractor, a man with a thick Texas drawl—and wearing the army symbols former combat arms guys stitch to their ball caps to display their army résumé—addressed the gaggle of soldiers who'd wandered over to his station. I pulled Lieutenant Tiffany Taylor down onto the concrete floor next to me as we gathered around for instruction. It hadn't taken us long to become friends, both of us realizing the only other female lieutenant in the brigade headquarters unit would be an important companion to have during a year deployed to Afghanistan. When we learned we'd be rooming together, it seemed natural, though we were total opposites.

Tiffany folded the long legs of her six-foot-one-inch frame under herself and arranged the rest of the gear we'd both collected as a pile of support behind us. "I wonder how we'll fit all this new stuff into the two duffels we're allowed to bring with us," I murmured.

"Just leave some of your makeup behind, Miss Thing." She laughed. Since the divorce and my move to Fort Campbell, I'd begun to shift out of what other soldiers degradingly called my "dyke" phase; my previously buzzed hair was now blond and bobbed, a style I could wear down in uniform. I also spent time at the makeup mirror putting my face on every day, trying hard to look both professional and just a bit older than twenty-three. Tiffany couldn't have been less concerned, her brown hair pulled back in the ubiquitous army bun and her fresh face ready to take on any challenge.

"I'm impressed they actually issued us sports bras for war," I added. "Remember how in basic training they gave the men free underwear but we had to buy four sports bras for the equipment lay-out with our own money? Didn't matter how many perfectly good ones we brought with us."

She shook her head.

"Oh, I forgot you went to West Point and didn't do basic train-ing," I said. "How will I ever forgive myself . . ." I trailed off, feigning a worshipful bow, my hands raised, paying homage to the intense rivalry between West Point and Officer Candidate School graduates, and kissing the ring. Like most West Pointers, she was used to being mocked by officers from the "lesser" commissioning sources, and re-sponded as they all do, with the confident smile of those who know their worth.

"All right, all right, guys," the contractor said, then started his brief. "This is a twenty-minute block of instruction on how to wear your new armored vest and carrier. Please lay the combat vest in front of you . . ."

Leaning some of my weight on Tiffany, I zoned in and out, know-ing that the first several times I put the equipment on would be a di-saster. Then a sergeant or someone else on the intelligence team, great at the "roughing it" parts of soldiering, would step up and "square away" the poor lost second lieutenant. Sweating through layers of winter gear, my eyes started to droop closed as the stuffiness of the old warehouse set in. Scared of falling asleep in front of everyone, I shook myself and tuned back in to the speaker.

"So, the thing is," he said, holding up a heavy square plate the size of a laptop computer, rotating it lengthwise in front of his chest and then pulling it snugly against himself. "When you put your vest on, and this is mounted correctly, y'all'll want to make sure that this piece of Kevlar is sitting no more than half an inch away from your center of mass. In a firefight, ya gotta protect yer vital organs, and that's how. When you lose weight—which you will, because the food in the sandbox is shit—y'all need to make sure you get a new vest from Damage Exchange. This is the most important thing any of y'all will hear today."

He paused briefly and stamped his foot, the universal army gesture to command special attention. "If there's too much space in between the plate that stops the bullet and your big old bellies, then the impact of the bullet hitting this here Kevlar can concuss your insides and they'll be sending those Purple Hearts home to your families instead of pinning 'em on you. Y'all hearing me? The fit makes a big difference in whether you get killed by a fucking raghead over there or not."

I had stopped cringing a long time ago at words like "raghead" that everyone threw around constantly. Like anything, if you hear it long enough, you stop hearing it. *Don't hate,* I reminded myself.

Around me, everyone sat up a little straighter, holding their own bulletproof plates tighter, examining the measurement. I didn't need to hold mine up to realize I had a problem. So did Tiffany, and every other woman.

"Excuse me, Sir." I raised my hand even though I didn't want to, knowing how this conversation would probably go. "Can you explain to me how this is supposed to work for the females?"

He blinked two rounded eyes at me, all pretense of joviality gone. "Come again, El Tee?" He drew out the letters. "This here is armor, doll, it has nothing to do with your gender. You are gonna want it to stop bullets, not buy you dinner."

"Yes, I understand the whole not wanting to get shot part," I said as I rose. "But can I demonstrate one issue, a rather small one in my case?"

I shed my fuzzy green overcoat and army combat uniform jacket and turned to face him. Nothing ever fit a woman right in the army: I wore my extra-small men's uniform pants hiked up to the narrowest part of my waist, to prevent them from falling off me when I walked. "Even for a girl like me, no curves at all," I said, ignoring the tightening feeling inside my chest as I drew attention to my bust, "a plate like this"—I pulled it tighter—"is gonna give a pretty wide gap between my vital organs and the Kevlar. I've got boobs, a bit of a blocking system built in here."

I pivoted to the right, showing him the gap of nearly three inches between the plate and my midsection.

The contractor scratched his head. "I see what you're saying, El Tee, but I don't know what to tell you. I've never had a soldier whip out their boobs during a briefing, you know?" He laughed, his eyes darting around the eighteen men in my group, and they all chuckled with him. *Fuck, I'm not gonna live that one down.*

"But in all seriousness, darling, I don't think you really have to worry about it. You women are not going to be in combat getting shot at, now are ya?"

I eyed Tiffany, and we didn't need words to exchange the same questions: Why even bother lugging around a thirty-pound weight if it wasn't even guaranteed to keep us alive? Did anyone even care?

After a year and a half in the army, I knew that women were an afterthought, always. Everything was designed for men, and women were considered scaled-down men, when we were considered at all. The attitude, no matter what part of the army it came from, was: You ladies *asked* to be here, so don't complain about anything. *Ever.* If a man has an issue, he can raise it, but a girl? Come on, doll. *You knew what you were signing up for.*

As if anyone can ever know what they are signing up for when it comes to war.

And war was where we were going. I'd arrived at my unit made up of three thousand helicopter pilots, crew, and all the staff who supported them, responsible for troop movements, close air support of troops in combat, and conducting medical evacuations or body retrieval of wounded troops and fallen Heroes.

Not that I knew any of that. I'd be going off to war on a team whose mission I did not completely understand, to do a job I knew I had only the faintest idea how to do. I'd arrived after the unit completed all the pre-deployment training, as the intelligence soldiers and officers were all heading out on leave. While my new unit, trained up and ready, was spending time with loved ones they wouldn't see for a year, I spent my days on the base, same as I'd done with any free time I'd had during the intelligence course, binge-watching popular American TV shows from the aughts that I'd never seen. I threw myself into *Gilmore Girls, The OC, Smallville, Lost,* and, of course, *Law & Order: SVU*—relishing seeing the bad guys finally get what was coming to them, sometimes. Danielle would have recognized my loner behavior as depression, but she was deployed to Korea. And I didn't. Not yet.

I spent time trying to prepare myself for what a deployment environment might look like—especially for a woman. I suspected, like so many times in my childhood, that I would have to figure out what role to play to survive. I needed to learn all the normal things a second lieutenant did: what to actually bring versus what was on the official packing list, what to do to prepare to leave the real world for a year, and what life was going to look like for twelve whole months over there. Before basic training, officer school, and even the intelligence course, Jeff helped prepare me for what it might be like—though always from his perspective. I'm sure he'd thought, like everyone else seemed to, that men's and women's experiences in uniform were identical, or at least parallel. I was finding out how wrong that was. I needed to know if I would have access to tampons, what our facilities would look like, what security would look like. What did I need to know to keep myself safe? Was there anything I could do to keep the gossips from whispering about me—whispers that could affect my career? How could I hold up under the mental stress of being one of so few?

I took to Google, hoping to find tips, stories, anything that could teach me what to expect. There wasn't much, except the suggestion to bring colorful underwear and nail polish to paint the toes—the only color besides variations of brown and tan I'd likely see in a year, self-care items for my eyes only, to help me feel like a girl in the sandbox. Mostly, I'd found other women expressing the same crushing lack of community that I already felt, and warning how amplified it would become downrange.

I wasn't prepared for the vitriol. The vetbros who'd served a tour or two spewed words that should have been unspeakable at anyone who dared to suggest women might be capable of serving in combat. Their arguments were always some version of "men are the best, down with all the rest," that quickly devolved into "somebody should rape you to put you in your place." Rape threats also came from men still in uniform, their identities conveniently masked by social media handles. Like in spy school, I found myself horrified by my difference from the rest, by how many of these men—the ones who were supposed to be my battle buddies—shared these same heinous beliefs. I wondered which of them were behind usernames just like these.

It wasn't just the men. I suppose I shouldn't have been surprised that women who have never been in the military look down on those who serve, but I was. I had always thought we weren't that different—we were all just women who'd picked one job over another, selected a career we thought would appeal to us. But they expressed how we were overly masculine, traitors to our gender. Some of the military wives, women whose husbands I might be serving alongside, called us hussies, whores, dyke-bitches. And "camp followers."

"Just like armies have always had camp followers as they go off to war, the US Army has blond Lieutenants," read one comment online. "I'm just lucky my husband's a combat guy, so he doesn't have to work with any of those dangerous sluts."

And then, buried underneath, were the warnings. Be careful. Be aware. Have a buddy. Don't walk alone. Most people are raped by someone they know. But have a buddy anyway. Maybe you'll get lucky, maybe you'll choose the right big-tall-scary-looking guy to keep you safe, and maybe he will *choose* to do so.

And even more blatant: Don't get raped. Just don't get raped. As though it was that simple. As though it was something we could control. According to the Department of Defense's own numbers, my odds of being sexually assaulted were one in four—and those were just the numbers that had been reported. Don't go anywhere without your rifle, never mind that they'll have them too and be better trained to use them. Keep your head down. Don't draw attention to yourself. And whatever you do, do not question the system that makes it this way.

My boss, the brigade's senior intelligence officer, Captain Dickson, threw a magazine in my lap one day when we sat around the office with everything packed, counting down the days and hours until we got on the aircraft to leave. "Here, read this," he said. "Let me know if you have any questions."

The article was about the sexual assault of women in uniform, how dangerous it was for those deployed to Iraq and Afghanistan. Words like "rape alley" jumped off the pages, numbers swam in front of my eyes, forming word problems as though there would be a test later: *If approximately 150 women have died in Iraq/Afghanistan, but 100 of them were noncombat-related, what percentage of deaths were from sudden illness? Murder? Rape? Suicide? Suspicious accident?* My hand slowly came up to cover my mouth, as I realized he was trying to prepare me for a hazard of duty that would only apply to me.

Don't get raped. Don't get raped. Don't get yourself raped.

■

"HEY, EL TEE, you know how you're always blabbing all that girl power shit?" Sergeant First Class Krizinsky, who we only called "Sarn't K," strolled into our intelligence office in Kandahar, Afghanistan, waving his four-fingered hand in the air in my general direction, as if there was any question to whom he spoke.

"Sarn't K," I quipped, "are you still pissed that nobody has been able to prove to me that they can do a push-up with their penis, and therefore have fundamentally failed to defend any reason there should be a combat ban against women according to the army's own physical standards?"

"Now, now, don't get your panties in a bunch, Ma'am." He raised his fingers in the air, pantomiming surrender. "I just came over from Task Force Pale Horse, where they're putting together some kind of girly, tough, experimental combat team and I thought you'd be chomping at the bit to go show off all your freaking HOOAH! I told 'em you're the baddest bitch we got in probably the whole unit."

He took a breath, smirking. I tried to hide the giant grin spreading across my face at his compliment. Technically, I outranked him, but like any good second lieutenant, I knew I wasn't actually in charge. Ever. It was an honor to have a sergeant first class say anything positive to me. I guessed my hard work was paying off. "Anyways, that's my old unit," he said. "They're good guys, the Pathfinders, for the fucking infantry. Ask Captain Madison for permission, though, 'cos Captain Rodriguez will be pissed."

"All right, Sarn't," I said, still trying to control my excitement. "I'll check it out. And yeah, I think you're right about her."

I knew that Captain Gillian Rodriguez, the only other woman on our intelligence team, would be far more jealous than supportive of a woman for standing out—in anything.

"I've always thought it's important for intelligence professionals to know the situation on the ground they're supposed to be the experts on," Captain Mike Madison said to our boss, Captain Dickson, recommending they release me from some intelligence duties to participate in the patrols. "Plus, you know she's never gonna shut up about equality and running fast and all the shit she thinks girls can do. Best we let her do it. She'll figure out pretty quickly that there is nothing cool about being 'allowed' to go on deliberate combat operations."

"What about the others?" Captain Dickson asked as if I wasn't in the room. "Don't you think our two male lieutenants will be pissed that she gets days off to go play soldier in the sand while they're stuck here manning their desks twelve hours a day?"

"I don't think I care much about their bellyaching," Captain Madison said. "They had every opportunity to be infantry men if that's what they'd wanted, whereas fucking Daniella, arguably as fast and strong as any of them, didn't have that choice. Now they need women, so she gets a shot. If it were me, I'd tell them to stop whining and go be in the infantry when we get home if that's how they feel."

It was settled. Captain Dickson understood the need for women in combat, especially in that war. And in intelligence, we understood counter-insurgency fights need the trust of its people. When we busted down the doors of conservative Muslim Afghan homes, we needed women to cordon and search families who didn't allow men to even look at "their" women.

Captain Madison was a good partner to Captain Dickson. He focused on training his lieutenants to value what different perspectives and viewpoints could bring to our business of predicting where things would blow up and where bad guys were most likely to hide to shoot at our helicopters. He'd wave his hands in large gestures learned from a long line of Italian ancestry, saying, "Men and women together make the best intel teams, 'cos we see different shit."

Alone, on the four-mile hike over to Pale Horse's Tactical Operations Center, the knot in my stomach grew larger as I approached the Pathfinders, the infantry attachment that works with a combat aviation brigade. Would these guys be married to the idea of their own superiority too? Were they like the vetbros online? Or would they be like the captains in my office who at least understood the need for us women to be there, all while doing our best not to bleed to death, wounded by the shards of the glass ceiling we were trying to shatter?

Walking up to the Tactical Operations Center, I saw men lounging on a step outside, cigarettes hanging from their lips, sleeves unbuttoned and flapping loosely about their wrists. No mistaking these guys for anything but the Pathfinders, with their cool confidence and Ranger tabs glinting off every left shoulder.

Their badass reputation was earned. They lived in 24/7 readiness to deploy a team—within ten minutes or less—to the site of any downed aircraft in the southern part of Afghanistan. They'd work giant equipment to cut open the belly of an army bird, rescue or recover souls and sensitive equipment on board, and destroy what could not be saved. Teams that were not on standby for this mission would do other infantry operations as required, and those deliberate combat missions were where the women would come into play.

Swallowing hard, I placed my hand on the door of the Tactical Operations Center, ready to introduce myself.

"Hey, El Tee!"

I turned around slowly. If I could discern who was addressing me, I'd know how to respond. If it were a low-ranking private or specialist, I could be outraged by the tone, and speak up, make them address me with a bit more formality. But anyone higher on the officer chain and *I'd* have to muster up the respect and deference. Just my luck, he was wearing rockers, the bars added to rank someone as a staff sergeant, and the levels above. It was impossible for a lieutenant to know how to respond to a sergeant, especially a staff sergeant, without knowing more about the power dynamics of the group.

The staff sergeant, a guy with blond hair cropped close enough to look nearly bald, sauntered over in my direction. I walked toward him, hoping I was successfully feigning an equal amount of disinterested confidence.

"Well, you're a pretty young thing," he said. "You're here to be in the infantry, I'd guess?" He cocked an eyebrow, like he was daring me to run away with my tail between my legs.

My heart dropped. I plastered on a giant smile and steadied myself for what I feared was going to be just the beginning of the hazing.

"I sure am, Sarn't Mills," I said, glancing at the name on his uniform. "Are you gonna be the one to teach me?" I hated how girly and young my voice sounded.

"Well, I'm gonna try," he said, replacing the cigarette between his lips.

He might be the guy who would train me, but I still needed to report for duty. I turned back to the door.

"Hey, El Tee."

"Yes, Sarn't?" I said, pivoting back to face him.

"It's about goddamn time!"

He smiled, before casually turning his back on an officer and walking away.

I quickly opened the door and slipped inside. "I need to find Lieutenant John Runkle, please," I said to the soldier at the front desk.

"Well, you found *me* instead," boomed a voice from somewhere in the cramped waiting area behind him. "I'm Sergeant First Class Z, and you must be my last fucking infantry recruit. It's nice of you to join us . . . Maaaa'aaaam."

A large man wearing sergeant first class rank and "Zanetti" across the right side of his chest rose from a desk in the corner. He nodded his head in the direction of five other women wearing all their gear and looking like the beatdown had already started.

"So y'all wanna be in the infantry, huh?" he asked. "Well, you'll probably be a sight better than some of the fucking girls on my team out there."

I understood he meant the male Pathfinders lounging outside. Resting soldiers, slow soldiers, weak soldiers. Soldiers we wanted to mock were always called girls.

"Well, c'mon, El Tee. Whatcha waiting for? Get your fucking gear on, we've got no time to waste. You ladies will meet Lieutenant Runkle when I say you're ready."

As we followed Sergeant First Class Z outside, he called over his shoulder, "Baby Ranger, General-Fucking-Patton, and Sergeant Blowhard, fall in. We're going to smoke some girls!"

The three men in question, Specialist MacGregor, Specialist Patton, and Sergeant Bohall, scrambled to their feet from where they'd been lounging, not bothering to put their fatigue jackets back on. "Smoking" someone, a ubiquitous army phrase for making someone work out so hard and long that smoke comes out of their ears, meant we were the day's entertainment.

"All right, ladies," Sergeant First Class Z drawled, "I want you to take your right hands, place them in front of your fucking chests, pull your precious rank off, throw it in the dust, and then get down after it."

We didn't hesitate. On the ground in front of us now lay one set of black captain's bars, my gold second lieutenant rank, two sergeant rockers, and two specialist chevrons. Rankless, we all assumed the push-up position, noses inches from the ground, waiting for the next command.

"Now push!" he yelled, motioning his guys to crowd around and give us a hard time. "Anyone here that can't manage to push with a little twenty-pound weighted vest on can stand up and go home."

I saw nothing but men's boots, the dust, rocks, desert scrub, and the occasional cactus as the morning passed in a blur of endless push-ups, burpees, and running in full gear—combat vests that didn't fit right, heavy packs, M4 assault rifles, and ten-pound helmets loaded down with night-vision goggles. All six of us were near the point of physical and psychological exhaustion, the brilliant purples and reds of new bruises blooming all over our knees, palms pockmarked with deep impressions from the gravel-packed sand. I'd stopped caring about anything other than keeping the burning sweat from blinding me completely when Sergeant First Class Z's voice rang out.

"Halt! On your feet!" We scrambled up. "I have to say, ladies, I'm fucking impressed. I'd bet you could give all of your fellow Fobbits a run for their money."

He spat out the derogatory word infantry guys have for anyone who is not "boots on the ground" at all times, the ones who stay on base and never face any danger more significant than the occasional rocket attack. We all puffed out our chests, standing a little straighter at his praise.

"All right, *females,*" Sergeant Mills said, walking up lazily, an old energy drink can in his right hand to spit tobacco juice into. "It's time for some bound-and-shoot drills. I hope y'all's knees ain't too dainty."

I groaned to myself. I suspected my knees looked as bad as my hands and imagined how prominently the bruises would stand out in my workout uniform. I could already hear the jokes from my colleagues back at brigade, how El Tee can't spend a day with the guys without coming home with bruised knees. Shaking my head and relegating that to a later problem, I tried to focus my attention on Sergeant Mills's explanation.

"Baby Ranger and General Patton, why don't you show these pretty young things how we move toward the enemy, down a corridor of fire without getting our heads blown off."

I was paired up with the other officer on the team, tall redheaded Captain Carmel. She could have posed for *Vanity Fair,* but stood there instead, sweaty, dirty, and exhausted. We'd both been through these kinds of drills in other training situations before—where they drain you completely before sending you to do the more dangerous tasks, a test to see how you can operate under conditions of extreme stress. We knew we'd take this training more seriously than we ever had before—this time it would be for real.

All six women watched as Specialist Jon MacGregor—a kid adopted from Russia at six who had only ever dreamed of being a US soldier—and Specialist Adam Patton—going through a nasty divorce back home and in love with one of the air traffic controllers I knew up at brigade headquarters—showed us the proper procedure.

"All right," Specialist Patton said, while Specialist MacGregor demonstrated on the ground. "One of you will jump up for a three-to-five-second rush forward while your buddy is laying down metal to make sure that damn Haji keeps his head down."

So many slurs. Training to kill people sure involved a lot of racist insults.

From his position on the ground, Specialist MacGregor said, "Only three to five seconds, you hear? Every second you're on your feet is a second you are a big, broad, juicy target for the bad guys. It's get up, rush, get down, and shoot."

He demonstrated, going up and down with an alarming alacrity that I wasn't sure I could meet.

"And don't let me see any of you trying to be delicate or lady-like," Staff Sergeant Mills commanded. "I promise you, blood and bullet holes will mess up those pristine never-been-out-of-the-tactical-operations-center uniforms more than a little mud."

Pairing up, we assumed the position to practice the drill. I sighed heavily when Sergeant Mills called out, "Officers fall in on me," and we stomped off to find an unoccupied piece of sand and gravel for us to practice on.

Captain Carmel looked at me. "Shoot or run?" she asked.

"Run," I said, thinking it was better to start with my strongest skill. Without waiting a second, I took off, my rifle at the ready.

"Hey El Tee, slow the fuck down! Where the fuck is your buddy?"

I paused mid-sprint. My heart sank. Lowering my rifle, I looked back to see how badly I'd failed my first test. Captain Carmel was getting to her feet from her shooting position, at least twenty to thirty yards behind me. In my haste and obsession with proving myself as good as any man, I'd forgotten one of the first rules of soldiering, written into our creed, shouted at the tops of our lungs in every training scenario I'd ever been in—never leave a comrade. I dropped my head and dragged my feet as I returned to them.

Was this it for me? Would I be off the team?

"El Tee," Sergeant Mills said, sitting down on a large rock. In his hand, I recognized the timer that noncommissioned officers used to time our physical fitness tests. "Look, I'm never gonna say it's okay to leave your buddy behind." He hemmed for a second, then continued, "When we get out in the sand, don't fucking do that, okay? Not the least because you don't want to find yourself fucking alone out there with the Taliban. Got it?"

I nodded my head, my face bright red and hot, and not just from sprinting.

"But, fuck, Ma'am, let me see you do that five-second rush over again! Captain, take a seat and relax, huh? Fuck it. Sergeant Blowhard, you wanna race her?"

So I ran. Hard. Once, twice, and then more times than I could count. With every return sprint, more guys ambled over from their shack to throw themselves down on the dust and watch the show, waiting for their turn to see if they could beat the girl. As tired as I was, every time I heard a hardened Airborne Ranger say, "Damn, girl!" or "I never knew there were skirts who could run like that!" my motivation soared and my exhaustion seemed to melt away. My assault rifle felt light as air, and my boots and vest only propelled me forward. With some exceptions, nearly every time I turned around at the sound of the whistle marking the five seconds, I saw a man sprinting his hardest, nothing heavy on his body, still behind me.

On what must have been my fifteenth round, I noticed a smaller man standing next to the sprawled-out guys. Unlike the others, he wasn't in fatigues. He wore the gym uniform: nylon black shorts, tennis shoes, a gray T-shirt with the word ARMY written across it, and a neon yellow reflective belt, bright in the hot sunlight.

"I've got next," he said, with a calm authority.

"Oh Sir, I'm gonna warn you now," a defeated Sergeant Bohall said, still smarting from his own race. "If she beats you, a hundred pounds soaking wet wearing half her weight in gear, and you in those tennis shoes, we ain't gonna let you live it down."

I prepared myself for another race. I didn't dare to look at the other women, not sure if they'd be cheering me on or rolling their eyes. We lined up, awaiting the whistle, and I hoped it'd be the last one.

Thankfully, it was.

"Well, now that we know that a fucking girl in all her gear can beat our majestic platoon leader running slick, I think it's time to end the Mess-tee-ah-neck show and introduce you all to the rest of the team," Sergeant First Class Z said. "I'm the platoon sergeant, if you haven't already figured it out. When we're outside the wire, you do what I say . . . or you die. It really is *that. Fucking. Simple.*" He dragged out his words, inhaling a puff of smoke with each pause. "This is Lieutenant John Runkle, our fearless commander, who clearly can't run to save us from mocking him for the rest of his goddamn life."

Lieutenant Runkle, in a voice so quiet I first thought he was only talking to me, said, "Gentlemen, these six women are on the team now. Got it? When they're attached, they're our guys as much as any of you. Period. Do wrong by them, and you'll answer to me. Now, let's get some chow."

As I ripped off the brown top of an MRE, First Lieutenant Runkle plunked himself down next to me in the dust. "Daniella, right?" He chuckled. "I don't guess I'll be allowed to forget your name."

"Well, then I'd best square you away on that last name—it's 'Mest-uh-neck,'" I said.

"You can call me John," he replied, nodding to our lieutenant ranks.

I nodded. "I'm sorry if I embarrassed you." I didn't want to get off on the wrong foot with him. "When I get into competition mode, I just run, all politics aside. Especially if I'm racing guys, you know . . ." I trailed off, unsure how to explain that I was always, *always* aware of how much I had to prove myself—to show I wasn't just one of "those" blond lieutenants.

Waving my concern away with one hand, but looking pensive,

John dug into his own cold meal. "I don't know if it's clear enough, 'cos we can all be a little rough around the edges, but we're more than happy to have you ladies here. We're going on ten years fighting these messed-up wars where we have to follow all the rules but the terrorists don't, all the while hamstrung by an archaic rule made by politicians who've never spent a day in uniform, never even seen what women like all of you are capable of. And who don't know how it's affecting the fight, not having you out here."

I knew he was referring to the combat ban, the reason that women weren't allowed to be in the infantry, or on anything that was considered the front lines, though even the lowest-ranking soldier knew there was no such thing in these kinds of wars.

"Well," I said, patting the combat vest I was now using as a seat, "maybe once we prove ourselves, they'll actually make some armor that works for girls. I hope none of us have to die before they realize it, but you know, Big Army." I shrugged.

I told him the story of the Texas contractor. He winced and admitted it wasn't something he'd thought of either. John promised me that he'd make sure I didn't get shot, as best he could guarantee, anyway.

Near the end of our meal, John asked me the question I would learn he asked everyone on his team, "Daniella, what makes you different? Tell me your story."

I laughed aloud before I could stop myself. I flashed back to high school and the last time I'd been asked that same question, and how much it had changed my life when I'd written that essay in response. *I grew up in a cult.* The truth no longer seemed easy enough to wrap into five tidy paragraphs.

"It's a bit of a long story."

John nodded, then got to his feet, brushing the dust from his shorts. "Well, your first mission is tomorrow. We'll have some downtime in the middle of the desert waiting for our ride, if you want to tell me then." He motioned at the helicopters parked neatly along the flight line. "I have a feeling that what you girls are doing here with us is going to be the start of something big. And I'm sure honored to be a part of that."

Without another word, he bounced up to his feet, and walked away.

"What is it about him?" I asked Sergeant Mills, sitting to my left. "I've never seen any lieutenant command the kind of respect that you all clearly have for him."

I expected the usual sarcasm and swearing, but Sergeant Mills raised his head to look me in the eye.

"Ma'am," he said, "it's really quite simple. Every man on this team knows one thing—he would die for any one of us, any of y'all too now. So we love him, and we'll follow him anywhere."

It felt like I'd seen real leadership, the values they talked about in officer school but seemed impossible to teach. The kind of leader I wanted to be but didn't know how. It was a good moment, one I decided to tuck away and hold on to like all the little thoughts in the secret jeweled box that still lived in my head.

But on the desert sand, peace never lasts long.

"All right, on your feet, bitches, and uh . . . ladies," Sergeant Mills roared. "Time to go plan tomorrow's little daybreak jaunt to hunt some bad guys."

21

A DAY MEMORIALIZED

■

Kandahar Airfield, Afghanistan, 2011

There's nothing fun about a birthday in Afghanistan, even sur-rounded by friends. But we tried. I walked the mile across dusty un-paved roads with Tiffany and Captain Madison, a couple of other lieutenants, and a few of my soldiers who were off duty after the 6 P.M. shift change from where we all worked in the Tactical Operations Center, to reach the Kandahar Airfield boardwalk. It was nothing like the vacation images that typically come to mind with the word "boardwalk." Sure, the boards were there—a kilometer of wooden slats built on a circle of Afghan dust and gravel, bedecked with little shops selling teas, Persian rugs, jewelry, kabobs, and American fast food. But there were definitely no soft ocean waves lapping anywhere in the hard, landlocked country. Nevertheless, it was an hour to sit around at Mama Mia's pizza joint, laugh with friends, and pretend to forget where we were, despite our uniformed bodies and ever-present rifles in our hands.

"I wish John was here," I said.

I knew by then infantry guys didn't get time off for jaunts to the fun side of the airfield. Being on standby 24/7 meant the team came before any person, always. Still, John made sure his people—even me, a woman-shaped tool deployed to show the locals we respected their culture—felt they were more than just part of the team. We were individuals, celebrated for who we were in addition to what we contributed to the group. A few weeks earlier, I'd been surprised when he made the time to attend my promotion to first lieutenant.

"We're out here fighting a new kind of war, Daniella," he'd said. "The kind those guys who write the doctrine don't know anything about. We need to be agile, questioning, and responding in the moment. We do that here the best we can, while still sticking to doctrine and everything the army has taught me and the guys—we'll teach you all of that. You give us the outsider perspective."

I could relax in his company, treated, finally, as a fellow lieutenant. Not a slut or a dyke or a bitch, not a female or a conquest or a competitor, or any of the other labels that seemed to stick to me along with my rank. Like the rest of his men, I understood he was the boss. During missions, both his confidence and humanity showed; he was respectful in his language and how he carried himself, and I understood why his team, my team, would listen and follow him into danger—no questions.

As he'd asked, I told him my whole story, and he did not judge. No one-upmanship for who had it worse. No tongue-in-cheek jokes like my friends from the unit who heard a bit of my story and teased me for joining the army, a second cult. He didn't stare at me like I was un-American, nor treat me like what I said was shameful. He looked at me with the thoughtful expression I saw on his face so often, and said, "Gosh, we need to schedule time for some more conversation. You must have some interesting and useful insights."

Over the next few weeks, during all the waiting that happens before and after missions, we had some of those important conversations—about leadership, culture, group psychology, motivation, combat, and each person's uniqueness and ability to contribute to the whole, as an individual. I told him a bit about how the group behavior in the army, while different, reminded me so much of growing up in the Children of God, at times. I chafed at all the limitations that were placed on women—how it was impossible to know what we were even capable of, because nobody let us into the room to try. We marveled at how the actions of this small group of women, unnoticed by most, might change the face of the US Army—one of the oldest and largest organizations in our country. He told me I had what it took to go all the way, that the army didn't know what they had in me, and he begged me to stay in long enough to make them see it. When I was talking to him, I wanted to promise him that I would—for myself and for all the other women, too. But I knew I couldn't.

"You sure are bonding fast with those grunts," Captain Madison said in response, leaning back in his chair, plates full of crumbs and pizza crusts on the table between us. His pointed use of the quip for infantry soldiers mirrored the criticism clear in his eyes. "Daniella, I know you're new, but you need to be very careful. People are already talking about you and the guys you hang out with. Be careful with John."

This topic exasperated me. Maybe it was the familiar salsa beat echoing in the restaurant, but I had just enough stamina to attempt to navigate it.

"Sir, I appreciate the concern, but who should I hang out with, honestly?" I gestured to Tiffany. "Tiffany and I are on opposite shifts, so is Captain Rodriguez and the two female battle captains in operations, and there literally are no other female officers in our headquarters unit. I go to salsa night to make friends and have an hour away from the unit, and the job, and thinking about work and war—and y'all don't like that, either. So, am I supposed to sit alone in my room for a whole year? Is that the only thing a woman can do to 'be respected'?"

"We tell all of our soldiers to 'watch out for their buddies' as a way to guard against depression and suicide," Tiffany added, her voice barely audible over the music. "But the female officers are just supposed to be fine on our own?"

"I mean, I get it. It's hard for you ladies," Captain Madison said. "You know, before I got over here, I used to think that the women who said they were scared were just being dramatic. But the more I get used to what it's like over here, the more I think that you probably *will* get raped on this deployment."

For a moment, I thought maybe I misheard him. But he barreled on, completely unaware of my shock or the stunned look on Tiffany's face. "Be careful out on those patrols," he said. "You really need to watch your back with a group of twenty-five armed guys like that."

I stared at Captain Madison. Mike, as he told me to call him when he'd unabashedly hounded me after hours and we'd started sleeping together not two weeks into the deployment. I knew these warnings had nothing to do with his concern for my career or my safety. He'd chosen to risk all that when he made a move on me, knowing I'd be the one to pay the highest price if it went south. The concern was nothing but possessiveness.

I looked at the face I had studied when we were alone, in secret. Handsome. Bold. Charming, in a New England kind of way. A thinker, a reader, and a good conversationalist. If I said that we were a twenty-three-year-old girl and a twenty-six-year-old guy, it didn't seem as bad as the power imbalance between a second lieutenant and captain. If I thought about us as friends, I could distract myself from the fact that he could ruin me without a second thought. That he was married. And that, as a lieutenant on his team, he was in charge of every facet of my life for the next 365 days. Of everything and anything that could make my life tolerable or intolerable for the next year. But no matter what I told myself to justify it all, I could never forget the fact that, legally, I had to call him "Sir" and do whatever he said during the day. And under the cover of darkness, I hadn't felt at all powerful enough to say no.

I didn't know which statement I should react to—the promise I'd "probably be raped" by some soldier in a dark corner of this base, or the indication that I needed to protect myself from the twenty-five American soldiers who were supposed to have my back in a firefight. I also knew, in my core, all the risks he'd mentioned were terrifyingly real.

My mind raced in different directions. Out on the sands, there was rarely more than one woman embedded with the Pathfinders. The infantry guys had already become like brothers to me. They circled around me, turning their backs and rifles so I could squat and pee, so different from the marches in basic training when we had to hold it for hours. As we trudged through booby-trapped sand in the middle of the Afghan desert, Sergeant Bohall, who we'd decided would pose as my brother, tried ad nauseam to explain to our partnered Afghan soldiers, "No, Lieutenant Mestyanek cannot be traded for twelve camels, though we do certainly appreciate the high value you've assigned to her."

These were the men that multiple senior officers were warning me about. And even though it was the best team I'd been on, my question was: Why weren't they warning the guys not to rape us? Where were the penalties for that?

I didn't know what to say. Where could I even start? I mumbled, "Sir, John's my friend. He gets why women in combat is an important issue. He has a vision for what we are doing here. I'm going to be his friend, and I don't care if that looks bad to any of you." I took a deep steadying breath, put out more bravado than I had in me, and said, "I'm not breaking your precious General Order One, Sir, because I'm not doing anything wrong."

General Order One, the military's ridiculous attempt to legislate sex, was, like everything else in the boys' club, used against women to keep us in line. The general officers who dreamed it up said the ban was for the purposes of "Good Order and Discipline," the army's catchall for anything they didn't want to have to justify too much. In the end, banning sex while deployed didn't make the sex taboo, it made having a vagina taboo. It made me a target for people like Captain Madison from day one. I stood and put on my resting bitch face so nobody could see how deeply Mike's words had affected me. "Now, if you'll excuse me, Sir, it's time for salsa practice with the USO right down there—" I pointed down the boardwalk. "And you know that's my jam."

Tiffany scrambled to her feet, knowing better than to sit alone at a table full of guys. I was always trying to get her to take salsa lessons with me, or hang out for one of the Saturday dance nights, but she only wanted to do her job, chat with her fiancé back home, and get through the year of horrors intact.

"I said that to get away from him," I explained, as we walked back to our room. "I don't feel like dancing tonight."

"Nothing like having threats of rape thrown in your face to teach women how to act right, huh?" she said, her voice sounding as wobbly as mine. "I'm sorry that I have to go back to work—night shifts are no fun. I wish we got to hang out more." After walking me to the door of the shipping container we shared that had been converted to a dorm, she'd head out for her night shift, but at least we each had a buddy for part of the way.

"No worries. Hey, try not to think about all those rapists in uniform waiting for you on your walk back," I tried to joke.

"I'll try. At least I can probably take a couple of 'em," she said and beamed, patting her rifle before shutting the door behind her. Tiffany was one of the best marksmen in the unit.

"Happy birthday to me," I said to myself, unlacing my boots and sinking into the thin twin mattress of my bunk.

That night, I tossed and turned, listening to the loud drone of the air conditioner. I finally fell asleep near dawn, only to find myself back in Uncle Jerry's basement room. But this time, he was wearing the uniform of an American soldier and the rank of captain—as untouchable as he'd always been.

■

I COULDN'T RUN fast enough. I tried to focus on putting one foot in front of the other but my mind traveled faster than my leaden legs. I watched Captain Carmel's red bun bob up and down as she led me and our other Female Engagement Team members to the Pale Horse Tactical Operations Center from the classroom, our lessons abandoned.

Just minutes ago she had received the text message that changed everything:

Six Pathfinders dead. Come now!

I didn't want to think about who it was, what it was, why it was, but tears began to spill from my eyes anyway. With the cadence of each footfall, I saw my guys: Mills, Patton, MacGregor, the rest of the Baby Rangers. John.

The Tactical Operations Center was pure bedlam. Captain Carmel broke away from us and demanded to know which helicopter she should fly. "Those are *my* guys, I'm going up," she shouted.

I felt like she did, wanting to do something, and saw the same looks on the faces of the other women. But unlike Captain Carmel, we couldn't pull rank. The rest of us didn't fly helicopters, we were all just support. Instead, we stood together, forgotten in a corner, listening to the radio chatter dominated by the sounds of our friends dying.

There are fragments where my memories should be: static, flashes, images seared into my brain. There are the sounds I heard over that radio and there are the scenes of what came after. But I don't know where my own memories stop, where they crash into the firsthand accounts of the survivors who were out on the sand that day, where they tangle with the words that were written about it later.

Did I hear the battalion commander, shouting his panic from a routine mission gone so fatally wrong? "GET ME A DAMN LEADER ON THE LINE!"

Did the room crackle with the response of the Private First Class who came on the radio when the bombs seemed to have stopped going off? "Sir, I'm it."

Did I hear the horrible silence that follows a massive blast?

I dropped to my knees, and I wasn't the only one, silently praying to every deity I didn't believe in. *Don't let it be my friends. Please don't let it be my guys.* It would be hours before they would tell us the names, officially. The first wave of guilt swept over me as people turned into numbers, a fatality count: Six dead. Eight dead. Nine. Ten humans, gone.

They were all our guys. If they weren't my friends, they would be someone else's friends. The husbands, brothers, sons, fathers, and teenagers who should have had whole lives ahead of them.

Finally, all nonessential personnel were cleared from the room, and I ran alone the four miles back to the brigade Tactical Operations Center, the higher command where I worked. I dragged my feet, sobbing in the dust, not caring who saw or what they would think. For the first time, I wasn't afraid of what a man could do to me. I didn't care.

When I entered my office, my face red, Captain Madison shot out of his chair. Throwing all formality to the side, he pulled me into a hug and said, "I'm so glad you weren't there. That none of you girls were with them today."

I wanted to punch him in the face, along with everyone who kept repeating the same sentiment. All I could think, over and over to myself, like a chant or a prayer, was there wasn't a single thing that made my life worth a cent more than any of theirs.

I sat at my desk watching the clock move, the second hand somehow slower with each moment. I stared at the screens transmitting important information, but I couldn't make my eyes focus enough to read them, even as I told myself I'd never leave those monitors again, that as an intelligence officer, this was my fault, that I should have known what was going to happen. I failed them. I should have protected my guys.

Captain Gillian Rodriguez approached me, speaking woman-to-woman for the first time in our turbulent relationship. "Daniella," she said, "there's nothing you can do for them here. The names will come out soon. Why don't you go back to housing, be with the rest of your Female Engagement Team girls?"

I could see the understanding in her eyes. She knew I needed sisters-in-arms at that moment, that this grief would be too much to handle alone. I ran every step, but hurrying did not make the news come faster. It was almost midnight when Captain Carmel arrived. The broken way she walked in told me it was going to be as bad as I had imagined. But nothing prepared me for the way that each name would feel like a punch straight to the face, or how none of us had any tears left to cry.

Instead, we stood, holding hands, sisters-in-arms, as she listed off the names by heart:

Sergeant Louie Ramos Velasquez.

The Puerto Rican jokester who always teased me about my "Mexicanista Spanish." He was our medic. I would later learn the home-made bomb that took his life flung his first responder kit toward the team, as if he was trying to take care of his men, even after he was gone.

Staff Sergeant Ergin Osman.

The guys used Velasquez's kit to sustain Sergeant First Class Osman long enough to make it onto the medical evacuation helicopter, but he couldn't be saved. Osman had just come in from a sister base to replace Sergeant Z for a few weeks. He was always trying to convince the Baby Rangers to go to college when they got back stateside, warning them they wouldn't want to be "still doing this ground-pounding shit as an old man, like me, with two little boys."

Staff Sergeant Edward Mills.

I don't know why, but I kept picturing Staff Sergeant Mills's chew can. I know he would have had one on him. Was it ever recovered, or was it obliterated by the blast that took his life?

Sergeant Thomas Bohall.

Sergeant Blowhard, my brother in the desert. The first guy I raced when I joined the team, when I so desperately needed to prove I belonged. Quiet, sweet, thoughtful. Gone.

Specialist Adam Patton.

Before he died, Specialist Patton waved at his best friend, Specialist MacGregor, who was part of the rescue team coming over the sand hill toward him. As he waited to be rescued from the trap of radio-controlled IEDs laced throughout the sand all around him, Specialist Patton lay down in the prone position behind his rifle, squarely on top of a hidden bomb.

First Lieutenant John Runkle.

As I heard John's name, I finally exhaled, realizing I'd been holding my breath, and my hope. I'd known deep down that he couldn't have lived through that explosion I heard, but the confirmation was final. There was no going back. He was gone.

I didn't hear John's final radio call. He had squatted down beside Patton, calmly talking to the helicopter rescue mission overhead, relaying the information his battalion commander needed. A leader, beside his men, until the very end.

There were four others, I would learn later—both of the air force explosive ordnance technicians who'd been on the mission, killed doing their job as the first to respond to suspected bombs. Two of the partnered Afghan soldiers. Others on our team had been badly wounded and were evacuated to Germany, then sent home to recover.

Half our team was gone.

My friends hugged and rocked each other, sitting on the stairs outside our rooms for hours. As morning broke, we agreed to the pretense of going our separate ways, knowing that sleep would elude us. I hoped Tiffany would be in our room, that maybe she'd come back early from her shift, but it was empty. I sat at my laptop and opened Facebook, hoping I'd get some salve of normalcy before the communications blackout that followed most fatalities. The little red notifications caught my eye. Birthday messages had continued to roll in from the day before, the States twelve hours behind us.

Nestled among them was John's message, the one he'd written as he went to bed the day before, after prepping his gear and his guys for the next day's early mission.

"Happy birthday, Daniella. Sorry I couldn't be there."

THE SUN WOULDN'T stop shining, for just one damn minute, to let us mourn in peace. Back home, it was Memorial Day weekend. On Kandahar Airfield, we stood, lined perfectly in rows, shoulder to shoulder, heads bowed and tears falling. The Pathfinder ambush had been the highest casualty-producing event—ten dead and many more wounded—in all the previous three years of war, since the 2009 troop surge in Afghanistan. Everyone at Kandahar Airfield who could get the time off had shown up for the memorial service and to honor the Heroes, the official army term for those killed in action. Those of us with a personal connection to the deceased stood together in the front row, trying not to break rank and grab onto each other for support.

Over the previous few days, I thought I'd cried myself dry. Squinting against the bright sunlight, I tried to hold it together as the words washed over me, the words we always say over the coffins of dead soldiers: *They are heroes. They died for what they believed in. We are fighting for justice and freedom. We are on the right side of history.* It wasn't that I believed the words were wrong, not exactly. It was just that, as I stood there, I could almost picture an invisible line cleaving my brain in two. On one side, there was the American patriot, the woman literally fighting for her country in a war zone, the one who believed in the promise of America and American freedoms, the woman who joyfully paid her taxes—because that's the price of American comfort. I loved America, the American Dream, all of it. It's what I'd been striving for my entire life.

But on the other side stood Daniella, the little cult girl who vividly remembered deaths being explained away as "part of a bigger plan in God's Army." There was the teen who felt the horror of 9/11 and the disconnect between what she saw with her own eyes and the empty platitudes of every authority figure in her life who said things were all right. That girl knew somebody had to be lying.

I had the intelligence officer perspective behind me this time, too. I knew what had happened in the aftermath of that fatal day—what always happened in the aftermath. The Pathfinders, Rangers, and other related special groups had been given a day off missions—to cool down, to grieve, to rage—and then they'd been unleashed. I'd seen the pictures of what happened afterward, had stared at every single dark-skinned man lying on the ground, faces blown half-open, teeth scattered around heads. I knew what nobody dared to say out loud: It had been an ambush. We had no proof any of those dead guys had anything to do with our dead guys. But man, hadn't it felt good to get some revenge on someone, anyone? They were all the same, weren't they? All bad guys. The enemy. The *other*. The reason our friends were gone.

The end that justifies the means.

At that moment, tears falling for my brothers, I thought about what other funerals might be going on at the same moment somewhere in the sands. Afghan Muslims will not allow a body to lie for more than twenty-four hours without burial, even the bodies of known terror- ists, even the corpses of those who have threatened and killed their own children. If we had gotten the "right" bad guys, the ones who'd watched our missions and learned the patterns, who'd set the bombs and booby traps, who'd hidden somewhere nearby with the radio-controlled trigger and waited until Specialist Patton had lain down right there, John prone beside him—what was being said at their funerals? Wasn't it possible, even likely, that it was the same kinds of things, the same grief, the same vows for revenge, the same belief in the rightness of their cause?

The booms of the twenty-one-gun salute silenced my thoughts. The terrible, soul-marking, death-signifying finality of each shot. As I rocked backward with each deafening burst, three separate volleys of seven, perfectly timed shots, I realized I was openly sobbing, snot running down my face, shoulders shaking in a rhythm all their own alongside the sickeningly sweet keening of the Taps bugle call. I locked my hands to my sides at the position of attention, determined to give my men this final respect no matter what it cost me. As the rituals of the ceremony concluded, I felt a sense of peace, against all odds—they were on their way home now, on to their final resting place, where there would be no more war.

Sergeant First Class Z, our platoon sergeant who'd been home on R&R when it all happened, told me he had threatened, cajoled, and begged his way onto the military transports that got him back to Kandahar in time for the ramp ceremony, the culmination of the memorial service when the eight coffins were loaded onto the aircraft. "I was at home preparing a Memorial Weekend barbecue with my family and friends that I hadn't seen in forever, when I got the worst visit you can ever, ever—" He paused, swelling hard, crying without any sign of shame. "—ever imagine. I never wanted to go on leave. A platoon sergeant should never be forced to. Leave. His. Guys," he choked out.

I broke protocol to lay a hand over his, looking around briefly to make sure nobody was watching to misinterpret my gesture. We nodded at each other, a promise to one day say the unspoken words we couldn't yet.

As we walked back to the unit headquarters, groups of officers and enlisted walking together, rank less important than ever, Captain Mike Madison approached me from behind. I flinched as his large hand landed on my shoulder.

"Daniella, I overheard some of the senior staff talking. People are asking a lot of questions about why you are taking this so hard."

"Mike," I said, my voice lowered as I used his first name. "Ten humans are gone. Forever. For nothing. From *my* team. And people are asking why I'm *upset*? Do you get how fucked up that is?"

I knew I could be in serious trouble for addressing a senior officer in that way, for letting my anger show through, for criticizing the actions of the American Army. But I didn't care. I refused, this time, to put my head down, to show respect to an Uncle, without question, the way I had in the past.

"Daniella," he said, his voice soft. "I know what they meant to you. I know that was your team, I know you cared. I've lost friends too."

His sentiments didn't stop him from issuing another warning. "But you need to be careful. I'd hate to see a promising career destroyed by rumors of an inappropriate relationship." He finished without a hint of irony in his voice.

I was done with him.

"Thank you, Mike," I said through gritted teeth. Of all the things he could say at that moment. Of all the times. Of all the people.

My fury turned to numbness. I knew it was the only way to survive. "You're right, Sir," I said. "I'll be careful."

had been out on the sands by choice for five years straight, with the Canadian army deployed to Kandahar, which he'd started right after his tour with the US Marines. Like me, he had no real home. And because he was a civilian, it caused no drama with my work. When I started hanging out with him after hours, I felt safe—at least that's what I told myself. But mostly it felt easy. A distraction. He didn't ask me any hard questions, and I didn't tell.

We'd been kind of a couple for months, friends publicly, but folks knew the real deal. He wasn't risking nearly as much as me—contractors were basically bulletproof, not under the Military Justice System, but so far away from their countries of origin that they didn't really fall under their rules either. I ignored the sinking feeling that told me to be careful. But as long as I was hanging out with a civilian, and I kept it to the boardwalk, salsa night, a game of Scrabble and tea at the British soldiers' hangout, or donuts with his Canadian colleagues, I believed nobody really cared what we did in dark corners. They were all doing it too.

Then one night he confessed that the ex he'd mentioned wasn't really an ex. She was actually his girlfriend back home, where he would soon return, finally cashing out the millions he'd banked during his contractor years to move back to Colorado, buy a house, marry the girl, and enjoy the American dream. He wouldn't be back. He wished me the best and held me while I cried. I felt so alone, left behind on the interminable sands.

I couldn't bear one more person falling away from my life. That night, I sobbed for hours, sitting beside him in his truck and listening to the melancholy music he played while staring at the shipping containers that dotted the landscape. I thought I loved him, or at least was falling in love with him, but it didn't matter. He was kind to me, but also firm. He had broken up with me. It was over.

I don't remember why we ended up in his room, but it had to have been on purpose, because getting there wasn't easy. We had to sneak into the building, past many other rooms, and slip in quietly. The army didn't allow civilian clothes even off duty, and if anyone saw me in my uniform, I could be reported, and my career would be over.

As a woman, I stood out wherever I went, everyone watching to see where I might be headed in the dark.

In his room, we talked all night long. Like I did all the time for laughs, I fake-begged him to leave his giant bag of "pogs" with me. Instead of having to deal with a variety of coins on base, the coalition of sixty-six countries who'd signed on to support the war in Afghanistan paid change in pogs, little cardboard poker-type chips that could be traded in for real money before going home. They took time to collect, but were useful for tea, ice cream, and other treats enjoyed in the short hours off duty. He had almost eighty dollars' worth, and I wanted that bag. I could be the queen of our salsa-club social circle, buying everyone rounds of chai over our endless games of gin rummy. I regularly teased him to fork them over without any seriousness at all, and he regularly refused, a smile on his face.

But that night was completely different.

At some point, we began to argue, and I moved to the bed, wanting to be physical, wanting to be held one last time. I'd taken his shirt off, and he'd put it back on, but he'd looped his arms around me anyway. We were fighting but also making out. When he pinned my wrists, I thought it was a joke. When he'd begun to move on top of me, I didn't get upset. Wasn't this what I'd wanted? When he began to tear at my clothes, I helped him take them off. But when he turned me over and held me down, face pressed hard to the pillow, and began to do things to me that I'd never given him permission to do, I opened my eyes and my gaze was drawn to my boots on the floor. My combat boots, my one thing made for women, meant to stay on base, but which had already been out on so many missions in the open sand. They had already faced what the men thought was danger. And there they were, unlaced and haphazardly tossed into the corner. I stared at the way the laces pooled on either side, one boot standing straight up and the other slightly tipped over, leaning on its buddy. I realized I didn't have a buddy, didn't have anyone I'd be able to tell, anyone I could lean on. I thought that person had been him. The same man on top of me, holding me down as I tried to struggle. There they were, the evidence of my crime, the only thing any investigation might care about—I had taken off my boots, I had sat on his bed, I had wanted him to touch me. No one would ever believe that I was being raped by a man I had been trying to sleep with. And nobody would care.

So, like I'd been trained in my youth, I stopped fighting. I knew there was no point. I stared at the boots until they began to blur in my vision. I stared and stared until he was done.

And then I sat up calmly and put my clothes back on. Somehow, I still had a voice. I asked him why he hadn't asked me. I asked why he'd forced me. I asked why he didn't stop when I told him to. "I don't know. I don't know. I don't know," he repeated again and again, his hands covering his face.

He got dressed as I put my boots on. Hole by hole, I laced them back up, the evidence that I'd deserved it. I had been telling myself for years that if it ever happened again, I'd be fierce, I'd fight, and I'd certainly report it. I wouldn't be like that fourteen-year-old girl who'd lain there and taken it, certain that it was her fault. I was protected now, I was somebody. I existed.

But I didn't report it. And I couldn't. I'd been breaking the rules. I'd gone with him on *purpose*. I'd taken my boots off *intentionally*. I knew nobody would care that I'd been raped, and I knew no one would believe me. If I walked out of his room and reported anything, it would end my career forever.

He picked up his keys and I picked up my assault rifle, and we walked to his truck in silence. I noted the ultimate irony of *this* assault: that I'd been armed, while he had not. He drove me to my room and before I could open the door, he tossed something in my lap. The bag of pogs. Eighty-three dollars and fifty-seven cents, I would count later, over and over. He hugged me and told me to keep my chin up. Then he drove away, and I never saw him again.

I felt the blood pulse in my body and heard it in my ears, along with Captain Madison's warning:

You'll probably get raped while we're here. Now that it had happened, maybe my constant fear, always waiting for the attack, would subside, I thought.

But the words continued to echo in my head:

Watch your back. Don't get raped. Don't get yourself raped.

◼

THE INCREDIBLE STARS of Afghanistan twinkled overhead, but my body, oblivious, shook as I climbed the unmanned guard tower in a corner of the airfield. I knew from my long runs that this place was totally isolated and I wouldn't be disturbed. My gloves slipped on the metal rungs, still hot from baking all day in the sun, though it had long since slipped over the horizon.

"I can do this," I said to no one.

It felt freeing to hear my own voice outside my head. I wanted to believe that this time I'd finally have the guts to go through with it. The M4 rifle slung across my back banged against my butt with each rung I ascended. It seemed a long way to the top, but probably not far enough, a nagging voice kept telling me.

I wanted it all to be over. This miserable deployment had been the worst months of my life, worse even than my childhood somehow, and I couldn't imagine living through whatever horrors the next half of the year contained. I had spent my life trying to gain control over my circumstances, but it amounted to nothing; and there I was again, falling victim to more abuse. No matter what I did or how hard I worked, it followed me.

I didn't understand what I was doing wrong. When I'd broken free of the Children of God, I never looked back. I thought that's what I was supposed to do, the only way to outrun the trauma of my past. I'd put my head down and worked and worked and worked, and it seemed to pay off, at least for a while. I thought I had gained complete control over my own destiny. But then I tripped up. I gave all that control back, one piece at a time, trading my future for the security of a man, for the army, for a clear and predetermined path. I told myself the trade was worth it. What I lost in freedom, I gained in safety. After all, I didn't have the tools to make sense of this world, did I? And who chooses the struggle of trying to decipher the world on their own when there's already a map in front of them?

But Kandahar broke everything wide open, especially those quiet pieces I'd hidden deep within myself. I laughed with the guys about how the place reminded me of my childhood, but it wasn't funny. The communal living on base reminded me of Family compounds in other parts of the world, some not too far away. The unpaved roads and open sewage running through haphazardly created offices and living quarters made me see the slums of Brazil. The walls, high, heavy, and topped with razor wire and armaments, felt all too cloyingly familiar—keeping me safe; keeping me in. Once again, fear had become my constant companion, always with me.

But more than anything, it was the men. There were men everywhere. I'd known that I'd be outnumbered on deployment, but I never could have imagined what the experience would *be* like, what I had signed up for. When Captain Madison joked about the certainty of my rape, it was like he flipped a switch in my brain, opening the floodgates of everything I had been stuffing in the dark corners of my memory. My body was the strongest it had ever been, and no one knew there was really a six-year-old girl inside it, small and terrified, her heart jumping at every unexpected sound, every footstep following her. My body was certain what had happened to me as a child could and would happen to me again. The nightmares returned, and every night I had to go back to those basements and back rooms. I didn't want to be six and trapped. I didn't want to be fourteen and out of control. I didn't want to be me, here, in this body that could never forget and never escape, no matter how hard I tried.

For a little while, with John and the guys, everything had seemed like it might get better. But even on that team, I couldn't escape the whispers and the constant propositions. I could never outrun the rumors that I was sleeping with one sergeant or blowing another as he gave me a ride home after our missions. When I did manage to find a friend, he'd get pulled aside and told to watch out. Being near me was bad for a career.

I had to be careful about how close I got to women too—it was so easy to be accused of being a "dyke," still illegal under Don't Ask, Don't Tell. Devastatingly, Tiffany had been moved to another base, and Captain Rodriguez had no desire to befriend other women. Danielle was deployed to Korea, and busy schedules on both ends never allowed us to chat in person. So the only time I could get any kind of human connection was with men who *were* willing to risk their careers, the men who wanted me naked, no matter the cost to them—or to me. Every time they took off my clothes, my skin tore away with it, exposing the raw insides of that six-year-old girl, and who she'd become. And every time, what I saw there made me sick.

I was broken and used and unsavable. It was better to be nothing, weightless, light enough to float off of that tower and out of this world altogether. I was tired of existing.

There was no such thing as safety, not here or anywhere. I was once again immersed in a world where predators not only survived, but thrived, where they were rewarded for the very qualities that made them good predators. Once again, I'd been powerless to protect myself. From my earliest days, I'd been nothing but prey. Even after I'd escaped the sex cult, I'd become an unprotected teenager in America—to be used by the people who lie in wait for those like me. I couldn't escape it. What was I even doing? Why was I even still alive? No matter how strong I was, no matter where I went or how fast I could run, I would never have enough power to keep men from using me for whatever they wanted.

At the top of the watchtower, I marched straight over to the edge and looked down. I could just keep walking. But was it high enough? I couldn't tell in the dark. I should have Googled how many feet you need to fall to be sure of death. The only thing I wanted less than I wanted to live was to fail at dying and break every bone in my body in the process.

In my uncertainty, I slumped down onto my backside and looked up at the stars. There's nowhere in the world to see stars like Afghanistan— not in the hills of Brazil, the southern tip of Germany, or the plains of Mexico—darkness all around, barely an electric light anywhere except on base. I looked up and thought about how many times in my life I'd sat on a roof in the blackness, eyes up, mind flying through scenarios of my final moments before death. I had been chasing it for as long as I could remember. I wanted to close my eyes under the stars and never open them again.

I didn't believe in God. I didn't believe in Hell. I didn't believe in *any*thing. I was alone and had nothing left to lose. And I knew I couldn't survive here for six more months. I didn't want to survive another six minutes. I couldn't do it anymore, the us versus them. I was so very tired.

There aren't many good suicide options at war—by design. Just that year, the army had made the news for losing more soldiers to suicide than combat in a single month. I remembered that article Captain Dickson had made me read, how female soldiers had always been at a higher risk of death by suicide or "suspicious circumstances" than by combat. I'd wondered why then, but up on that guard tower, I understood.

I'd brought a razor with me, a silly plastic thing that had kept clacking in my cargo pocket, as if daring me to go through with it. But the thought made me queasy, plus with no bathtubs or large bodies of water anywhere, who knew if it would even work? Large slash marks on my wrist and top secret briefings don't go together. If I failed, I'd lose my clearances, and my career would be over. I could never seek behavioral health services either, for much the same reason.

And there was the desperate soldier way of committing suicide, the one we all heard about in whispers or jokes, the one nobody ever imagined doing—until they did. I looked down at my leg and then at my boots. Those boots again, those constant reminders of both my powerlessness and my shame. As I pulled at one lace, then the next, I imagined the scene. I could pull them off, yank down my long, drab-green sock, see the hot pink of my painted toenails—that would give me one last smile. I could use the elastic strap from my pant leg to help hold my foot in place next to the rifle, my big toe right next to the trigger. Leaning forward, I'd place my mouth over the barrel, and the angle would be just right—no aiming involved. I knew there would be a moment of fear as I flexed my toe to pull the trigger, but then there would be nothing. Peace. Blackness. Over. That was the way to do it.

I lifted my hands to my face. Why couldn't I beat this thing? Depression, mental illness, suicidal ideation—whatever the hell it was called. This conviction that I should no longer be living, should maybe never have existed. By every definition in the world, I was a success. I had survived so much—all those predatory adults, in The Family and out of it; graduating with honors both times, as the fucking college valedictorian; commissioned by General Petraeus; honored for fitness and badassery, for playing the boys' game as hard as I could at Fort Benning School for Boys and since then. Hadn't I already proved to all those Aunties and Uncles that I was something, that I had made it in the outside world?

No. One shot and the cult would win, I realized. There'd be the *tsk*, just like little Davidito. She'd pursued all of Satan's glories, but couldn't save herself.

Nobody in my unit would have understood either. Maybe they'd blame it all on my troubled childhood if they discovered it—a convenient way for the army to pass the buck, never at fault. I'd be another statistic, another woman who couldn't hack it in this hard life.

I was so fucking tired.

I lay back, staring at my boots, laces in hand, trying to get up my courage, hugging that rifle like it was my best friend. But then my actual best friend popped into my head—Danielle had made an effort to stay in my life even while she was deployed to Korea; she knew my history, and she loved me anyway. No matter what anyone else said about my death, she'd know the truth—that I'd failed to outrun my demons, despite all the miles I had put in. Somehow that thought comforted me, even as it devastated me. Marching through my mind behind Danielle came the other women who'd made me: Merry, Auntie Jade, Michaela, Ms. Raibon, Heaven, and others. And Mom. I thought of each of them, struggling in their own ways to make their way through a world that wasn't made for them, either. And in that moment, I knew I couldn't let them down.

My old desire to prove everyone wrong awoke in me. I sat up, hugging my knees instead of my rifle. I wouldn't let anyone beat me—not the Uncles, not the army, not the rapists, or all the bad men in the world, and certainly not my fear.

I have survived so much.

I grabbed my boots, determined to see them as friends and not traitors. I tied a second knot on each bootlace, securing them into place. I knew it wasn't gone, my desire to disappear. I knew I hadn't beaten those demons—they'd be back. There was always another battle, always another war. But that would be tomorrow, or the next day, or the next month or year. All I needed to do in that moment was climb down the tower, put a hard face back on, and keep walking.

23

COMBAT BARBIE

■

Kandahar Province, Afghanistan, August 2011

I kept walking that dark day I came down from the tower. After the mission that took the lives of so many of our guys, we wondered if missions with women would be put to an end, but the pace only increased. We spent time doing roadblocks and searches of the Bedouins in the surrounding areas, stopping vehicles of suspected smugglers, and visiting villages to hang out with the local leaders, and their women and children, hoping to win over hearts and minds. A lot of our time was occupied patrolling all around the area surrounding Kandahar Airfield—outside the wire. All deliberate combat operations would now have women attached to them, the generals had decreed.

Overhead, the noise from the two giant army helicopters was deafening, their rotors spinning in unison as they lifted off from the concrete landing pad. After the birds were gone, the absolute silence was worse, leaving me and twenty-five male colleagues alone outside an Afghan village. As the dust from the rotor wash settled, we all got up from our kneeling "at the ready" positions, and I looked around, on the alert, squinting against the harsh glare of the desert sun.

I saw the village about five hundred yards in front of us. A single narrow path, the choke point, would make us targets if bad guys were around, as we crossed from the open desert into the center of the small town. Sergeant Jon MacGregor, promoted after his role in the rescue missions that tragic day three months prior, pointed out that the rains from the night before had caved in part of the path. We needed to be on our guard.

The guys got this, I told myself. *They know what they're doing.*

We assumed our practiced patrol position and began to march forward. Our intelligence briefs told us there wasn't supposed to be much danger, but nobody on this team took anything for granted. I eyed First Lieutenant Andy Huang, the new platoon leader who'd been brought in to replace John, and felt grateful he didn't look nervous. I settled my face, careful not to show any emotion in front of the guys. I clicked into being Combat Barbie, a slur some male soldiers hurled at us women who dared to play their game. But we leaned in and decided to claim the term with pride. Combat Barbie was perfect, professional, and proudly serving. So what if she was pretty too?

We moved ahead, slow and steady. Out in the open country of Afghanistan, it took us nearly four times as long to cover ground as it did during training drills because we never knew what part of the road would be rigged with bombs or which rocks might hide snipers. That's asymmetrical warfare, and what fighting terrorists is like. If it were a chess game, the Americans would be just moves away from a checkmate, when the insurgents douse the board in gasoline and light it ablaze. Winning, but not by any of the rules the rest of us have agreed to play by. It's hard to replicate scenarios in training because the fear, the almost buzzing alertness of being out on their sand, is impossible to mimic. I didn't think my constant fear could be heightened any more than it already was, but with each step toward the village, my heart tightened and I battled my mind whispering a barrage of unhelpful questions—would this be my last day on earth? Or maybe the day I lost a limb, or three?

From near the back of the patrol, I could see First Lieutenant Huang, up front, put his arm up in the air—a hard-closed fist. That was our signal to stop dead in our tracks. It was too dangerous to move. We'd barely been on the ground for a couple of minutes, but already something was wrong. The explosive device technician near me carried a radio to communicate with his partner up front. I heard the warning crackle: "We're picking up something, but we'll need some time to verify. Move slowly. Everybody be on their guard."

Fear gripped me, and I could feel my body threatening to flare into fight-or-flight mode. But my training kicked in and I forced my rational brain to take control: The guys with the right machines, the ones that detect bombs, were up front and on alert. I reminded myself that I was mostly safe, that what I was feeling was a physiological response to fear, one that kept me aware and alert when helpful, but could turn to panic if I let it. I would not let it. This was just an Afghan village after all, one we'd been to before. Nothing to worry about.

But something was wrong. I could feel it niggling on the tip of my consciousness, and my brain spun hard as I tried to puzzle it out. War is like chess, except with real consequences. As I was the only woman on the team, John and then his replacements always encouraged me to speak up and speak out. But I needed something more to go on than my Spidey-Sense tingling.

Then it hit me: Where were all the children? Usually they were swarming out of the village, racing toward the helicopters as fast as their little feet could carry them. Where were the six-year-old girls toting baby siblings on their hips as I'd done so often as a child? Where were the boys with their slingshots made from sticks, always scaling nearby rocks and cliffs, as nimble as the mountain goats they ran around with? Where were the children with the bright reddish-purple hair that I had thought was dyed, until I learned that it is a phenomenon found only in the deserts of Afghanistan, some DNA leftover of Genghis Khan, or so the legend goes. In the back of my mind, I scrambled to connect the dots. I was an intelligence officer even though I was playing infantry at the moment—I knew the answer was somewhere in my brain, but I couldn't think of it.

Suddenly, like the flash of a bomb, there it was.

"Stop!" I said, with a certainty I didn't know I had.

Doubt crept in. What if I wasn't supposed to be doing anything, noticing anything, saying anything? What if no one wanted to hear my thoughts? I was just there to engage with the women and children—the ones blatantly absent.

I shifted my weight and stared ahead at the endless miles of sand, steeling myself for the criticism and ridicule as everyone looked my way. I knew that I'd never live it down if I was wrong.

"There are no children," I told First Lieutenant Huang. "Anywhere!"

I gesticulated around, stared at the raised eyebrow on the lieutenant, trying to read his expression. I hoped he didn't think I was trying to step on his authority. But then both of his eyes widened.

"Everyone hit the ground!" he yelled. That was the moment I knew for sure that I wasn't wrong. The men hadn't seen it—at least not all of it. The experienced group of Airborne Ranger–qualified Pathfinders, and explosive device experts, men who did this day and night without rest, men who had been primed, who had already noticed several other indicators that could have been nothing—or could have been an ambush waiting to take ten more of us to early graves. The children were the last piece of the puzzle, an obvious sign—once combined with everything else—and one I always briefed troops about in my day job. It had only ever been in theory before, but now the reality of their complete and utter absence hit me with fear that left my hands and feet tingling.

It would take twenty minutes for the explosive device technicians to verify the bomb, in a spot they'd identified about one hundred yards in front of our group. It looked pretty small, but still deadly. We wouldn't continue on the mission. Clearly, drinking tea with these village leaders would have to wait. We'd call in the "suspected IED" grid marker, and base operations would send a team over to deal with it more officially. By later that afternoon, the children would probably be back outside. We'd never find out if it had been a terrorist who had booby-trapped the village, or if one of the men we'd had tea with the last time we were here had been paid to lay the bomb. Maybe it was someone who had his children's lives threatened if he didn't cooperate.

The Afghan villagers may have been ambivalent about the American soldiers in their country. They may have wavered between supporting us or helping clothe and feed the terrorists who tried to take our lives, depending on whose mission they related to more. But one fact didn't change: They loved their children as much as any other parents anywhere in the world. If they know something is wrong, they won't let the children out to play. I'd briefed this to teams of soldiers going out beyond the wire. We called them indicators, signs of danger.

I realized the reason why I noticed *this* indicator. I loved seeing the little girls. I felt flattered they could always tell I was a woman, even in my full combat kit—the ill-fitting body armor, helmet and bullet-proof eye-protection, loaded M4 rifle and six extra 30-round magazines clipped to my load-bearing vest, gloved and booted. And as much as I stood out to them, they stood out to me, too. Most soldiers on my team would try to win their favor with Beanie Babies and candy. The guys talked about the joy of making them smile, though I'm sure our commanders didn't mind whatever positive influence may have been gained with their parents by the gesture. But I saw more than kids happy to see American saviors. I saw a version of the childhood I'd survived: hungry faces wearing brave smiles, callused bare feet, and the fear hiding behind their eyes. That day on the sand, I didn't see girls laden with too much responsibility, along with the toddlers and babies they struggled to balance. That day on the sand, I saw their absence instead. I can't say for sure what anyone else experienced. All I know is that when we were walking back to the helicopters, mission aborted but no casualties this time, First Lieutenant Huang said to me, "Man, I love having you girls on the team—you notice the silliest things." But he didn't say it like it was silly; his face didn't crack a smile at all. Just a silent nod and he was off, a sign from a quiet professional: Keep doing good work. You're a valued part of this team.

On the birds taking us back to relative safety, all I could think of were the many people who'd said to me, "Daniella, I'm so glad you weren't there," the day John died. But what if I had been there? What if any of us had been there, the women our country so strongly believed needed to be kept out of harm's way? What if, as John had once pointed out, our being so different, with such divergent life experiences, and all the *silly,* little things we notice, was the entire point?

What if we could save lives, just by being women? What if I could have saved him?

■

SOMEHOW, I SURVIVED that grueling year in the desert.

After I stopped sleeping with Captain Madison, he made my work life intolerable, as suspected. I didn't think I could talk to anybody about what was really going on, not even Tiffany. I asked my commander for help navigating the increasingly toxic work environment, and the captains made the sudden decision to move me into a role inside the central part of the Tactical Operations Center, to put some distance between me and Captain Madison, where I was "causing trouble" and "flinging accusations." I chose to see it as a promotion. It was the opportunity to be the boss of my own little team, away from all the captains and other lieutenants of the intelligence team, away from all the political machinations and jockeying for favor. I learned more about what our analyst soldiers did in real time, got some great mentorship from the sergeant first class who was my counterpart, and tried to learn to be the type of leader John had been, connecting with my team as people, as individuals, learning about them as we sat next to each other in parallel little seats for twelve-hour shifts. We scanned thousands of reports a day, tracked intelligence, briefed officers, launched medical evacuation helicopters in response to injury reports, sent gunships out to the reports of troops in "contact" with the enemy—when our guys were being shot at—and dealt with downed helicopters, the biggest deal of all.

I enjoyed it there, in the center of the command cells, overseeing and supporting some of the action that I'd observed from the other side, rather than just making PowerPoints and briefing colonels and generals. I learned so much about tactical level operations, and maybe even a little about strategy, both in the air, and of the ground troops we supported. In theory, that would set me up for a great career afterward, especially paired with my Female Engagement Team experience—which we'd been assured would get us awards or some kind of recognition, as the army started to see how valuable women were on the team. The award never materialized, our unit arguing that it wasn't right for lieutenants, sergeants, and specialists to get accolades higher than the captains for whom they worked. The army didn't carefully track our names, or build a record for our experiment, likely out of plausible deniability, should something happen to one of us. I wondered in the back of my mind if it had been an experiment intended to fail, to prove what they all "knew" about women at war, that had gone so differently than anyone had expected. Instead of proving that you needed to be a man to be good at war, we'd begun to show them the truth: that when both men and women are trying to kill you, it makes an awful lot of sense to have both men and women on your team trying to stay alive. Instead of a medal, I valued the Female Engagement Team certificate I'd been given upon completion of our forty-hour block of cultural sensitivity training as much as a Bronze Star.

A few months after we'd begun, Big Army had set up a whole new program called Cultural Support Teams, realizing that, since it seemed women were in combat to stay, they should get at least a modicum of special operations training, too. Even if nobody ever knew what we did to lay the groundwork for those teams, it felt incredible to be part of the army's very first Female Engagement Teams, knowing we were a part of making the service equal for women. I could feel the crack in the brainwashing beginning, and I was right there, in the middle of it. I hoped that the combat ban and everything else that kept women secondary, in support roles, lesser by design and then oppressed because of it, would come crumbling down. It was an exciting and promising time to be at war, as much as it almost broke me.

One day, I was out running sprints in the heat of the day—because it was hard, and *why not?* I was still punishing myself, putting my body through the most extreme workouts to make me forget where I was for a little bit, to maybe exhaust me to the point I could sleep at night.

I heard a man shout, "Stop that female!" and then two men started running to catch up to me. *What the fuck was happening?* I couldn't process it, so I dug down deep to sprint even faster, to outrun them, never giving them the satisfaction of looking anywhere but straight ahead. One of the men was faster than me, relatively rare, and I think he realized he'd frightened me. He throttled back, but not enough to give up the pursuit entirely. Matching me pace for pace, he introduced himself, "I'm Sergeant Major Blaise, recruiting for Special Mission Units Command. Can we talk?"

If tennis shoes could make a screeching sound on sand, I'm sure mine did. Special Mission Units are the James Bonds of the US Army, or at least that was my understanding. And Sergeant Major Blaise wanted to talk to *me*. Maybe this would be my chance, finally, to prove myself. To maybe even have a little fun. I followed him back to the shipping container that served as his on-base office. He said he'd caught sight of me and thought any female crazy enough to be racing sprints in the Kandahar noonday heat would be a good fit for the team. I asked him to please not chase deployed women anymore. He apologized profusely, likely never having considered our fear. The unclassified part of the Force's mission, the only part he could tell me then, was, "highly trained units of one to four personnel, deployed around the world to *find, fix,* and *finish* the enemies of America. You stay until mission complete."

When I mentioned I'd be perfectly suited for that kind of work, that in addition to being fast and "crazy," I'd also grown up internationally as a missionary kid and loved globe-trotting—the easier version of my story—he smirked.

"You know," he said. "I've heard they call the CIA 'Christians in Action' for all the missionary kids recruited who do very well with globe-trotting. With fitting in anywhere. With disappearing."

He sized me up and down and then offered me a glimpse of a life I could choose, laying out the next five years. "Look here, El Tee, I'm heartbroken to know you're just a lieutenant, or I'd take you from your unit today. I've only got room for captains and sergeants, can't do nothing with you for another year or more, depending on how your cohort promotes. What I can tell you is that I know everyone. Special operations is a very small world. With your Female Engagement

Team experience, I can get you a slot in a Cultural Support Team assessment, which, from the looks of you, you'll fly through. You do a fun deployment with the Rangers, or the Special Forces. Six months, combat, door-kicking, shoot-'em-in-the-face, all the fucking fun shit a badass like you has always wanted. Then, you pin your railroad tracks," he said, tantalizing me with the colloquial term for captain rank. "And the Cultural Support Team will hand you right back over to us, after getting you a faster version of the captain's course. From there, you do your years with us, then you write your ticket. You wanna be CIA? FBI? Run the joint? Sky's the limit."

It felt like the kind of opportunity John had foreseen, the dream that the army understood my worth. Combat Barbie, a real-life James Bond girl—was this the route for me? But it was still army. I looked for the catch.

"How many women do you have?" I asked, almost under my breath, embarrassed how much I cared.

Looking me dead in the eye, seeming to intuit what I was really getting at, he said, "We recruit almost 50 percent women for this team. Women increase our safety, hands down. You know, there's a reason it's James Bond and a James Bond *girl,* after all."

He'd clearly given that line before and knew its effect on someone like me. "I hope you'll think about this path," he said. "You're the perfect candidate for the Force—no family, no husband, no kids, free to travel, nothing really tying you to that world back home. You're perfect. We could easily make you not exist. It's a lot of *fun,* too."

As I sprinted back to the headquarters building, I thought about all the things he'd said. In so many ways, it sounded glorious. The Force was the toughest, baddest thing out there, and they *wanted* women, knew what we could do, unlike these bozos in Big Army. I could imagine myself alone in a faraway country, headscarved and ambling through an aromatic street market, all my hard-earned childhood acting skills, language skills, interest in other people and cultures coming together to play in a high-stakes game of chess where the prize was life or death. This time, I'd have a concealed weapon to protect me, not just laser-fingers and Jesus. It sounded like an adventure novel, like a movie, but I wondered if I could fit in on those teams any better than I did on the Big Army ones. Could I ever fit anywhere? What if I was still too different? Too broken?

Or what if I fit perfectly—like he'd told me I would—because I had nobody? Because leaving home and never looking back wasn't a big deal? Because I'd never had a home, and maybe never would? Was that the life I wanted?

These were the thoughts I carried to the end of my deployment. As awful as Kandahar Airfield had been, I looked at homecoming with trepidation. While everyone else was giddy, looking forward to seeing their partners and kids, excited to return to their homes where they would be surrounded by familiar things, I packed up my meager belongings in my drab-green army-issue duffel bags and booked a room in the barracks for when we got back. As Sergeant Major Blaise had deftly pointed out, I had nobody and, more importantly, I had no idea what this next phase of my life would look like.

I descended the staircase of the 737 we'd chartered back to Fort Campbell as slowly as I could without holding up the line of soldiers behind me, all of them eager to catch the first glimpse of their families in the holding area. I stood there in a stupid formation, everyone staring straight ahead, trying to pretend they weren't dying to run to loved ones they hadn't seen in 365 days, that they couldn't hear their own children's voices calling "Hi Daddy!" cutting through all the others. It hadn't occurred to me to invite Mom to be there when I got home. She wouldn't have been able to afford it anyway, managing on a combination of government welfare and the meager sum the Children of God still paid Dad for his artwork. Even if she had the money, she wouldn't have been able to take the time out of court reporting school, away from the baby and other kids to make the trip. I didn't have that kind of family, I thought, the kind who showed up for important moments.

Some general, probably the post commander, droned on about the importance of our mission, our valor, and how important we all were to the country. He said a few solemn words for our fallen. Everyone bowed their heads, a perfect excuse to let a few tears fall. But it would be impossible to stop, so I stood there, trying not to lose my composure.

As soon as we were released, I fumbled my way through all the happy, hugging bodies, my vision blurring from the tears. The noise of their reunions enveloped me as I kept my head down, trying not to show my embarrassment. Around me, some people stared in surprise, then pity—the poor first lieutenant, just back from war, who has nobody. Ducking into a side nook in the hangar, I pulled out my phone.

"Hi, Mom, I'm home." I dissolved into sobs.

I cried for myself, for my friends who couldn't ever come home again, for the innocence I hadn't been able to lose at war because I'd never had it to begin with. I cried because even though I'd chosen to go on living, I wasn't sure if I could keep making that choice every time I hurt this badly. I cried because I didn't want to be an officer anymore, because I wasn't even sure I wanted to be an American these days, or if I ever had. I cried because I knew that I could easily choose to ditch it all. I could finish my army sentence, move to a beach in Brazil, and take a job teaching English, like a friend from my earliest years was doing happily. I cried because I knew I wouldn't belong there either. It would never be that simple. I cried remembering the only home I'd ever known, the Children of God communes and its people who weren't my people anymore. I cried because I was a girl from nowhere, and all I wanted to do, like any soldier just back from war, was go home.

24

I'M THE BITCH

■

Fort Campbell, Kentucky, 2013

Redeployment—coming home from war—had not been as much of a tonic as I expected. For at least six months, I struggled with the intense anger and grief common to many soldiers returning from a war zone. I wanted the time on my contract to expire so I could leave the army. I felt if I didn't get out of the United States and find somewhere to fit in, I'd die, and likely at my own hands. I kept a personal gun because that was what we all did in the army, especially as a woman living alone. Danielle was often unreachable, on her own deployment now, so I would often call Mom, needing someone to sit with me on the phone, a heightened awareness of the loaded gun in the safe just steps away. I didn't *want* to die, but sometimes it seemed too exhausting to keep going. It felt like Mom was the only person on the planet who cared if I lived or died, and she never tried to talk me out of anything, to guilt me, to tell me to think about the people around me. She sat with me, understanding, and we talked, getting to know each other as adults.

Mom saved my life so many times.

In a moment of despair, after attempting to find connection with another human the only way I knew how—with my body—a sometimes friend, sometimes lover, and always army superior said a few words to me that changed my life:

"Daniella, I think you need to get the fuck over yourself, and like, soon. You aren't as different as you think you are."

I hadn't known how to respond, so I said goodbye. But his words didn't vanish, they only formed into a bolder font in my mind, emerging whenever I was alone. *Get. The. Fuck. Over. Yourself.*

I decided he was right. I had been running for almost a decade, fighting every day, every moment since I left the cult. To establish myself, to get an education, to feed myself, to keep living, to succeed. But nothing I had ever done was good enough to convince me I belonged, that I was "normal." Despite the shine of my accomplishments, I was breaking inside.

The day I saw my name blazing out at me on the army captain promotion list, I felt a temporary high, almost like a drug. *Maybe this is it,* I thought. If I made it to captain, maybe I could relax my obsessive drive toward success, and maybe I'd get over myself.

I knew what else I needed. In order to figure out this culture, this country I had fought for but didn't feel like I was "from," I needed to figure out relationships with people.

Channeling my honor-student days, I set my mind to the task of studying—myself, others, Americans, and specifically, a phenomenon I learned about called "Third Culture Kids." Reading the book by that title, and then many others, I began to see myself in a whole different light: not as a misfit from a cult, a girl destined to be lonely and alone, but as a member of a significant group—there were a lot of us, apparently—who grew up in cultures not their own. Third Culture Kids were studied by experts and understood, President Barack Obama being a famous example of one. There were things I could do, steps I could take, and, most comfortingly, books I could read, to reach across the divide between me and everyone around me.

I realized I didn't want to be a Combat Barbie or the James Bond girl after all, the perfect soldier with nothing to lose, with nobody worrying if I ever made it back. I wanted people to know me, I wanted to see if maybe I wasn't that different after all. Slowly, I began to make new friends, in my unit and out, and I started translating myself to the world around me. I started saying "I grew up in a cult," the first step in acknowledging the truth of who I was, and, like Danielle had asked me what seemed like a lifetime before, to allow people to see the *real* me, to not hide myself behind a sheen of perfection that was never more than skin deep, covering my secrets and shame. A shame that had never even been my fault.

Bit by bit, I came to life. Allowing myself to show a sliver of who I was gave me a confidence I hadn't felt for a long time. What had seemed impossible months ago suddenly seemed viable—and sensible. I devised a plan: I'd stay in the army until I found something better, sharpening my expertise in intelligence work. I'd use the time, and the captain money, to improve myself. *Who knows?* I thought. Maybe I'd even be able to forge a career I'd enjoy in the service.

Immediately upon getting back from Kandahar, I was offered a job promotion: senior intelligence officer for a battalion in our brigade, which would include managing my own team and serving as a subject matter expert advisor directly to the battalion commander, in charge of about a thousand soldiers. In the army hierarchy, this job was the next big level up for me. And it was coming a year and a half ahead of schedule. I was nervous about failing; I was still so new. On the other hand, if I did well, I could write my ticket without having to write off the idea of a family or people to call my own. Maybe I could have it all, the dream career and the life outside it. Maybe, when I was the one calling more of the shots and setting the culture on my own team, it would be tolerable. Maybe, if I went into the scheduled deployment having already earned a team's respect, I would be able to keep it. With the speed of the army—only two hours to make a decision—I said yes.

My two-levels-up boss would be the battalion commander, Lieutenant Colonel Scott Halter. One of the first things he told me was that I wouldn't need to prove myself to him; he trusted the chain of command who put me into the role well above my rank and grade. It had been a long time since I had good models of leadership, but when he named the three values he required of his team, I liked him immediately.

"Candor—always be honest with me," he said. "I know I look frightening because I'm so serious, but this is just my face." He did have a serious face, attached to a thin and wiry body. He was average height, the few gray hairs scattered around his temple belying the fact that he was only thirty-eight, with dark, contemplative eyes.

"Come to me when you have something to say. Competence, I know you have already." He tapped the folder holding my yearly evaluations that each commander received every time I made a move. "Competence is the one people will catch a break on—you don't always have to be perfect. We'll work over the next year as a team to establish our competence before we head back to war, but you will be allowed to fail and recover. That matters to me."

I nodded, feeling both relieved and surprised that he said I would be allowed to fail, something I'd never heard in the army. I couldn't help but fixate on that one sentence: *You don't always have to be perfect.* I wasn't sure I believed him.

"Character is the one thing you can't mess up. If I find your character isn't up to snuff, you'll be off my team."

I realized from his words that day, and later on from his actions, that he was a good man who cared about being a good leader. I had seen so many times how rare that was in the army, and in the larger world too. It had been so long since I felt truly hopeful, and I believed I could be safe and supported on his team. He was a real leader, and I desperately wanted to be good enough for him.

■

IN THE HEAT of a midday run in the Kentucky summer, I scanned the crowd of men. In my non-army workout clothes, more of my legs were visible than the normal knee-length, which would mean more ogling.

I'd been advised to take a coveted spot on the brigade commander's lunch running team. The all-male team gathered around Colonel Johnny Maxwell, a man we jokingly referred to as "King Maxwell," a nod to his King Henry the Eighth leadership style. He was someone who had defied the odds to succeed in the officer corps, after coming from poverty in the South. Running had been his way out too, and he'd even been a professionally competitive runner. Colonel Maxwell loved to hear Colonel Maxwell talk, and of course, we all obliged with smiles on our faces. I'd been playing that game since birth. I knew how to smile and nod, how to appease the Uncles at all costs. And like the Tudor king of old, Colonel Maxwell loved his favorites, usually runners or young women officers, and showered them with attention and political capital. I was becoming one of them.

I stood next to the guys from my Lieutenant Mafia, as we called it, the operations and intelligence officers I worked and socialized with, the guys who knew me as more of myself. Most of us competed on the 101st Division's competitive running team and, twice, had traveled together to Washington to compete in the Army Ten-Miler. These guys had my back. We had spent the previous two years building what felt to me like a real team. I saw our battalion commander, Lieutenant Colonel Scott Halter, standing quietly to one side, always watching people. He appeared to be as obsessed with running as he was with teambuilding and leadership.

As we began to move, the pace of the supposedly leisurely run picked up, even as the heat climbed to over 100 degrees, everyone needing to impress Colonel Maxwell, knowing it was the price of being one of his elite. Finally, I had something in common with the top leaders; most did their business on the golf course, a world where I—and most women—were excluded. In this unit, running was my in to the people in power.

Ordinarily, I would have been pushing myself hard to be up at the front of the pack. Both Colonel Maxwell and Lieutenant Colonel Halter often bragged about me as if I were their own daughter, proud of the trophies I kept accumulating. But that day, I wasn't feeling it. I'd slowly become wary of Colonel Maxwell, of the sycophantic behavior he seemed to need from his followers. Army culture was as obsessed with appearance and youth as Hollywood. The colonel was forty-five, and his constant bloviating about the good old days made me wonder if he feared that he was slowing down, that his days of relevance were numbered. I also knew the rumors about how he acted toward the women he liked. "Be careful, don't find yourself alone with him," said the women who pulled each other aside to whisper, like we did as children, giving warnings about the creepy Uncles. As always, my safety relied on *my* behavior, never theirs. It was my responsibility to never make a wrong calculation about whom to trust.

In the year and a half since we'd been home, I'd guarded my reputation fiercely, knowing I couldn't take much more of the gossiping and backstabbing that had characterized my first deployment. It was easier to be respected back home at Fort Campbell, where work and lives were somewhat separate, and where General Order One, reserved for combat only, didn't exist to paint a target on my back. Though I'd begun to share more of myself with friends, I had to continue to be careful. It took me a long time to realize what it seemed like Danielle had figured out from the get-go: You can be a woman in the army, even an officer, and be successful—but only if you can present as genderless as possible. Look too good, or have any hint of a private life outside of work, even so much as a dog or quirky hobby, and it could go south. As a woman in uniform, dedication and constant sacrifice was what was required. I decided to go all in.

I had bought my own small town house, drove the hour into Nashville on the weekends to hang out at the one salsa club with friends, and concealed any appearance at work that I might have a personal life. Back home, I could spend my free time as I wished, putting my hard face on along with my uniform and relegating them both to a heap at the foot of my bed at the end of the duty day. As I settled into this double life, I began to relax, make friends, and share my real self with them, but only far away from work. I started dating, and even had one or two lovely relationships that ended amicably when the other officer moved to a new station or deployed for a year. It was never worth the risk of trying to hold on to these relationships, for any of us. We were incredibly young, our lives full of possibility, our futures so undecided. And of course, the pressure and scrutiny were only magnified for women.

That day, running with my brigade, I let myself fall back, trying to find shade and drink water. I noticed a man who looked vaguely familiar take the place beside me, but I couldn't place him. He was very tall, and *very* handsome. His piercing blue eyes were the first thing that jumped out at me, even before I noticed his rugged jawline. *Swoon.* I looked for a wedding ring and didn't see one. I pulled my eyes back to the road, sighing. The fact that he was on this run meant he was in *this* brigade, and very much off-limits if I hoped to keep my stellar reputation. We chatted casually as we ran together, keeping time.

At the end of the run, I stuck out my hand. "I'm Daniella," I said.

"Yeah," he said, taking a step back instead of completing the handshake. "I know who you are. I'm Tom Young, and I've been in this unit for five years."

As he waited for a sign of recognition, my mind ran over everyone in my unit—my Lieutenant Mafia; the other staff officers like me; the platoon leaders and commanders down at the company levels. I knew all of them. And I knew all the runners in this unit, even the enlisted ones. Who was this guy?

"Chief Warrant Officer Two Tom Young," he said. "I'm one of the pilots you brief all the time, Ma'am."

Well, that explained it, then. He was a warrant officer—never would I have imagined catching one of them on a "voluntary" lunch run. Warrant officers are a whole thing in the army. There are the enlisted soldiers, sort of like line-level workers and first-line managers, then the officers, the mid- to senior-level executive ranks. Warrants fall somewhere in between. In the power structure that belies it all, though, they are in the perfect place—they are the subject matter experts, and he who holds the knowledge holds the power. There were rumors of how warrant officers could chew lieutenants into pieces, and, of course, uglier whispers for what they wanted from women. I'd kept myself apart, being friendly, but always professional.

"I'm sorry to break it to you, Mr. Young," I said, emphasizing the "Mr." title given to warrants, "but as one of the *only* women on battalion staff leadership, and as the intelligence officer, I might be a bit more visible than you." Then, I made sure to laugh so he knew I wasn't "being a bitch." "But I'll make sure to remember you from now on in all the briefs, okay?"

∎

OUR UNIT MOVED to the army's Joint Readiness Training Center in Fort Polk, Louisiana—an oppressively hot and humid bog of over 3,400 square miles that Eisenhower had given the army in 1940 to train for operations during World War II. We were there for our culmination exercise—to prove to ourselves and our commanders that this unit, this team, was ready to do it for real in war. Every unit does culmination exercises—war games—every time, no matter that all we did was go to war, come back home, just to turn around and do it again. As the unit's intelligence officer, it would mean interminable days and little room for missteps—everything we did wrong could mean a life once we deployed, so we had to get it right. I felt every bit of my position's gravity, carrying a weight that felt heavier than my twenty-six years.

During the first week of the trip—the leaders' summit—I'd been locked away with the seventeen men on my team in a conference room for fourteen hours a day, crafting the battalion-level operations orders and intelligence products the companies under us would have to work with during the field exercise. It was a time that brought us all closer together, almost as if rank—and in my case, gender—didn't matter as much as it did back home. Importantly, General Order One didn't apply yet, and so neither did the scrutiny it brought. We'd work our butts off all day, and then wind down with six-packs of beer, which would also be off-limits to us soon, and someone on a guitar; all together in the same situation, with only each other for companionship for the upcoming weeks out in the swamp. I realized I was lucky to be the only woman on the team. If there'd been even one other, we'd have been expected to keep to ourselves by default. It hadn't occurred to anyone to isolate me, and I'd been treated like just another member of the team. It reminded me of how I'd felt patrolling with John and the guys.

The rest of the unit arrived a week later, and as exercises began, the officers at the top slept less, the lines in everyone's faces becoming more and more visible. The Keurig I'd brought from home ran day and night to keep up with everyone's demand and gave me power in my own little corner of the Tactical Operations Center. I worked around the clock, often eighteen-hour days, trying to get my team

ready, including a brand-new girl, Private Parker, who had no experience or training at all. I knew from my first deployment how hard
it could be to deploy with a team without enough time to get to know
them, let alone gel with them, and though she struggled to grasp the
intelligence work, our team did our best to get her up to speed.

Days blended into each other, and ten-mile runs at midnight with
three or more of my Lieutenant Mafiosos became our only time to
decompress and do something other than work, eat, or try to catch a
few hours of sleep. I swallowed the knowledge that these men, who'd
become like my brothers, would be warned away from camaraderie
with me, despite my record of professionalism, the instant we touched
down on the sand. I had already warned them that our long runs,
so well-known throughout the battalion, would become suspect as
soon as we fell under General Order One's restrictions overseas. They
didn't believe me, laughing at what they thought was my exaggera-
tion.

"Everyone knows you're just another bro," First Lieutenant Mark
Ackman, the hippiest guy to ever graduate from West Point, was fond
of saying. "Besides, nobody will say shit about you. You're fierce."

"They will, though," was all I ever had the energy to mutter in
response.

I asked them to watch my back, told them which men scared me
the most, and which left me feeling uncomfortable. They nodded that
they would. I was part of the team. They promised me I'd be safe.

As my exhaustion deepened, my responses to my subordinates
grew shorter and snippier, my smile disappearing out of conversations with my peers. I knew I was sometimes called "the Ice Queen,"
and, in that moment, even I could understand why. Two weeks into
our exercise, the warrant officer I worked most closely with, Mr. Simmonds, came to me, an impish grin on his face.

"Hey, I found something perfect for you at the shoppette, El Tee.
Redecorated your office. Enjoy."

I walked into my little clapboard makeshift space to find literally
every available surface covered in hot pink, Hello Kitty duct tape. I
cocked my head to the side, amused and confused.

"I thought it might help soften you up a little," Mr. Simmonds said behind me. "You know, because everyone thinks you're so mean and such a man-eater. Thought we should show them your softer, girlier side."

"Touché, man. I appreciate it," I said, my grin reaching my eyes this time. I reminded myself that my soldiers were all feeling the stress as well. Everyone was doing the best they could.

The days passed in pure monotony, all of us going through the motions of our jobs, waking up from a dead sleep to respond to downed aircraft drills and sudden missions, a small reminder of what the long nine months of our upcoming deployment would be. I couldn't help but see the similarity with the drills of my youth, when we'd be awakened in the middle of the night and timed on how long it took us to grab our flee-bags and line up in formation. I came to find that walking into a bright pink office covered with the face of a strange Japanese kitty made me smile, and I saw others smile too, so I guessed Mr. Simmonds had been right about that softening effect.

One morning, another warrant officer came to my office, an Apache gunship pilot attached to us from another battalion. Striding into my office with the swagger common to attack pilots, he stopped short seeing the bright flash of pink and kitty.

"Well, well, what have we here?" he said, speaking out of the side of his mouth with an accent so strong I could only guess he was from Louisiana, and backcountry, probably from nearby. "A pretty little pink missy in a pretty little pink office with a pretty little pink . . . kitty . . . how perfectly loooove-ly."

My eyebrows and my hackles raised. I wanted to punch him.

"Excuse me, Mr. Boucher, is it?" I swiveled around, trying to temper the harshness in my voice when I saw his rank, chief warrant officer three. Lieutenants are always warned not to get into a battle of wills with a chief warrant officer three or higher. But I was about to be a captain, and I was more than a little tired of putting up with harassment—all the time and everywhere. I knew his comment wasn't that bad, compared with hundreds of others I'd heard over the last four years, but I was tired, and I had lost all my patience.

"That's Ma'am to you," I snapped, my voice steely and hard. "I'm gonna need you to turn right around and examine how inappropriate that was while you are on your way out of *my* office, *Mr.* Boucher."

"Aw, c'mon, *Ma'am,*" he said. "I didn't know who you were, I'm just here for my brief, and I'm sure that you and I can get along."

"I'm sure that we can, too," I said, an insincere honey coating my voice. "But right now, you need to walk away and we'll try again when you have a little more respect. Oh, and in the future, the color of someone's office, anyone's office, does not give you the right to say whatever you want to them." With that, I swiveled my chair back around, making it clear there was no room for argument. After a moment or two of shock, he slinked out, and I could tell by the sound of his footsteps that his swagger was gone.

I sunk my head to the desk, my heart beating rapidly. I felt like an animal, prey—the way a deer shakes with adrenaline after escaping a predator. When I calmed down, I stood up and decided to find Mr. Apollo Simmonds, my closest colleague, and tell him what had just happened—I thought he'd be proud of how I'd handled it, and as a chief warrant officer three himself, he could tell me if I'd overstepped. I came face-to-face with Lieutenant Colonel Halter mere inches outside my door—the man we called "the Ninja" for a reason. He'd heard the whole exchange. I swallowed hard as he motioned me to follow him.

"I have a story to tell you, Daniella," he said, expressionless as always, his voice steady, as we walked down the hall to his office. Was I in trouble or not? There was no way to tell. "When I was a young lieutenant, we deployed to Iraq and I was made the unit intelligence officer, because, well, there really was no one else to do the job."

He told me all this as we walked down the hall together, like this was some casual conversation between colleagues on the way to the office. I had no idea what he was getting at.

"I had a sergeant who worked for me, like your staff sergeant does for you. She was super squared-away, and she taught me a lot about intel work. One night, she came banging on my door long after I'd been asleep. She said, 'Sir, I've gotta tell you what happened before you hear it from someone else.' I didn't know what to expect, but my

mind was racing. Then she told me that one of the battle captains had been harassing her, consistently, on the night shift. Finally, he'd made one comment too many, and she snapped. She was coming to me because she was sure she'd be court-martialed for the disrespect toward an officer, but she wanted me to understand. She told me, 'Sir, I'm gonna tell you what I told the captain.'" He became more animated than I'd ever seen him. He continued, "And then, not missing a beat, she looked me dead in the eyes and said, 'There are two types of women in the army: bitches and sluts. Sir, I'm the bitch!'" He raised both of his thumbs to point at his own chest.

Then, after a small smirk and no further explanation, he turned and walked away. I stood, stunned, wondering what had just happened. Second Lieutenant Steven Wilson, my right-hand lieutenant and mentee, a late witness to a part of the exchange, was equally puzzled, as I could see from his confused shrug. Mr. Simmonds walked up, and I burst out, "Apollo, I think Colonel Halter just called me a bitch . . . and I think it was a compliment."

As I replayed the strange encounter, inwardly I glowed. It had taken me four grueling years, but I felt like I'd finally arrived. Lieutenant Colonel Halter—a leader I looked up to—respected me, and maybe everybody else did, too. Maybe, just maybe, I was no longer seen as a threat or a liability. Maybe this time I wouldn't have to be worried about being the slut or the dyke. I'd finally grasped the coveted title that army women all must strive for: I was officially a stone-cold *bitch*.

Back home, our sergeant major tasked me to give a pre-deployment brief to about fifteen women, all privates and lieutenants, like Private First Class Parker on my own team, who were headed into their first deployment. He didn't tell me what to say, but he knew I'd been in that situation less than two years before. He wanted me to communicate to them, somehow, what to expect as women in that environment.

"We're 5 percent of the population over there," I told them. "It's hard, stressful, emotionally draining, and often scary to be a woman on the sand. But you're not alone, and if anyone so much as hints at something to you that makes you feel uncomfortable or unsafe, you

come to me. I've been in this unit for four years now, and nobody fucks with me!"

I had hoped that my "Queen Elsa" status, the ultimate Ice Queen, would protect me and that it could carry over to the only girl who worked for me too. I caught Private Parker's eye as I closed my presentation and I was certain she heard my silent message: *I got you.*

■

I GLANCED AT my watch: Five minutes to go. Time for the top to bottom inventory—hair, perfect in its French braid, twisted and pinned to severity despite the headache I knew I'd get; medals and ribbons perfectly aligned on my sharply tailored dress blue uniform, 101st Airborne combat badge pinned in its place of honor over my left rib cage; the yellow stripes boldly embroidered on my sleeve, showing that I'd been to war and come home to train and go again, this time as a real leader; then the skirt, stockings, and pumps, shiny and black. I swallowed hard and walked out, rehearsing my speech in my head.

From up on the stage, I saw Mom waiting for me to walk up and take my place between her and Merry, at the place of honor, where I would become the US Army's newest captain and they would pin the bars on my shoulders. Mom had been at my high school graduation, but this was the first professional achievement I asked her to attend.

In the intervening years, Mom and Merry had both started their own lives, struggling hard to juggle school, motherhood, and the Systemite world they had entered. I don't know how they did it, but they excelled, each in their own way. Mom had become a court reporter, which only took an associate's degree, but it was a career that she could eventually earn more at than the judge; Merry got her GED after her son was born, then attended both community and a four-year college, and, at twenty-four, was a grade-school teacher, specializing in early childhood education and English as a Second Language. That day, they stood with me, and I could see the pride in their eyes that is born out of struggle. Dad had remained with the kids back in Texas; he'd sent word that he was proud of me. That felt huge.

Scanning the room, I wished Danielle could have been there, but she'd just returned from Kuwait, where she'd been deployed immediately after a year in Korea. She was in Washington, getting set up at her new posting. I smiled, thinking about how she was probably out at the Jefferson Memorial, pinning on her captain's bars at the same time I was. I hoped to see her when I got back stateside after war.

Lieutenant Colonel Halter stood out in his sharp blues amidst a sea of army green as he raised his hand in front of mine and recited the oath I then repeated, swearing once again to defend the Constitution of the United States against all enemies, foreign and domestic. I'd never told him the real story of my background, but he'd picked up enough details from the lieutenant chatter to know it was unique, and he spoke about the unconventional upbringing I'd had, fluent in several languages before joining the army, raised alongside fourteen siblings. He touted me as one of the most skilled intelligence professionals he'd had the privilege to serve with and bragged about my running. I looked at my friends around the unit and felt an overwhelming sense of pride and joy—I did this, I mattered, I believed in myself and it had paid off. But maybe even more importantly, I had real friends, people with whom I'd been able to stop being closeted about my past, people who saw me for who I truly was, who knew my hopes and fears and had my back.

Taking center stage for my speech, I thanked Lieutenant Colonel Halter for his mentorship and told a few stories that demonstrated how great I felt his team was coming together—*our* team, the one we'd all worked so hard to build over the previous year and a half. We were ready to go overseas and do great things. We were Task Force Lift. Even though I felt it was all a little over the top, I was swept up in the emotion—like everything in my life had been leading me to that single moment. I told them how happy I was to have a mission, a purpose, a real team, and a leader we all loved.

In front of me stood Colonel Maxwell, and I could feel the displeasure radiating off of him. I knew there'd be hell to pay for not talking more about the brigade, for not paying homage to him. At the end of the ceremony, as everyone lined up to shake my hand and that of Mom and Merry, Colonel Maxwell paused with my forty-one-year-old mother, and said, "You look far too young to have so many children. What were you, fourteen?"

My mother, an expert in cult Uncles, the woman I had always seen as shy, looked my commander straight in the eye and said with her chin high and a confident, unwavering voice, "Yes, I was. That was Daniella."

■

AT 10 P.M. on December 23, seven weeks after I earned my captain's bars, I heaved my overly stuffed duffel bags into the hangar. Nothing like spending Christmas deploying to Afghanistan. I scanned the hangar, looking to see who else would be on our flight, the first of many that would take our unit from Fort Campbell, Kentucky, to Leipzig, Germany; to Manas, Kyrgyzstan; to Bagram, Afghanistan.

And then I saw him.

"Hello there, Mr. Young," I said, trying to sound casual. "I did promise to remember you, you may recall."

"It's just Tom now, *Captain,*" he said, acknowledging that I'd been promoted, was now owed more respect, and that I could in turn be much more casual with the warrant officers. "Come on over, Ma'am." He held out a welcoming hand and guided me to where another warrant officer was crouched on the floor. "Hank, scoot over, give the Ma'am a spot."

His colleague moved over and Tom gestured to me to sit. "You can be in the cool kids' group for the trip, if you want," he said. He smiled at me in a way that made me feel warm, though I tried to ignore the feeling. It was like he saw me, like he wasn't afraid of me. Like there was no need for me to be afraid of him.

I was grateful. For everything.

And I was ready for war.

25

TAKE ONE FOR THE TEAM

■

Bagram, Afghanistan, 2014

By the sixth month of my second deployment, I was skinnier than I'd ever been, and the lack of sleep and good food had taken its toll on me. Alone in my single room, yet another storage container masquerading as a living space, I took down my bun and untwisted my braids, massaging my scalp so that maybe my head would stop pounding, which I knew was a futile gesture. I did what we always did in the army—take a Motrin for anything that hurts, drink water, and carry on.

I flopped down onto my metal bunk, a Disney Princess blanket hung from the top like a curtain, a small reminder to myself that I was still a girl. Taking off my boots, I wiggled and stretched my toes, forbidden pink nail polish winking at me, the only person who would ever see it. But none of my usual small comforts could make me smile. How had it all gone so wrong? This deployment had started out with so much promise.

On the battlefield, Lieutenant Colonel Halter had made good on his word. Surrounding himself with people who fit with his own leadership values of character, competence, and candor, he had built a team of dedicated professionals. He had reassured me that competence could be developed, and that technical failures would always be okay, which he demonstrated during my first training mission brief to him and brigade commander Colonel Maxwell. My first brief to the big boss had not been to his liking, and Colonel Maxwell had been angry, even though he hadn't given us specifications in the first place. But Lieutenant Colonel Halter reassured me that it was okay to mess up the first time—just not the tenth. In contrast, I watched him fire and decommission a junior officer who he'd thought was a good man, until the complaints rushed in from women he'd harassed. Character seemed to matter to Lieutenant Colonel Halter as much as it mattered to me.

Tom had become my running buddy and, as we got in our daily ten miles, our friendship blossomed. For the first time, I told a guy about the cult right away, sending him off to the Family International Cult Wiki page, letting him know I'd be open to talk about it. I thought that alone might scare him off, but instead, he came back with thoughtful questions that deepened our discussions. I started to get to know him, too. He was five years older than me and from Seattle, a place I knew little about, and had joined the army at seventeen, just prior to 9/11. He'd been in the army for fourteen years, first as a helicopter mechanic, and then a pilot, and was expected to get another promotion. At the top of his craft, he'd join the famed 160th Special Operations Aviation Unit immediately after our deployment.

We fell into a comfortable routine of long, hard runs at 6 A.M., getting to know more about each other with every step. After our workout, I'd head to my desk for a twelve-hour shift, and he'd put on his flight suit, armored helmet, and bulletproof vest, climb into his bird, and fly all over Taliban country. I knew the danger he faced better than anyone—it was my job, after all—but I tried not to let it get in the way of our times together.

In early February, I received the first report of a possible shoot down. One of my soldiers ran up to me yelling, "Ma'am, the Chinooks got shot!" My heart sank. Not more of us. Not Tom. Not again. I whirled around. I needed to get to my station. I had a job to do. But then there he was, tall and bright, his hair still matted from his helmet, striding into the Tactical Operations Center. It was the most beautiful sight I'd ever seen. "Don't believe it, Ma'am," Tom said. "Q here just means to say that some bad guys took a few pops at us. We're fine."

I couldn't admit to him how badly I'd been scared, so I yelled,

"Mr. Young, you failed to report kinetic enemy activity in real time? C'mon!"

After that, it became impossible to hide my feelings, though they had taken me completely by surprise. How had I let this happen? I was always so careful to maintain my professionalism. One day, when I couldn't hold it in any longer, I sent Tom a text message telling him how I felt. He responded quickly: He felt the same. The next day, we walked together to Green Beans, the coffee and chai shop on base, for our first "date," wondering how much time we'd have to get to know each other with no pressure, without the ever-watchful eyes around us catching on. A relationship would be complicated and I didn't think I had it in me, especially on the sand, so I tried to scare him off, using a tactic that sometimes worked with White men who'd been born and raised in America—the ones who wanted to marry the perfect girl next door and briefly mistook me for her. I told him how much I loved to salsa dance, expecting his smile to falter, the recognition to leave his eyes, and for us to go our separate ways.

"Well, I don't know how to dance," Tom said, looking me straight in the eyes. "But I can build you a dance floor." And then he grinned.

Oh crap, I thought. *I'm gonna marry this guy.*

I smiled because I knew he knew it too. I'd seen it in his eyes. Somehow, though we were such different people in the details, there was something inside us that matched. Though we hadn't known each other for long, we were already fitting together, already becoming a team. I tried to fight the fantasy of what a life with him might be like, a life with someone I trusted to always have my back and to never get scared away, no matter what darkness of mine I let him see. I steeled myself, trying not to get too attached, preparing myself for the loss that would inevitably happen. Experience had taught me the price of finding Heaven meant there'd be hell to pay.

But I also knew I was not willing to let him go. I was willing to fight for us. So with the candor I had asked of my team, the candor that had been asked of me, I shared our relationship status with my subordinates and my command. We'd consulted another couple in our unit who'd been in the same situation. She was a captain, he was a warrant, and they'd fallen in love during a deployment and married soon afterward. They advised us on how to navigate a burgeoning romance during deployment, under the increased scrutiny on women and pressure of General Order One. There were very specific rules to follow, and we'd be under the strictest watch, the leadership constantly worried that we'd mess up, that they'd have to deal with the downsides of having a woman on their team at war. The rank made a difference too. Warrants are commissioned officers, so there was technically nothing wrong with any warrant and any captain, as long as one wasn't in command of the other. But, there's a clear class system in the military, and while men often "date down" the ranks, when women do it, it garners a lot more attention. Our friends advised us to be as open as we could to make sure there could never be a question that we were aboveboard and honorable. So that's what we did.

The Lieutenant Mafia loved it—finally someone had tamed the independent Captain Mestyanek. "You can finally just be one of the bros, now that people know you're *taken*," First Lieutenant Mark Ackman, one of my better friends in the Lieutenant Mafia, said to me, clapping me on the back. What wasn't said, but was so obviously implied by my being "taken," was that I'd also have less to fear from "rape alley," which existed on this deployment too. With everybody knowing I was "Mr. Young's girl," I was even safer from harassment than I was as the bitch, and a captain, under my own rank and stature.

As we had hoped and expected, our leaders grudgingly agreed there was nothing against rules or decorum about a single captain and warrant officer hanging out in their free time, having declared a romantic interest in one another and an intent to be a couple, so long as we observed the rules. But we had to be careful. A major warned me that it could be bad for my career regardless of how well we handled it; it wasn't worth it, and better to walk away. Another female captain chided me to watch out for any warrant officer who might be in pursuit of the "Captain Mestyanek trophy." Everyone knew the swagger of the warrants, even on the sands where sex was outlawed.

I knew Tom wasn't one of those warrants. And from the way he'd referred to us as "we," from the very beginning, I knew I wasn't a trophy to him. I thought about how close I had been to leaving the army, how close I had been to leaving everything. And suddenly I was with a boss I respected, a team I loved, and the beginning of a relationship with someone who felt like he might be the one.

The hope I felt carried over into my role as a leader, too. Private Andrea Parker, who had been placed on my team back at Fort Campbell with less than two months to prepare for war, had been struggling since the beginning. But I wanted to believe in her, wanted to be something like the mentor I never had when I was in her position just two years earlier.

"Think Private Parker will be trouble in Afghanistan?" the headquarters unit commander, another captain, had asked me one day before the deployment, casually sitting next to his first sergeant.

I remembered the brutal start with my first unit, the late arrival to a team without the knowledge of their mission nor the understanding of the unwritten rules of being a soldier seen as desirable by a sandbox full of men.

Don't get raped.

I felt enraged, on her behalf, on my own. "Do you know that's what my bosses whispered about me before my first deployment?" I asked him, somehow managing to keep my tone professional. "Then they treated me like I was trouble. A threat, all the time. I won't have this discussion. No."

He looked at me for a moment, head cocked like he'd never even considered that, like he couldn't comprehend anyone seeing me as anything other than the professional he knew me to be, with the iron-clad reputation I'd worked so hard to establish. "Okay, fair point, my bad."

At least he seemed a man willing to listen. Willing to try to understand women were fighting an additional war invisible to him, one damning in its brutality, in the harm the army caused its women every time we deployed to serve our country. With Lieutenant Colonel Halter's leadership and the high value he placed on character, coupled with my rank and stature, I started to believe it was possible to get the men like this to see it—to see *us*—and, if I could do that, then, just maybe, I could enlist their help to fight it. After all, fighting for our brothers and sisters was what we were supposed to be about. Once they understood how the gossip, harassment, and rape culture were hurting us, wouldn't they want to stop the fratricide against their sisters-in-arms?

I wanted Private First Class Parker's first deployment to be so much better than mine. I wanted her to not fear the men she served alongside, to not get tossed a pamphlet telling her that rape was inevitable and her fault. I wanted to make sure that, at just nineteen, she didn't become one of the statistics, like I was. But the army operates under an "it's better to be feared than loved" paradigm, especially when it comes to officers, and I had to be careful about not appearing to dole out preferential treatment. I did my best, before we ever got on the plane, to make sure she knew I had her back.

In Afghanistan, Private Parker worked the night shift at my intelligence station. One morning, just weeks into our first deployment, as I walked through the door, she said, "Ma'am, can I talk to you alone?"

That was the first mistake.

That was when I didn't follow military protocol. Protocol I'd been trained on. Protocol designed to protect officers from their soldiers.

The thought of bringing in a witness never crossed my mind. Not even for a second. I saw a scared, teenage girl, one who I'd sworn to do my best to protect, one who was under not only my command but also my protection. I didn't see a threat like the ones I'd been trained to assess. I saw a girl who needed my help.

We walked into a borrowed office and closed the door. It took her a while to get the words out and she had a hard time meeting my eyes. "Mr. Albright has been sending me text messages," she finally said. "It's making me uncomfortable and I want it to stop."

I needed more information. I could think of no circumstances in which Chief Warrant Officer Three Hank Albright, a married warrant officer and one of our senior pilots, should have been engaging in any sort of nonwork-related conversations with a married, nineteen-year-old Private First Class.

"What kinds of text messages?" I asked.

"Here they are," she said, handing me the cell phone with the text thread. "Nothing sexual, but I'm concerned. My husband wouldn't like it, and I want him to stop. Mr. Albright keeps telling me that I'm too pretty to be in the army."

I sighed and opened the phone. It was my phone, one I had given her for emergencies, because I was worried about her walking alone at night. Too pretty to be in the army—how many times had I heard that *ridiculous* line before?

I scanned the text messages, knowing that I'd need to get a feel for what they contained, as the command would ask a lot of questions once—*if*—this was reported. That part was up to her. The messages were friendly and casual and not work-related, therefore inappropriate according to the army regulations, but, as she'd said, I didn't notice anything blatantly sexual either. I did see that some of the messages had been deleted, the text thread progressing in a way that didn't make contextual sense in some places. From the way the thread read, I assumed those had been messages where she was complaining about me, her boss, and she'd deleted those before coming to me. Nothing about that seemed strange or made Mr. Albright's actions less serious. She was a nineteen-year-old kid, and deployments were hard—of course she complained about her boss sometimes. Everything she said added up.

"Parker," I said. "What steps would you like to take next? Let me explain your options."

I paused briefly, making sure that I recalled all the information I'd been trained on. I was our unit's Equal Opportunity representative, a position I had asked for, to the surprise of those who didn't see it as an officer's job. I thought of the many Sexual Harassment and Rape Prevention classes I'd taught. I took a deep breath and began.

"The first thing I want you to know is that no matter what you decide here, I will make Mr. Albright stop texting you—this is what we call the third-party approach. You reported to me and I'll go to the lowest level that I can, which is to Mr. Albright directly. This is what we are taught to do. It seems like you participated in this conversation at first, but you will never be in trouble for that—he's the senior ranking person so he's the one responsible. I outrank him by a lot, so you don't need to worry about that."

Then I had to say the part I neither liked nor agreed with.

"When you leave this room, you can do one of two things. You can file either an official or an unofficial complaint of harassment. The official complaint will be investigated and will likely have negative impacts on Mr. Albright. The unofficial complaint means that I, and the rest of your chain of command, will be informed and aware of what happened, we will make sure it never happens again, and will do our best to protect you, but no formal investigation will take place. That would mean no negative actions will happen to your harasser." I paused again, making sure I was being extremely careful not to influence her opinion. "I want to be very clear; you need to tell me what you want to do, and I will do it."

"But Ma'am," she said. "Don't you think that because I'm just a private and he is one of the most important helicopter pilots in the unit, they'll protect him?"

In that moment I saw a scared young woman, like the one I had been so many times, in so many situations. In any other time and place, I would have offered her a hug.

"Andrea," I said softly, breaking protocol by using her first name. "To be honest, I don't know what will happen. The army is trying to change the way it does things in regard to sexual harassment. Back when I was a very junior officer, things weren't great for women, especially in these situations."

My mind flashed back to Kandahar, to the boss who'd put me in an impossible situation, to all of the men who propositioned me nonstop, to the ex-marine who'd pushed me down into a pillow and taken what he'd wanted from me. I remembered my boots unlaced in the corner, the futility I'd felt thinking about trying to report that rape, in getting anything that resembled help and not condemnation. I thought of the friends I had told years after the fact, the ones who implied that it had indeed been my fault for breaking the rules in the first place.

"You are right," I said. I could hear my voice shake. "He is an important officer in this unit, and you are a private." I took a deep breath, wanting to make promises, but unsure of which ones I could keep. "But believe me when I say this—I will protect you. I'm an important officer in this unit too, and you work for me."

"What if he claims that he was just trying to be friends?"

I knew she was worried she'd be the one accused of stirring the pot. I hoped General Order One, the rule I despised so much, would help protect her.

"Private First Class Parker and Chief Warrant Officer Three Albright are not allowed to be friends, the same way that you and I are not allowed to be friends. Hank can be friends with me, but not with you. It's not *allowed*. So it's not a defense available to him. Especially on a deployment."

I emphasized the word "allowed" to create no room for any misunderstanding. I was on her side, and so were the army regulations.

Gazing directly into my eyes with what seemed like increased confidence, Parker said, "Ma'am, I want to file an official complaint."

"Okay," I said, proud of her, while mentally gearing myself up for the fight ahead, reviewing the order I'd been trained to handle this in. "I'm going to go and talk to Mr. Albright, and then I'm going to talk to the command. You go home and get some sleep. I'll keep this phone to address the situation. It will be at my desk, which always has someone manning it, and you can pick it up there tonight when you show up for shift."

I got up to leave, and she rose to her feet as protocol dictated. And then I asked the question the entire chain of command would ask of me.

"Andrea, tell me this, before I confront him. Did he ever touch you?"

"No," she said, without hesitation.

"Okay, thank you. Relax and don't worry, I've got this."

I was confident I did, in fact, have it under control.

Eight hours later, I was ushered into a shitstorm. I'd gone immediately to the room where the Chinook pilots planned their missions. It felt weird to me to be basically back channeling, going to the source of the harassment to tell him to stop, instead of going to the headquarters commander, or Lieutenant Colonel Halter, or anyone else in the chain of command, but that was the protocol, what every class on the topic told us to do, and what the victim had requested. I asked Mr. Young to give us the room. *Why did it have to be his friend?* I thought to myself.

Once we were alone—though I was careful to leave a door open so I wouldn't be breaking General Order One by being in a room with someone of the opposite sex—I'd told Mr. Albright, with whom I had a professional and friendly relationship, in no uncertain terms that he was forbidden from having any kind of nonwork-related conversation with Private First Class Parker. His response came as I'd expected—he was just trying to be friendly with a lonely girl, that he had a daughter nearly her age so he couldn't be the bad guy, he was just being fatherly.

"Hank, you are allowed to be friends with me, we're both officers, but you are not allowed to be friends with her. No matter your intentions, you need to drop this now," I remember saying. He agreed, he apologized, and I left the room.

I spent the rest of the morning, in between my work duties, talking to other women, our HR officer, our doctor, and a few others who I knew had some stories and insights into Mr. Albright's personality. He'd been talked about, it turned out, at the lower levels—the creepy Uncle, be careful. I was pretty sure it was a cut-and-dried case, and I knew that by Parker's evening shift she'd talk to the command, make her complaint. Then, at lunch, I received a phone call from the headquarters commander, his voice full of anger. "You need to get to my office right now, Daniella."

In his office, face-to-face with an angry company commander and first sergeant, I learned that Parker had indeed filed a complaint.

Mr. Albright was mentioned. And so was I.

"Private First Class Parker claims that she came to you with a complaint of harassment," he said. "And that you confiscated her cell phone and then tried to dissuade her from filing a formal complaint. She also said that you said Hank Albright is an important pilot in this unit, he is your friend, and most likely nothing will happen to him because the military is not good at protecting women."

I raised my hands to my face, rubbing them briskly over my eyes and cheeks, as if trying to wake myself from a bad dream. Everything I'd said and done had been taken out of context.

I spent the next hour carefully explaining my words to the best of my recollection, even showing them my journal entries from that day, a book I carried with me constantly, needing somewhere to sort out my thoughts in this environment where I wasn't professionally allowed to have friends. I'd written down some notes after I'd spoken with Parker and after I told Mr. Albright to back off. When I went to look for the cell phone to show him the text messages that I'd left secured in our intelligence office, manned 24/7, it was missing.

"Daniella," he said, a nod to our shared rank even though he was my commander, as he rubbed his giant hands over his face in much the same way I had done. "Why didn't you have a witness in the room? Don't you know better than to go behind a closed door with a soldier alone?"

As I looked at him, he suddenly appeared very different to me than ever before: His jaw squared off and his Ohio State linebacker physique loomed over me. Hard. I could see that, this time, he wasn't going to try to see it from my side at all.

I sighed in resignation. "When a scared, young girl I've promised to protect came to me and asked to speak alone, especially when no other women were even on shift, it never crossed my mind that I needed a witness for myself." Looking down at the floor, I said, "I guess I fucked up."

"Yes, you did. You need to be very careful now. This is probably not going to break in your favor." Pulling himself to his feet and re-inforcing his position as my commander, he said, "You are dismissed."

War marched on, and we continued to balance working and leading in a dangerous and draining tactical environment. The investigation marched on too. More and more women came forward to accuse Mr. Albright of inappropriate actions, including the wife of our first sergeant and an air force woman on our weather team, and a case progressed against him. Tom was caught in the middle, neither defending Mr. Albright nor completely breaking contact with the man who'd been his friend for years, who some had begun to worry might hurt himself. As far as our developing relationship went, we did our best to keep a wall between the investigation and what we discussed as we got to know each other. I knew this: I was under scrutiny, and he could be forced to testify against me. I tried to protect him from knowing too much.

In the months that followed, Private Parker continued to struggle at work. As her boss, and as the only woman anywhere near her in the chain of command, I wished I could have been able to do more to help her cope—especially with my background—but I knew I couldn't talk to her without a room full of witnesses. To say things were awkward between us would be an understatement. I felt frustrated that she had misrepresented our conversation to the chain of command, and I spent much of my time that spring thinking about what had gone wrong, how scared and lonely she must have felt to lash out like that. I remembered how much I had hated the army labels for women on my first deployment, how she might have been wrestling with being married but seen as the 'slut' because army culture always blamed women for being the objects of harassment, but not the men harassing them. I tried to help in the public ways I could. We moved her to the day shift so she'd be able to meet with her lawyers, and my senior sergeants, her direct supervisors, attempted to discern and manage her comfort level at work, reporting daily to me. Lieutenant Colonel Scott Halter would take the time to personally check on her, every single day, to see how she was coping, and ensure that she felt supported by her command at every level. Still, there was no appetite from the command to ask why these things happened so often in our units, in our vocation that was supposed to be about things like honor and integrity.

Stress and grief take their toll. As Private Parker began to miss work, showing up hours late to relieve her shift partner from his already twelve-hour-long night shift, my hair started falling out. When she started wearing her hair or uniform in ways that purposefully broke army regulations and snapped at the sergeants who corrected her, I began losing so much weight that my already-too-big-pants fell off my body. Lieutenant Colonel Halter's posture seemed more stooped by the day, pressed thin under the invisible weight I knew he carried. The lines in his face deepened, and even though I knew he was still not even forty, I saw more white hairs popping through every day. Tom showed the strain too; his superiors were trying to warn him away from me, scared of what any association with me would do to his reputation and if he'd get pulled into the sprawling investigation. All the lieutenants felt the tension too, and none of us allowed ourselves to have conversations about any of it.

Private Parker's story started to change. She claimed the text messages—missing with my cell phone that had never been recovered—had been blatantly sexual, that Mr. Albright had cornered her in the offices, touching her around the hips and waist, all claims that seemed in direct contradiction to what she had told me on that first day. At some level I understood that victims come forward in stages sometimes, when they come forward at all. Like I also knew victims sometimes lashed out against those trying to help them. It hurt, but I tried to lean into my understanding of psychology, to remind myself that it was normal, to not take any of it personally. As usual, I tried to cope by running, adding even more miles to my punishing daily routine as Private Parker's behavior became more erratic and unaligned with Lieutenant Colonel Halter's values of candor, competence, and character that I tried to exemplify for the team. The migraines I'd suffered from occasionally began in earnest, and I'd started lactating, a crazy symptom none of the doctors could figure out. They'd checked my blood and chalked it up to wartime stress and girly hormone imbalance.

Then I made my second big error in judgment.

Colonel Johnny Maxwell appeared on my screen late one evening on a video call, explaining that he wanted to look into my eyes and ask me for my honest opinion on the case. He wanted to know who I believed in "this messed-up case of he-said-she-said." He assured me this wasn't about me, and from the seriousness on his face, I believed him.

I thought he valued my opinion, as one of his senior intelligence officers, the one who briefed him on some of the biggest decisions our brigade faced. So, I looked at the man we jokingly called "King

Henry the Eighth," and told him the truth with a candor I hoped would make Lieutenant Colonel Halter proud.

"Sir, all I can say is I've never known Mr. Albright to lie. I don't question that he is the kind of guy who has likely had inappropriate relationships with soldiers, but I do think his story has remained consistent in this matter. On the other hand . . ." I paused a minute, measuring the risk. But he'd asked my opinion, and it was my job to advise commanders, to listen to stories and reports and attempt to analyze, to give my educated opinion on which version of what I knew was more likely true, so I proceeded. "I know Private Parker is lying. I'm not saying what happened to her was in any way right, I'm only saying she has lied about some of it, so I couldn't say with any certainty where the line is."

"I'd really like to know what makes you think she's lying," he said. "I'm having trouble adjudicating this case."

There was something about the way he said it that made my childhood training with the Uncles kick into full gear. I formalized my demeanor.

"Sir," I said with respect, "I don't think she's lying, I *know* she's lying. She lied to our commander about her conversation with *me,* and she's told opposing stories about what was in those texts. I saw them with my own eyes, and I specifically asked her if any missing ones might have been sexual in nature, if he'd ever touched her. She said no then. Now she claims otherwise." I slowed down to make sure my voice sounded as measured and reasoned as possible, though I knew—from both the cult and my time in the military—this was dangerous territory. "But to be clear, that only means, to me, that she has been less than truthful about some things surrounding this messy case. I know victims come forward in stages. I don't know if that means she's lying about Mr. Albright."

"All right, Daniella, thank you for your candor." He switched back to his broad grin, the one he usually wore when talking to his prized runners, or women. "How's the running coming?"

"Training for the Shadow Boston marathon next month, Sir. I'm gonna give it my best shot, lack of sleep and proper training notwithstanding. It's the first Boston Marathon since the terrorist attack, and since I qualified last year, but can't be there, I'd like to represent well here."

"Well, remember what I've told you before, you wanna be good at the marathon? You need to lose some pounds. I want you to look like a bag of bones with a condom stretched over it. That's when you'll fly."

"Yes, Sir," I said and plastered on my obedient smile. My uniform was falling off of me, but I was never skinny enough for the army. "I'm down about fifteen pounds already, so only a few more to go till I'm condom-level skinny."

"Good girl," he said and clicked off the screen.

That was the last I'd heard until three months later, when Private Parker herself was caught in violation of General Order One—by being found alone with a soldier of the opposite gender. Suddenly, she became the one who would be on trial—an Article 15, a formal punishment where a soldier is reduced in pay and rank and given additional duties and physical labor. Also, she was married, and her husband would certainly find out. I felt bad for her, knowing full well the injustices of General Order One, of any organization getting involved in its members' sex lives. But there was nothing I could do to help her.

There was, however, something *she* could do, and much like how I'd pointed the Uncles toward the other kids as a child, hoping that someone else would be the one to get the bad spotlight and the punishment, Private Parker took her shot too. The army had recently decreed that any victim of sexual harassment or assault could request a reassignment if they felt their unit was retaliating against them, and they would be moved within forty-eight hours. Private Parker filed her complaint, and in the next twenty-four hours, the charges against her were dropped so she could be moved at her request, and like that, she was free of the flagged charges against her. I was happy about that, at least. I hoped she'd end up in a better place. I understood her strategy, as did my superiors, and still, I trusted that nobody in my leadership team would ever believe I was creating a negative environment for women. Mr. Albright was back home, already discharged from duty. It would finally, finally all be over, and we could focus on the war.

But late one Sunday night in April, five months into the deployment and three weeks after Private Parker filed her complaint, I was ordered into a meeting with the case's investigator who proceeded to read me my rights. Then he leveled a charge of "creating and fostering an environment of sexual assault, harassment, and *retaliation* in the unit." He explained that Private First Class Parker had requested a transfer, reporting that Captain Mestyanek was making her life a living hell because she'd filed a harassment complaint against her boyfriend's best friend.

If I hadn't been so terrified, I would have laughed out loud. That explained why I had been unable to shake the anxious feeling something was happening just outside my vision, that I was being set up to take a fall.

I refused to speak without a lawyer, and the investigator, a lieutenant colonel with all kinds of rank authority to pressure me, informed me that it was late on a Sunday, too late to contact one, as though he hadn't set the timing of this interrogation in the first place. I got the impression he was angered that I dared to make the request. He tried to bully me into making a confession, pulling out all the techniques of rank and surprise. But I wasn't going to play that game. I told him I would speak to an attorney, and we would respond.

But that didn't happen. I was released back to my room and then everything snowballed.

Our command sergeant major, the highest enlisted man in the unit, was suspended and banned from the unit area, and the rumor was that it was because he had asked whether there was anyone looking out for the rights of the accused, also a soldier of his, both accused and accuser under his care. Tom was removed from his senior position and transferred to another base with less than sixty minutes' notice. They told us he needed to be kept out of the investigation for his own protection, that he wasn't being fired. But he was being fired.

I knew the distance would be the only way to save both his career and the promotion he'd been expecting, even if his relationship with his friend was over. Maybe, if I was lucky, our leaders wouldn't see a ticking time bomb of trouble every time they looked at us together, at least in regard to General Order One.

And that made me wonder, as the investigation centered squarely against me, after they'd charged Mr. Albright and sent him home, kicked him out of the army: What had caused it to become such a witch hunt? Just that year, the army had started to increase pressure and focus on eradicating sexual harassment and assault among the troops, and I appreciated the intensity, though it was hard when it had become so misdirected—against the sergeant major, against me. As such a public advocate for women, I was shocked that anyone, let alone with the backing of a full-fledged investigation, could believe I'd meant to cause harm.

The headquarters commander leaned back in his chair one afternoon and explained it to me. "Daniella, you have to understand what is at stake here," he said. "Congress is overseeing these kinds of investigations. If they ask, we have to be able to give them something, to show them we did right by the victims. We stand by you as a leader and I wouldn't ask you to do anything differently, but sometimes you just gotta take one for the team."

Later that night, as I looked up at my Disney blanket, my tears blurring out the princesses so I couldn't discern Cinderella from Rapunzel, I wondered who was really in control of all of this? It was clear that someone higher up had an agenda, and if we were all just the puppets, then who was pulling the strings? My tears continued to fall as I realized how naïve I had been, thinking that the label of "bitch" would protect me.

■

THREE WEEKS LATER, I bumped down the road in a beat-up white Toyota with Lieutenant Colonel Halter at the wheel, both of us summoned to report before Colonel Maxwell to hear the verdict. I'd never been given another chance to speak in my own defense once I'd enlisted counsel.

"Whatever happens in there," my battalion commander said as we approached Brigade Headquarters, "just keep your cool."

Colonel Maxwell, always one for theater, was carefully staged at his desk, US and military flags displayed behind him, when Lieutenant Colonel Halter and I were ushered in. I immediately went to the position of attention as protocol dictates when formally reporting to a superior, a more serious stance than I'd ever been called on to adopt with him in the past. This time, there were no smiles, no sign of recognition on his face, no "at ease, Soldier." He merely snapped at me to put down my coffee, which I absentmindedly still held in one hand, trembling in front of my body. I understood at once why all us junior officers had fought so hard, grappled with each other, to stay in the favor of these few men in power.

He read the official letter of reprimand aloud, a nonjudicial move they'd decided on once I'd enlisted counsel to fight back. Like the type of divorce I'd filed against Jeff, it meant they'd left me nothing to fight. Though I wouldn't likely be *convicted* of anything, the letter of reprimand, if it stood, would almost certainly mean my hard-fought career would be over in disgrace. I would go from the golden child, an impressive military intelligence officer and decorated runner, someone who'd helped make military history for women, maybe with a chance to make general someday, to someone who maybe wouldn't even see her next promotion. After the reading, he folded his hands on the desk, and said, "Now, Danielle," and while I knew he'd misnamed me on purpose, my heart quickened at the reminder of my friend, and it gave me strength instead of depleting me.

"I don't think you quite grasp the seriousness of your actions here," he said. "Your failure to act correctly on a complaint of this seriousness, your failure to secure your soldier's personal cell phone, your ill-advised romantic relationship with someone in the unit . . ."

I ticked off the crimes in my head—the things Private Parker had said about me, the missing cell phone, loving Tom.

"Danielle," Colonel Maxwell continued, "I don't think there's any way that someone like you can understand what this girl has gone through. Think about that and submit your rebuttal. Dismissed."

Back in the car, tears fell silently down my face while my shoulders shook violently, my body ignoring every warning I'd ever heard to never let them see me cry. What did Colonel Maxwell mean by "someone like me"? How could he possibly think he understood what women went through on a deployment, or what constant and endemic sexual harassment was like, every single day in uniform, in our whole lives? What did he know about me and my life? And did any man really have the hubris to think he knew more about what women went through than another woman? I turned my head to the window, but I wasn't fooling Lieutenant Colonel Scott Halter. We didn't say a word on the fifteen-minute drive back to the Battalion Headquarters. After parking the car, we walked slowly toward the Tactical Operations Center. He turned to face me, his normally serious face softened.

"Sir," I said, voice hiccupping, "I won't accept an official reprimand for 'creating and allowing an atmosphere of sexual harassment' among my soldiers. I 'can't possibly understand what that girl has been through'?!" I mimicked Colonel Maxwell's voice disrespectfully. "I cared about Parker and I tried to help her. That was my phone that I gave her so she wouldn't be stuck alone at night in this crazy dangerous place with no way to call for help."

I saw the surprise in his eyes. That was new information that had never been considered, since I'd never been given another opportunity to speak in my own defense. How much more was there, I felt him wondering. Nearly hysterical and heedless of who might be watching from inside headquarters, I continued, "None of you could possibly understand what this means to me. I'll go to a court-martial if I have to, but I won't accept this." I sobbed, even though I knew I couldn't fight an administrative action with a legal response. "I didn't do it. I won't say that I'm guilty of harming that girl. I won't sign it. You and I both know the truth."

"Daniella, calm down," Lieutenant Colonel Halter said softly. "I know this seems bad. This may be the worst thing you've been through in your life. But, I promise you, this will pass. I know for a fact that he doesn't intend to give you a permanent letter of reprimand, and obviously, he doesn't have all the information since you refused to speak without a lawyer—which was your right."

He started talking about the rebuttal, about keeping it simple, acting calm, and giving the commander the information he needed. It would probably be reduced to a local letter of reprimand. It wouldn't follow me, he offered. I heard his whole speech, but my head was stuck on the phrase, "This may be the worst thing you've been through in your life."

It suddenly dawned on me that these senior-ranking officials had no idea who I was, or what I could or could not "understand" about what this girl had been through. In contrast, the lieutenants and captains who were close friends and colleagues, the ones who knew my backstory and the work I'd done to keep women in our unit safe, had been almost happy when the investigation had turned its teeth on me. "Good!" First Lieutenant Mark Ackman had exclaimed. "There's not a chance in hell anyone on earth will ever believe that Captain Daniella-fucking-Mestyanek had anything to do with an environment of harassment, and this investigation that is tearing us all apart will finally be over."

This may be the worst thing that has ever happened to you.

I walked away, my shoulders shaking in ironic, painful laughter.

Sitting at my desk, staring at a blinking cursor, I considered what to do. Should I obey Lieutenant Colonel Halter and write a simple statement? Should I trust my leaders would get it right if they had all the information? Should I do what the Uncles wanted, not roll my eyes, not talk back, not "justify myself," just take the punishment with my head down, grateful for the correction?

No.

I didn't trust any of that. Since when had Uncle Sam and the US Army ever done right by women? When had I ever seen a group of men in power make the choice to support a woman over the power structure that kept them in place? Private First Class Parker didn't deserve what had happened to her, but that didn't mean I deserved to take the blame and be the scapegoat. I wasn't afraid of Congress, either; I'd tell them my story too.

I began writing and didn't stop for a full ten pages. I started with a respectful rebuttal, providing information that had been missing, the justification for my actions, and my side. But where I should have stopped, I couldn't. I suddenly needed them to know how much I understood about sexual harassment and assault. How I'd fought against it my whole life. How I'd suffered from it. How I might look like the perfect all-American girl next door, but couldn't even remember the first time a man had hurt me. I needed Colonel Maxwell to know I wasn't his patsy for Congress. I needed Lieutenant Colonel Halter to know the levels of "worse" things I'd been through, what it had taken for me to get where I stood. I needed everyone to know that I wouldn't—couldn't—take one for the team, when I'd never been a part of the team to begin with, not really. I needed these men to understand. It felt like my life depended on it.

My heart thumped and my breath came in short spurts as I walked into the command suite. With my hand poised to knock, images of all the Uncles flooded through my mind—the ones who were supposed to have cared for me, loved me, the ones who hurt me, who beat me, who raped me. All my life I'd tried to be good. I'd tried to do the group thing, to play the game to the best of my ability. I'd fought hard for success in the male-dominated world, in one extreme group after the other. I gathered my courage, entered the room, dropped the pages onto Lieutenant Colonel Halter's desk, and turned on my heel, walking out without saying a word.

Back at my desk, I stared at my screens, intelligence information pinging constantly. I couldn't focus on anything. Every second I sat there, I wished I could take it back. I thought of all the people I'd shared my story with, the good responses eclipsed by the captain who'd told me that someone with my history should never have joined the army, the major who wondered aloud why someone as broken as me thought they could be a leader. Everyone who laughed about why I had escaped one cult and joined another, as if I myself was the joke.

I wanted to love the army. I wanted the army to love me, even though I was so different. I wanted the army to be better, to be a place where I belonged. Where women belonged.

And then Lieutenant Colonel Halter was at my desk, paper in his hands, tears in his eyes.

"Don't change a thing."

26

RUNNING FOR MY LIFE

■

Bagram, Afghanistan, 2014

The hardest lie I ever told myself was that I was strong enough.

In the aftermath of being in the basement with Uncle Jerry, staring at a bottle of bleach and wondering if drinking it was the solution I needed to end the pain, if that would clean me from the inside out and take me away, I told myself I could wait a little longer, one day I would get away, could run and never look back. Disowned at fifteen, feeling like I was from a different planet, being told I didn't exist and worried I'd broken with my whole family forever, I told myself I could power through. If I worked hard enough, someday I'd be normal. Someday, I'd fit in. Throughout my six years in the army, it's what I chanted to myself every time I was looked down on for my gender, for being small, for being young, for being different—suck it up and show them how strong you are. If you can prove it to everyone, they'll have no choice but to believe it.

The day I won the marathon was the day I stopped telling myself that lie. We'd prepared for months to compete in the Shadow Boston Marathon on Bagram Airfield. Before Tom was transferred, we'd get up before the crack of dawn, the only way to get ten or more miles, even at the punishing pace we'd been pushing ourselves, and still make it to our twelve-hour work shifts. There was a hole in my heart the hours with him used to fill.

The thought of running the race without him gut-punched me. I told myself I wouldn't compete. Someone else could get up at 1:55 in the morning and struggle through 26.2 miles of circles on desert sand and baked concrete. Someone else could feel their unit's pressure to perform, the same unit willing to let her take the fall for the team when needed. I missed Danielle so much, and I wished for someone to talk to. It was bad enough my brigade had turned against me since the rebuttal. At Task Force Lift, my friends and colleagues had waited alongside me with bated breath, silently on my side. But as the weeks dragged on and nobody heard anything, as Private Parker was transferred and life seemed to go back to normal for everyone else, as the investigation against me ramped up, I could feel myself turning radioactive, could feel an invisible force field growing that no one dared to cross. This was my team, these were my brothers, but as they each got pulled in to testify, for or against me, it made sense that a distance would wedge between them and anyone who smelled like scandal. Under official investigation, I could only speak freely with doctors and the unit chaplain; anyone else could be required to divulge our conversations. It hurt that I couldn't confide in them anymore, even though they'd all communicated their support. I told myself I was strong enough to survive the remaining three months of deployment on my own. Soon enough, even this would end.

Nevertheless, when the alarm went off on the morning of April 17, I hurled myself out of bed and into my sneakers, lined my toes alongside the feet of a hundred other women and five hundred men, with no expectations of doing anything other than burning off my anger and despair in a longer-than-usual morning run. This was one thing they couldn't take from me, couldn't taint with the investigation. I had worked hard to develop my running skills—eventually clocking my single mile time at five minutes and fifteen seconds. I'd run faster than the vast majority of the men I served with, to their dismay. For a long time, I'd thought that meant I could compete with them in their world, on their terms.

"Just get through this one," I told myself after the briefing on what to do if terrorists shot rockets at our base during the race. "Don't worry about racing, just keep steady, just do it for you," I coached myself after the gun went off. I thought of how, only a few days earlier, Meb Keflezighi had won the Boston Marathon, the first American to win in twenty-five years. We'd all gathered around the television in the Tactical Operations Center and watched Boston Strong, and America with it, come back together the year after the horrific bombing. The Boston campaign had been modeled after the well-known "Army Strong" recruiting campaign, the campaign I'd signed up under, and I felt the significance of the moment, what Meb was doing for the country and what we, on the other side of the world, felt we were doing for our country too. I ticked off the miles, passing one woman runner after another as I moved up closer to the head of the pack. I kept telling myself, "You got this, you are strong, you can show them all." But with every step I ran, my suspicion grew. I worried it was all a lie.

Nobody was more surprised than me when I broke the finish line tape, waving at the helicopters flying security overhead, wondering which of our pilots was flying that day and if they'd recognize me from up there. Surprise turned into brief elation, the proverbial runner's high mixed with the utter exhaustion of pushing my body to its extreme and walking away with the gold medal. But even then, I knew the lie for what it was when I walked past Brigade Commander Maxwell. As I held my head high and gasped for breath, my medal around my neck and a piece of the finish line tape in my hands, reporters following behind me, Colonel Maxwell looked through me like I wasn't even there.

I knew then it didn't matter how strong I was—there was nothing left for me to prove. At least not to him. True to his Henry the Eighth moniker, I knew I was a former favorite, fallen. I put my head down and returned to work, to complete the eighteen-hour shift I had traded with newly promoted First Lieutenant Steven Wilson, my second in command, in order to get the time off to run the marathon.

As my brigade ignored me, national-level magazines like *Women's Running* reached out to profile me for my wartime race win. The professionally shot photos show me running in perfect competition form against the backdrop of the gun-laden Chinooks on the flight line, framed by the ubiquitous mountains of Afghanistan. They were supposed to depict me as the picture of health, speed, and female power, but when I looked at them, I knew the truth. I'd stopped sleeping, spending nights in my bunk staring at the ceiling, the thin mattress always reminding me of my beds in the Family communes. The words "responsible for allowing an environment of sexual harassment/assault and retaliation to thrive" danced madly before my eyes. I knew women who did that, who truly fomented environments that harmed others, like Auntie Sara and her Davidito book, delivering her own three-year-old daughter for a child marriage. Those kinds of women were the Aunties who'd raised me. But I wasn't one of them. I kept hearing Lieutenant Colonel Halter say, "this may be the worst thing that's ever happened to you," with my maniacal laughter in the background, and then a slideshow of all the worst moments in my life—Uncle Jerry's basement room, the beatings, the hunger, the injuries and illnesses, the prayers, the deaths of friends, that final rape, those stupid, stupid combat boots, the time I climbed that tower and came so close to ending it all—and I couldn't forgive myself for working so hard to gain control of my life only to hand it all back to this organization of men. I didn't deserve sleep.

Nobody noticed how much weight I was losing—partly because I was dwarfed in a uniform not designed for anyone built like a woman—but even if they had, I wasn't convinced anyone would have cared. Colonel Maxwell *wanted* me to look like a bag of bones in a condom, after all. My hands started shaking so much I could barely hold the cup of caffeine that was my constant companion. I'd bitten my fingernails to the quick, cuticles torn and bleeding, medical tape always wrapped around the worst wounds. The lactation symptom that I'd noticed earlier got stronger, more painful, and impossible to ignore.

I recognized the parallel in my behavior to that of Private Parker. I showed up late and needed sick days due to an exhaustion so strong I couldn't make myself get out of bed. We couldn't afford anyone else on the team to step away, and I hated asking them to pick up my slack. How could I lead through three more months? I had always relied on being strong enough to endure and survive anything, but I had lost faith in that lie. I started asking myself the hard questions again:

What if I couldn't keep shoving it all down? What if I wasn't strong enough? What if I couldn't do my job? What if I couldn't keep going in this world?

One day in late May, the air felt even more charged and awkward than usual as I entered the office. The unit operations officer, my direct boss, stood beside my desk, as though he'd been waiting for me.

"Daniella," he said, sounding almost sympathetic for someone normally gruff. "Can I talk to you in my office?"

My heart began to pound, my perpetual headache tightened on its screws, and I knew I wouldn't be able to formulate a coherent response to whatever he was going to tell me, the headaches scrambling my ideas into a word-salad, as they'd started to do more and more. I set my coffee down carefully, preparing to snap to attention if necessary.

"Please, sit down, and—" He paused, glancing toward the door. I could tell he was trying to weigh the privacy he clearly felt I deserved against the prohibition of being alone behind a closed door, not with his senior intelligence officer, but with a woman. "Shut the door," he finally said.

"I want you to know," he said after another long pause, "that if it was up to me, I'd be writing up your Bronze Star award right now, and I know the boss feels the same way." He nodded in the direction of Lieutenant Colonel Halter's office. Looking down at his boots, unable to hold my gaze, he continued, "We've received direction from the top that nobody with a letter of reprimand will be eligible for any deployment awards this time around."

I felt the death knell of my career. It hit me in slow, stunning beats. I'd already cried so much, there was nothing left, so I just sat very, very still. In the US Army, it was near impossible to return from the role I'd held without a Bronze Star at a minimum. My records would silently condemn me anytime they were reviewed—at a new posting, at any trainings, and for promotion. Nobody would even ask, they'd pass me over in the sixty seconds they took to look at my records for a promotion board review, assuming I'd done something horrible—and for a woman I knew that meant they'd think I'd slept with someone inappropriate, and gotten caught.

I nodded and nodded, unable to say a word, and when he dismissed me, I silently walked out. My head pounded and my mouth felt so, so dry. It seemed like all my colleagues—my friends, my mafia—were in the hallway as I slowly passed, their concerned faces in my periphery. Despite the tension and distance between us, I still had faith they were on my side, still my team. But I knew, for their own good, they couldn't be close to me anymore, and I didn't blame them.

I pushed past them all, needing to get outside where I could breathe. I saw the tall weather tower and started climbing, no M4 this time, but feeling something eerily like what I'd felt three years prior—numb with pure and utter hopelessness. I sat and stared, looking down at the dozens of helicopters parked neatly along the flight line, the breathtaking mountains surrounding the Bagram Basin, and the incredibly huge sky, already tinged with the pinks and oranges of a desert sunset. My migraine raged, but the inability to see straight or form coherent thoughts was a blessing. I watched the colors swirl and let the tears fall.

My body remembered this numb feeling and found a certain comfort in it, easily accessing the place I used to go when the world seemed like too much to handle. Wouldn't it be so nice to fall forward into this beautiful scenery? Wouldn't it be poetic, so beautifully tragic, if the team I'd fought so hard to be a part of were the ones who finally did me in?

No—that was the old me. That was the suicidal, tortured little girl who was so tired of trying to fit in and pretending to be normal.

"That's not me anymore," I said out loud, trying desperately to get myself to believe it. "Fuck you, Daniella!" I almost yelled. "You're better than this." And with one last, wistful glance at the mountains and the beautiful hazy sunset, I started the climb back down. I marched over to Halter's office. I knew what I had to do.

"Sir," I began, feeling calmer than I had in a long time. "I think it's time for me to leave the army."

I WAS TOLD I'd be removed from my position as the senior intelligence officer—not fired, of course, but sent to work up at brigade headquarters, for Colonel Maxwell directly. I'd been around long enough to know that *meant* fired, and so did every one of my colleagues and subordinates, who looked at me speechless when I told them. To add insult to injury, First Lieutenant Steven Wilson, the one I'd been training for two years as my deputy, wouldn't be given the role as my replacement, but a different lieutenant, a mere two weeks senior to him, would be brought in from Fort Campbell to take over for the last two months. It was a bad joke, as we all knew it would take her almost that long to get up to speed, and it seemed specifically intended to punish First Lieutenant Wilson, who'd written a strong statement in support of my character. He'd tried to advocate for himself, explaining to Lieutenant Colonel Halter how dangerous it was to bring in a new senior intelligence officer only three months before the end of our tour—the most dangerous time of any deployment. Lieutenant Colonel Halter shook his head, telling Steven, "Thank you. I understand all you've said, but the decision has already been made since apparently I don't control my own staff." I was crushed for him, and for Lieutenant Colonel Halter too, but there was nothing I could do—my rank, experience, and record in the unit where I'd spent nearly five years meant next to nothing. Especially since I told them I planned to leave.

I remembered being fifteen and yelling at my dad that I wanted to leave The Family, how I was then separated from the rest of the group, all the adults worried I'd poison the others with my doubts, with my ideas of the world outside the group. It was the same message: You're choosing to leave the team; you're not one of us anymore.

Lieutenant Colonel Halter was one of the few who never adopted that attitude with me. Somehow, with a few sparse words, he always made it obvious that just because he'd chosen a lifelong career in the US Army, he wouldn't judge me for wanting something different. I realized throughout all his past support of me, he'd been preparing me to get out, if that was what I chose. He would talk to me about life "after," other career options, seeming to understand that if he failed to prepare his people for the validity of life *outside* the group, then he was failing to prepare them for life *after* the group. I'd even once requested a conference with some junior officers he knew who'd gotten out, so I could ask them what had influenced their decisions. He'd made it happen. He seemed almost excited for those of us moving on, as if it mattered to him that we chose paths that would make us happy. It was as though he knew the best way to prepare us for a life after the army was to acknowledge that we would all *have* one, sooner or later. It reminded me a bit of Mom, how when I was eleven we'd walked around the commune in Belo, talking about life outside The Family, her sharing what I now see were her doubts, her questions, the beginning of her recognition that there was maybe an equally valid life outside the commune walls, a way to prepare and encourage me, if I needed, to leave everything I knew behind. And, in the end, she'd encouraged me to go.

With headaches that became more and more crushing, I continued to try to show up every day to do my job. One day, I couldn't take it anymore. I scheduled a meeting with the brigade executive officer, second in command to Colonel Maxwell. I told him I felt I was being fired as a direct result of going public about being a victim of assault myself. I knew people had started to look at me differently, wondering if my past trauma meant I didn't have what it took to be a leader. I knew if I'd written a contrite statement, apologizing for my sins and *taking one for the team,* the situation would have been different. Carrying the values of candor and character that had become ingrained in me, I shared with him how the abuse I'd lived with since childhood had influenced the work I'd done not just to overcome but to help other victims. With that context, I asked him to see why I could not "just live with" an official reprimand and the words of the accusation. I asked him to consider, as my leader, what mental environment they'd be requiring me to work under. I mentioned doubting my own resiliency, that beloved buzzword of an army already thirteen years into an unwinnable war. I didn't want to be another sad statistic, and it was all becoming too much. I offered him a way out: Send me home.

It wasn't unusual to send individual soldiers home early, and I knew they didn't need me in the new role. In the perpetual chess game of the army, the brigade executive officer made a move that showed he knew I was seriously struggling: He made it my choice whether or not I'd like to go home rather than "finish out the deployment in a job above my rank." I didn't care what it would mean for my career; I was beginning to feel that if I didn't get out of that environment soon, it would kill me.

They agreed to send me home.

But the next morning, when I opened my eyes after another night awake more than asleep, I couldn't see. I stretched my hands out in front of my face, waving and snapping my fingers to be sure I wasn't dreaming—nothing. Actual blackness, like the wires connecting the camera of my eye to the machinery of my brain had been pinched shut. Panic rose in my chest as I struggled to keep breathing and tried to review my options. I was alone in my shipping container. Without a roommate, nobody would accidentally find me. I slowly placed my feet on the ground, completely blind, and my whole body trembled. I couldn't think straight; every thought in my head seemed to float away before it could land and make any sense. Words danced around in my head, and I knew when they came out they would be unintelligible. I picked up my phone, typing in the passcode from memory, unsure if I got it right, and pressed the dial button, trying to remember the last person I called.

"Help me," I croaked, and then a sentence I knew never to say to any man while deployed, certainly not someone subordinate: "Please come to my room."

By the time my friend and colleague Chief Warrant Officer Three Apollo Simmonds banged on the door of my room, things had started to get a little better. My vision had returned in swirls to my right eye and the pressure in my head felt like it was relaxing slightly. My breasts were contracting painfully, in what I would later learn is a milk release signal, usually in response to a hungry newborn baby. I was able to stumble to the door, still clad in pajamas, and tell him I needed a hospital. My buddy Mr. Simmonds, an Airborne, Air Assault, Ranger-qualified-infantry-guy-turned-pilot, always good in a crisis, asked no questions and set to work. Calling my intelligence office, he enlisted Lieutenant Wilson to get a van and meet us at the barracks, and we set off for the clinic, where my friend Captain Terri Weber, the unit's physician assistant, was waiting to see us.

When I told her about how my vision had disappeared completely, and about the pressure in my head and breasts, she was more concerned than usual. A quick eye exam told us all that my vision was completely gone in my left eye—I couldn't even see the largest E at the top of the eye chart. I begged for my usual shot of Imitrex, the migraine medication that kept me going, and orders back to bed, but she shook her head. Not this time.

"Daniella, something is wrong. You need a CT scan. Now."

There's nothing like walking through a war hospital with an invisible injury. I felt the smallest I'd ever felt in my life. As the vision in my left eye pulsed in and out, making me feel like someone was trying, poorly, to focus a camera lens inside my brain, I was led to the doctor. When he heard my symptoms, he *tsk*ed sympathetically and sent me straight past the eye station to CT, before turning his harried expression back to a group of marines brought in with shrapnel visibly embedded in their arms, legs, and chest plates, who were laughing and joking about their close call with death.

A few hours after the CT scan, I was back at my desk trying to focus on work, but I couldn't stop thinking about going home, getting out. Everyone who handled me that morning expected to find something bad, so it wasn't surprising when Terri called me to come in as soon as I could.

"They've found some lesions around your pituitary—as we suspected," she said. "There's some brain swelling too, so in my opinion this needs immediate attention. I've already got the medical side of folks working on your evacuation to the hospital in Germany. I'll let you tell the boss yourself if you'd like."

I numbly nodded my assent, and then began laughing, though it came out almost like barking. Terri looked at me quizzically, probably wondering how much the swelling had already affected me.

"You have to admit," I mumbled. "Self-diagnosing a brain tumor is pretty awesome." I'd been doing my own research for months, scouring the internet for whatever I could find about my symptoms, and had circled in on them being a pituitary issue. My blood had been tested after the lactation started, and I was being monitored for the ever-increasing headaches. But, until that moment, the doctors hadn't found anything concrete.

"It explains a lot," she confirmed. "And at least now you'll get treatment—that has got to be a relief." She leaned in to hand me some heavy drugs that would hopefully prevent any further swelling in my brain. Then quietly, under her breath so only I could hear her, she said, "Daniella, you're getting out of here. Just hang on to that."

Medical evacuations happen quickly in a war zone. I would be on a plane in a matter of hours to a day or two. When Tom informed his commander about the situation, he was given permission to see me, telling him to "Go with God, man," as he hopped on the next helicopter. And then I was in Tom's arms, and for once, nobody cared. Turns out, you're allowed hugs, even at war, when people think you might be dying.

The next day, I was on the medical evacuation plane. I sat amidst the friendly group of wounded marines, chanting Tom's parting words like a mantra that could somehow help me: "If there is a God, I know he didn't wait all this time to let me find you just to take you away."

■

BY THE TIME I got to the hospital in Germany, I hadn't slept in nearly three days, my normally hazel eyes were wide, black saucers, and my hormone levels were testing off the charts. The surgeon, a US Air Force lieutenant colonel, took me by the hands and asked me to relax and breathe.

"Daniella," he said, and I could hear the deliberate calming tone he used with me, "I promise we'll take care of you."

I was so wary of everyone at this point, and so incredibly tired, I kept staring through him.

"From what we know now, there is every reason to believe that your tumor is benign, although based on your symptoms it may be larger than we can see on the CT scan. I'm going to tell you a bit about the process now, because once the MRI comes in, things will likely move quite quickly.

"Brain tumors are a funny thing," he continued, "because we really don't like to open up your head more times than absolutely necessary. With a tumor anywhere else in your body, we would do a biopsy, then, once we knew if it was cancerous or not, we'd come up with a treatment or extraction plan." He paused, and his face turned more serious. "With the brain, we have to put you under with the oncologist standing by—she'll then do the biopsy and we'll figure out the treatment from there." He reassured me that they believed it was benign; pituitary tumors are relatively common, brain tumors in general are, and usually don't mean death.

I tried to relax, tried to trust that I would be okay in the hands of some of the best doctors in the world, but my old fear of doctors was still there, combined with new ones. "So, what does that mean for me?" I asked. "I don't really get a say in how much of my brain you take out, huh?"

"It means we talk about all your options before you go under." He turned on a giant screen with a picture of the human brain, every segment marked with words I still couldn't really read. "Your surgeon, which could be me or someone back home, depending on what we find today, will go over this image with you, and what parts of the brain the tumor is touching. If it's benign, which most pituitary tumors are, no sweat—we cut it out. If it's cancerous, we'd have to cut out everything it touches—or not, depending on what you and your doctor decide. If we can't get it all out, because it's touching a function that you don't want to lose, then it's not gone, and that's a whole other story." He quickly continued, "But we don't need to get into that today. I understand you must be very scared, and that's okay. But we are going to take care of you. You are not alone, okay?"

Sobs escaped my lips and wracked my body. I had not realized how much I needed somebody, anybody, to care, to acknowledge how scary it was, even if I was going to be "totally fine." For months—for twenty-seven *years*—I had been shoving my feelings down, all of my fear and pain collecting in the shadows, and with nothing left to lose, those feelings tumbled out.

The next day, everything changed again. The doctor told me I didn't have a brain tumor after all. In fact, the MRI had come back completely clean. They could not explain what had happened on the CT scan, nor what was causing any of my symptoms.

Rather than feeling relief, I was flooded with a sudden panic—if it wasn't a brain tumor, what the hell was wrong with me? Why had I lost nearly thirty pounds in two months on a frame that couldn't afford to lose ten? Why was I always shaking, losing speech and vision, and lactating? At least when Doc Terri Weber told me about the tumor, there was an explanation, a cause for what was making me sick. There was something that could be cut out, even if it meant opening up my brain.

"If it's not a tumor, what is it?" I kept asking the doctor. He did his best to explain, to calm me down and talk me out of my panic. I collapsed onto the chair in the corner of his office, my face drenched with tears. "Sir," I cried. "They're going to say it's all in my head. They're going to send me back there. I can't. I just can't."

My doctor, the air force lieutenant colonel, looked at me with real sympathy in his eyes, shaking his head back and forth with the slightest motion. Then, closing the door with the ease of someone who wasn't watching his back all the time, he sat at the desk across from me, poured me a glass of water, and asked, "Daniella, what is happening in your unit that someone as healthy as you showed up to my operating room with every sign of a brain tumor?"

As I sat there, the trauma of my life began to wash over me in vivid pictures and I knew then that my real diagnosis was written between the lines of his question. My mind could fool me, could tell me everything was fine, could tell me I was strong enough to just keep running. I could push everything down, never admit that trauma on top of trauma was just too much. But the body keeps the score. I couldn't keep running from my life.

Once more they carried me onto a C-17, the stretcher hooked into the floor with military-grade straps, nurses passing through with drugs to help everyone fall asleep. The marines, in their stages of disrepair from the roadside bomb that had jumped up and bit them, high on painkillers and adrenaline, talked and joked among themselves, tried to comfort me, to pull me into their camaraderie, but I couldn't handle even well-meaning bro-culture. I closed my eyes and let the drugs carry me into their comforting haze. When I came to, I was in the arms of the military nurses, loading me off the plane and into the bus that would take us all to the Walter Reed National Military Medical Center in Washington, D.C., famous for treating those who have lost limbs, eyes, or had unknown brain injuries coming out of a war zone.

Through a foggy haze, I saw the receiving unit's executive officer, the captain who was second in command for the unit that cared for all incoming Wounded Warriors. She walked toward me, steady and professional, checking in all her new soldiers, as she made sure she had the right charts and each service member would be sent off to the correct place. Then she stopped right in front of me, gave me a slow smile, and very calmly, in a voice that nobody else could overhear, Captain Danielle Reid said, "Hello, my love. Welcome to Walter Reed. I've got you now."

27

MR. PRESIDENT, WE'RE NOT LESBIANS

■

Walter Reed National Military Medical Center,
Washington, D.C., August 2014

Five weeks.

A blur. A whirlwind. Everything and nothing. Both at once.

I had spent five weeks on different brain medications, being evaluated by psychiatric professionals, undergoing more MRIs. Everyone tried to figure out why I'd shown up missing the brain tumor I was supposed to have. Or did I have something else? Diabetes, thyroid issues, and far-flung diseases were all considered.

Once I'd opened up to the colonels about my past, it seemed I couldn't stop talking about it, especially to the mental health professionals whose offices I was in nearly every day as part of my treatment. Something clicked when the surgeon had asked me, "What is going on that you showed up here with all the symptoms of a brain tumor?" I started to see all the ways every part of my life was connected.

I told them about the cult, about my hard childhood and teenage years. I told them about joining the army, about how I'd tried with all my heart to be a true believer. I told them about my assault from my first deployment, but it was too late to do anything. I told them how my health had declined so rapidly that I'd gone from winning a marathon to becoming this slip of a girl, shaking and always in pain, within a mere two months.

And I told them about the investigation—how everything had spiraled out of control, how I'd been pulled into its grasp and branded the enemy even though I'd tried so hard to help. It had been the perfect example of the double bind for women in the military: I had to be a bitch to survive, but once achieved, it had been so easy for Colonel Maxwell to use that against me, to label me a woman-hater. I told them why I couldn't accept the letter of reprimand saying I'd contributed to a toxic environment for women, that there was no way I could just take one for the team, that I wasn't the bad apple, that the problem went much deeper, down to the roots.

The environment had been toxic for women all right—that was true army-wide—but in this case, nobody had wanted to look deep enough to find the real, systemic causes. I recognized the familiar thread: It was like when the cult leaders had excommunicated Uncle Jose for his transgressions, then simply moved on. The army's values, our leaders, and the regulations like General Order One were supposed to protect us, but they put women at greater risk every minute of every day we were deployed. They wanted problems solved quickly, with tidy solutions. They'd wanted the case to be neatly put away. They wanted the fault not to be the army's. Someone had to take the fall, and they'd chosen me.

My future was in limbo. My paperwork to leave the army had been canceled the second I'd been medically evacuated. Seriously ill or injured soldiers cannot leave the army at will. We are their military assets and once we are broken, just like our helicopters and all the other machinery of war, we must either be repaired or damaged out—medically retired—to get us off the books.

I was stuck at the mercy of the medical process, enlisted against my will until the leaders above me decided I was healthy enough to make my own decisions again. My paperwork had been destroyed, my application to leave the army, but also the letter of reprimand against me, which would stay behind in Bagram.

A week after I got to Walter Reed, they checked me into an ICU where they ran twenty-four hours' worth of medications into me through an IV, trying to break the migraine that had lasted for nearly sixty days and caused swelling in my brain. My doctors were concerned, but otherwise, they couldn't find anything wrong. Without the expected tumor, the chain of command at Walter Reed discussed sending me back to Afghanistan, back to my old unit, and even through the numbness of all the pain meds, I was terrified. But Danielle would not let that happen, enlisting the help of Dick Winters, proud 101st veteran, nephew and namesake of the famous Dick Winters from the Band of Brothers series. After hearing my story, he used his political capital to get me permanently transferred to the Warrior Transition Battalion at Walter Reed, where all the soldiers with terminal illnesses, or those with significant and unknown recovery times, were sent.

In that unit, our only mission was to recover. With that transfer, Danielle was in my new chain of command, and I had a leader who I knew cared for me. But back in my old chain of command in Afghanistan, Colonel Maxwell was taking revenge against my Lieutenant Mafia, against anyone who had supported me or tried to speak on behalf of my character. This was the leader who privately told me he didn't believe I'd done anything wrong, then fired me after I'd been public about my own abuse. As I recovered at Walter Reed, the staff told me they couldn't remember another time a brigade commander hadn't called to check on *one of their own* who'd been evacuated from combat.

I told myself at least I didn't have to go back. But there was still a part of me down deep that wanted his acknowledgment, his approval. His apology.

■

AFTER A FEW weeks, I started getting accustomed to two nonmedical things—the mind-numbing boredom and the perks. Boredom because, assigned to the recovery unit at Walter Reed, I had the least regimented life I'd ever had in the military. Besides attending however many medical appointments I had in a week and learning the cafeteria schedule so I didn't miss too many meals, there wasn't much to fill my time.

I took up acrylic painting, card games, and entertaining fellow warriors with my storytelling during the day and karaoke performances at night. My brain still felt fuzzy, but the headache had turned into more of a dull ache instead of a constant throbbing. I also began to feel more at peace as the distance between me and the shitstorm that had happened back in Bagram faded by the day.

To ease my mind, I tried to focus on the perks of my recovery assignment. Walter Reed is smack in the middle of Washington, D.C. It reminded me of Bagram, how the Lieutenant Mafia called the missions we ran for the big brass "taxi driving the generals." The same politicians and senators we'd flown around Afghanistan, plus bigwigs from giant corporations, paraded through Walter Reed, shaking hands, giving out fancy coins with big, bold emblems on them, a uniquely military way of thanking us for our service, along with all the photo ops and the good publicity that come from boosting the morale of our nation's most cherished soldiers.

On a weekly basis, we could schedule ourselves into a slew of activities, like the limo lunch, when a Fortune 500 company rented a limo and took a curated selection of Wounded Warriors out to a pricey seafood restaurant overlooking the Potomac. I'm not sure how my doctors signed off on it, but the corporate executives poured us full of wine and seafood, and we paid them back with entertaining war stories and the warm feeling they'd checked the box of patriotism. I would get selected for almost all the trips—a convenient girl-soldier to round out the picture for the corporate storyboards. I knew the game, but I went anyway. It was something to do, plus I got to ride in a limo and eat good food. I smiled through my medicinal haze, I shook the hands, and I wore the swag. The next week, I did it all again.

Five weeks into my recovery, I sat playing poker beside five male soldiers, all fellow patients, most missing limbs, the exceptions being me and the private with terminal cancer. Danielle ran into the room, shouting and waving a piece of paper in the air, having lost all trace of professionalism. "We got in, we got in!"

She was talking faster than she usually did, which was already pretty fast, and I tried to focus, but my mind felt fuzzy through the haze of the anti-swelling brain meds. The other soldiers seemed to be getting excited about something she was saying about a house. Were we moving somewhere? I had no idea what she was talking about.

Then her words suddenly came through loud and clear: "You're going to meet the president! You're getting a private White House tour! And you're fucking taking me as your guest, woman."

Even with my cloudy brain, I knew this was a big deal. Every so often, the unit's cadre would be alerted that the president was ready to meet some warriors, and they each submitted packets on who they believed should go. When Danielle first told me she was submitting me as a candidate, I begged her not to. I already felt like a fraud, classified as a Wounded Warrior, being honored or given anything special, especially alongside those who had earned it for real by risking their lives. What had I done except have a nervous breakdown at war? I was the girl who begged to go home. Why would they celebrate my failure?

"Girl, please!" Danielle said. "My motherfucking best friend is one of the first motherfucking women on deliberate ground combat missions. We watched the first women graduate Ranger school a few months ago because of what you did in your 'little combat patrol experiments.' If that's not as good of a reason to meet the president as getting blown up, then I don't know what is."

Danielle was months into her posting at Walter Reed, and even though her five years in the army had done some work smoothing her rough edges and tempering her Jersey accent, she was still as colorful as always. She continued to persuade me, talking about "all those douchebags we went to officer school with," the guys who swore that women would never be capable of any of this, and how pissed they'd be to know I met the president. It made me laugh enough to seal the deal.

And then she took me shopping.

Since I'd arrived straight from a war zone on a medical evacuation plane, I didn't own much. The rest of my bags, armor, and military gear would come home with Task Force Lift, but there was certainly nothing in there appropriate for the occasion. Danielle and I enjoyed a day as girlfriends hanging out, away from everyone's watchful eyes, as if we were normal. But I could never fully relax. I felt like an imposter walking the aisles of Nordstrom Rack. I couldn't stop thinking of my team, still at Bagram Airfield, still in a war zone. I knew that when I had asked to be sent home, I'd chosen to quit the team, and I had betrayed them. If anything happened to any of them, I knew I'd feel like it was my fault. Tom was still out there, flying helicopters every day, getting shot at regularly. And there I was, buying a pretty dress to go tour the White House for being a hero.

The sedatives I was on didn't dull the dissonance I felt returning from war—the absolute shock, and not a small amount of horror, that life back home simply continued like the country wasn't at war, like our people weren't dying overseas. I vacillated between wanting to laugh hysterically or throw things, almost in equal turns. But I managed to keep my composure as Danielle guided me through the department store, and helped me settle on a conservative blue-gray Anne Klein sheath dress that would pair perfectly with the bright orange pumps I bought in Germany after being evacuated. It felt good to be a woman again, to be going somewhere as Captain Mestyanek while dressed unapologetically femininely.

A few days later, as we pulled up to the White House gates, I could feel my blood pressure begin to rise. Guards monitored us as we approached in single file, only the first level of security in one of the most secure buildings in the world. My chest tightened and my pulse quickened the way it always did when I approached security officials of any kind, the way I'd been programmed to feel as a child—the fear written into my bones that they'd find me, catch me, and haul me away for being an imposter who infiltrated into this level, a fraud with top secret clearance, still someone who didn't belong.

Danielle's calm demeanor comforted me as we waited. She had all the confidence of a born and raised American, cultured in a world where she never had to doubt her rights or her entitlement to them. Security waived us through the checkpoints right after they'd verified we were who we said we were: Captains in the US Army, with top secret clearances, wartime service, and invitations from the Office of the President to attend the day's event. Still, I was surprised every time we passed another level of security, some part of me believing I was there in secret, trying to fool the Antichrist's soldiers. I rubbed my temples and pushed my fingers into the deep depressions under my brow bone, trying to massage the throbbing source of the pain behind my left eye as we walked down the first hallway, trying to calm my shaking nerves, to stop always looking for the exits, but the bright lights and the stress of it all made my still-daily headache worse.

I'd always thought of the White House as "the people's house" and the seat of the world's oldest modern democracy, leading me to imagine it would be somehow humble, that there would be a greater difference between where the US president lived and the palaces of foreign dictators and kings. But there wasn't, not really; every room in the White House drips with opulence and wealth. As we were brought on a guided tour of the East Wing, I thought of the pictures I'd seen of Buckingham Palace, or the palace of the last Brazilian king I'd toured as a child in the mountains above Rio, and the stories I'd heard from more than one colleague about going into Saddam Hussein's palace right after his capture, with its rooms made from pure gold. The White House rooms weren't plated in gold, but I could tell everything in them was worth millions and millions of dollars. The message of the building was clear: We stood at the epicenter of power of the richest and most powerful country on earth, the place where the richest and most powerful men made history.

The tour was incredible, with the White House museum director giving us in-depth details about everything she showed us. At first, I felt disconnected, knowing only the barest minimum about most of it; the history classes I took in college were some of the only education I'd had on American history. But as I ran my fingers over the oyster inlays in the dinner service china of Rutherford B. Hayes, as I sat on furniture picked out by Eleanor Roosevelt and stood on the same rug where Franklin D. Roosevelt gave his fireside chats, I could imagine being a part of the larger American tradition, a bit more connected to the history of our country than I'd ever felt before. We kept coming face-to-face with the portraits of presidents—the great men resting forever in the hallowed halls, next to the smiling women who propped them up, forever destined to play the role of being behind a great man, never truly equal and certainly never out front. I thought about my own firsts, the reason, I knew, I'd been selected to be there. On those Female Engagement Teams, I'd had my own experiences of being out front, forging a path for women, hoping to maybe break the glass ceiling, but always coming just a bit short. *When will it change for us?* I wondered. Would it ever? The cracks were forming, everywhere, but it was still painfully, inexcusably slow.

After nearly two hours of seeing the sights, I was exhausted, worn out from the medications and still not used to that level of physical exertion, of being "on" for that long. We entered the East Room, used for ceremonial purposes and entertaining. It was stunning, all gold and ivory, with opulent area rugs and portraits of various First Ladies who've held court there in years past. I knew there was no guarantee we would meet the president himself; he was, after all, the most powerful and important man in the world—he could be called away at any moment for something urgent.

We lined up in some semblance of order, about twelve groups of people clustered around their "warrior," as we were called. For most, it was an injured young man, flanked by a wife, fiancée, or mom, sometimes a proud father standing nearby, and maybe one or two other family members who'd been invited. I knew once again why I'd been chosen to round out the group—as ever, one of the few women on the team. It had never crossed my mind to bring anyone but Danielle as my guest. She was my best friend, my person. She had been with me since the beginning.

Somebody of impressive military rank was brought out to present each warrior with the President's Volunteer Service Award, complete with a lapel pin that has no official place on any military dress uniform, but that we all knew we'd try to get away with once we were tailored again into our dress blues. *If any of us could ever wear dress uniforms again,* I thought, looking at all the soldiers missing limbs to my right and left.

The pin was about the size of a dime, with an America-tough gilded bald eagle holding an olive branch and arrows, potent symbols of both peace and war, and a bold shield of American colors centered across its chest. It glinted off my lapel, a visible symbol that I had every right to be as proud of my service as my Lieutenant Mafia and captain counterparts would be of their Bronze Stars—the award I'd been denied. It still stung, but as I looked down at my new hardware, I told myself that maybe it would be okay after all.

Then he walked in—the president of the United States of America. There was some ceremony, but it was somehow casual at the same time. President Barack Obama wore an understated black suit and had plenty of gray hair peppered around his temples. I was struck by how much smaller and older he looked in real life than on television. It did nothing to lessen the electricity of his charisma, his poise, and the empathy that seemed to emanate from him. I thought of Lieutenant Colonel Scott Halter, so young in such a weighty job, both of them carrying every bit of that weight on their shoulders at all times. President Obama walked with a grace and confidence most people never nail in quite that way, and I grabbed Danielle's hand to steady myself from the emotions I'd suddenly felt in his presence. A look from her told me she felt the same.

I realized there was a practical reason behind the ceremony where they'd pinned the Presidential Award on our lapels. It was a way to alert the president to who the warrior was and who were the guests. As someone who was more than used to being told that I "didn't look like a soldier," I appreciated this little bit of effort to help the commander-in-chief not jump to any easy-to-make but wrong conclusions.

I expected the president to quickly walk down the row of people, shake the hand of anyone wearing an award pin, thank us for our service, pose for a group photo, and get right back to his perpetually busy day. But that wasn't what he did. Instead, he spent real time with each group. As I watched President Obama work his way down the line, I could see the quiet power of his actions. For two to three minutes, he gave each person the gift of his time. I thought of so many Aunties I knew, who held on to the memory of the first time they'd gazed at their Prophet's face. We'd all treasure our time basking in the glow of our leader, cherishing the feeling that the most powerful man on earth stopped and listened to us, and cared about us and ours. They were completely different men, of course, but I wondered if my feelings, if those Aunties' feelings, came from the same place. I felt so much gratitude that the president gave us these quiet moments, validating our service in the eyes of our loved ones, and showing us a glimpse of the human behind the position. It made me feel special, as if I were being shined on.

Then he reached Danielle and me. In the picture I have of that day, I see a too-skinny blond girl, my broken nose in profile, wearing an ill-fitting dress and a poorly cut jacket, offering an awkward handshake as President Obama looks directly into my eyes with sincerity, his hand fully covering mine, pressing his small, regal, presidential coin into my palm. Danielle, on my left, looks on in attention and admiration, unwilling to miss even a second of the interaction.

"So, Daniella, what branch of service are you in?" he asked. "And what do you do?" He'd gotten my name right the first time, so rare, but with his complex cultural background and his childhood spent abroad, not to mention having a name like Barack, I suspected he knew what it would mean to me.

"Army captain, Sir. Intelligence."

"And where are you from, Daniella?"

My favorite question.

"Well, I'm from Texas, but I grew up in Brazil."

That's what my paperwork said, anyway. We chatted about his professional experiences in Brazil and the loveliness of the culture.

And then he said, "Who is this, Daniella?"

"Sir, please allow me to introduce Captain Danielle Reid."

And then he repeated the same part that always comes when Danielle and I introduce each other.

"Daniella and Danielle, huh? You two sisters?"

Literally everybody asks us this. Every. Single. Time. It's not that we look alike, but neither do we look unalike. I usually laugh, often snapping back with an acerbic but friendly, "C'mon, whose mother would do that?" This time, though, I responded with the necessary decorum.

"No, Sir."

"Oh," President Obama said, and he took a half step back, seeming genuinely surprised. Since everyone had brought 'their people,' I could see him contemplating who we were to each other as he looked back and forth between the two of us. Though it lasted only a few seconds, Danielle and I both felt we could see the thoughts ticking behind his eyes—this president, the man who'd repealed the military's infamous and unjust Don't Ask, Don't Tell policy, who'd made it acceptable for lesbian and gay soldiers to serve openly under their true identities, who'd removed the fear from what it could mean to a career to be labeled a "dyke" in uniform. I imagined he'd begun meeting more same-sex couples in the military by that time.

Then he asked, "Soooo, how did you two meet?" His famous playfulness danced through his eyes.

I was highly amused, and in no way planning to correct what I thought the president was assuming.

"Well, Sir, we met in basic training, then went to officer school together."

"Oh, wow!" he said, and his face lit up. "And you just knew it was meant to be?"

Danielle couldn't take it anymore. "Yes Sir," she chimed in. "We knew we would be army sisters for life."

The casualness of her tone did not fool me. She wanted him to understand us correctly, to know that, though we weren't, in fact, lesbian life partners, we did see ourselves as one of the most important people in each other's lives, that there was a reason she was the friend standing with me that day. She wanted to give a voice to the value that true female friendship held in an army designed to isolate us at every turn.

"Well, that is such a lovely story," he said, with what felt like genuine warmth. "Thank you for sharing it with me. It was wonderful to meet you, Daniella and Danielle, and thank you to both of you for your service. I mean that."

And then he was gone, on to the next group for handshakes and conversation, handing out his gilded memories. I could not stop shaking in silent laughter as Danielle's eyes shot daggers at me, trying to get me to calm down and stand still—we were still in the presence of POTUS, after all.

But on the bus back, I realized it wasn't funny. I had put on another ill-fitting form of equipment, this time irony, to detach from the situation. Even *that* commander-in-chief, a woman's ally if ever there was one, couldn't see past the stereotypes, the programming we've all been subjected to in this area of our thinking—in so many areas of our thinking.

And that's when I knew I was at another crossroads in my military career, in the rest of my life, and in who I told myself I was in the world. I was a soldier, a fighter, and I had truly believed in the US Army, at least for a while, in a way I never believed in God. After my first awful deployment, despite the trauma I'd suffered, I'd chosen to stay, recommit, rebuild my reputation, accept their limiting stereotypes, and play the game their way. And I'd almost won. For a while, I'd been genuinely happy, finally fitting in on a strong team. I'd been beloved by my unit and accepted by the group. I was the golden child I had always dreamed of being.

But the group hadn't been able to protect me from the senior leadership, who'd been willing to throw me away as soon as it was convenient. I hadn't fawned under the colonel's attention; I didn't worship him the way he seemed to demand. Like all of his elite soldiers, I carried ambitions, but maybe the same determination that drove me to win races looked too ugly when applied professionally while wearing a skirt. Maybe it was the times I'd tried to speak out to change the status quo for women. Maybe it was choosing Tom despite the colonel's decree that war wasn't a time for love. Or maybe I just made him uncomfortable. Maybe any of us strong women made the Uncles in the leadership uncomfortable.

Rolling down the street in that bus, going back to Walter Reed after meeting the president, I realized this game I'd been playing was designed to never let me win.

I needed to make a decision. My medical evacuation had changed things—I hadn't been fired from my job, and my paperwork to leave the army had been canceled. I had the rare chance for a do-over. For all anyone knew, I was another captain who'd gotten sick at war. Getting an award from the president would wash a bit of the perceived "sin" from the lack of a significant medal on my record. If I got better, I'd be sent somewhere else, where nobody had ever heard of me. Like in the Children of God, I could do my penance and be welcomed back into the group. I'd likely have to repeat my time as battalion intelligence officer so I could earn a significant award, but then I could maybe put it all behind me.

Back in Afghanistan, Lieutenant Colonel Scott Halter had seemed sad the army would lose me when I told him I planned to leave. Like my mom, I could tell he cared about me—the person, the individual—not just me, the group member. Like Mom, he'd always tried to help me, to protect me. Ultimately, he'd fallen short. But maybe so had I.

"Daniella," he'd said to me before I'd left Bagram, scared and helpless. "Tell your story."

Could I?

Exit. Excommunicate. Backslide. Leave.

Could I recover from the life I had lived? From the cults I kept joining? From never having learned to be myself?

I swallowed hard and remembered what he'd said. "Use your intelligence skills. Find the thread. Write it down."

Maybe there was a way out after all.

Maybe the way out was through.

EPILOGUE

When the wind blows through the bamboo and tropical flower trellis-work and hits the wind chimes just right, I can almost imagine I'm in a small beach town in the northeast of Brazil. That's my favorite vacation spot these days, alongside the friends we've adopted as family. I take my husband, Tom, now retired from his last role as an Army Special Operations pilot, and our little girl, who's been speaking Portuguese, Spanish, and English since birth. Up here on my rooftop deck on the East Coast, I've created what I lovingly call "fake-Brasil"—spelled with an "s," the Brazilian way, the way I say it in my head, the way it's written on the imprint on my heart.

Across from the pergola where I sit and write, there's a tiki bar that Tom built, part of the woodworking hobby he's exploring as he transitions from his own twenty years as a soldier, leaving the group he's known his entire adult life, uncovering his own traumas along the way. Displayed on the bar are the military challenge coins we collected in our combined twenty-seven years of service, along with our final ranks—captain for me, chief warrant officer three for him—locked forever in resin over a tricolor wood countertop. It's a good final resting place for the awards, the ribbons, valor citations, oak leaf clusters, air medals, combat patches and stripes, all the symbols that mattered so much when we wore the uniform.

Sometimes, I stare at the rocks I've brought from Belo Horizonte, the semiprecious gemstones from the country that, despite all the pain

I experienced there, bathes even the darkest parts of my memories with color and light. I think of all the places I've lived, all the different versions of myself I've put on like a uniform. I think of all the men outnumbering me, encouraging and rewarding me for these versions of myself that were not mine. "Good" men, like the "good Uncles" who didn't rape or beat us but who nevertheless upheld the system that abused us. Men who stayed silent or agreed to tepid changes that never thwarted the power dynamic they held, locking us in groups that fail the whole. I think of the groups I've left, and the ones in my life now. It's not just army and cult. It's professional groups, alumni associations, veteran's organizations, even the homeowners' association in the neighborhood we love. The groups-within-the-groups, like my Lieutenant Mafia buddies, our text chain still going strong after all these years even though we've all gone on our separate paths in life. I think of the support groups I've attended over the years, for cult survivors, for military sexual trauma survivors, and how they've taught me how to feel my pain and mourn my losses, to live with both my emotions and myself, to understand my fear and how it's changed me. Sharing my story with others like me has helped me to find a sisterhood, and even a sisterhood born from the worst kind of shared trauma is better than going through life alone.

I think of all the groups of amazing women—women like Danielle, like my childhood friend Michaela, like my sisters Heaven, Merry, Reyna, Jamie, and others. The strong girlfriends of all ages, races, backgrounds, and creeds who have come into my life throughout my journey. Women who test my thinking, hold me to standards, and illuminate the world. Women who both love and accept me unconditionally for who I am and inspire me to be better.

And I think of the cult and the army. The similarities between them. How both required me to give up more of myself than they ever gave me. How both indoctrinated their members to think and behave according to an unquestionable set of values, in isolation from the wider world. We were always ready for the next set of orders, worshipping at the altar of mission before self. In all those marathon Bible studies, in all the punishments and isolation, in all the Children of God's dogma of persecution; in the hell of army basic training, the hazing of officer school, in all those official ranks and hierarchies, in the intricate dance of medals and demerits—both groups achieved dedication and obedience through their programming.

Wherever there is programming, the code can be written wrong.

Like it went wrong for my ex-husband who, when I married him, was the best of the bad relationships I had been in. In retrospect, I can see the nascent seeds of extremism, control, and violence in his beliefs and actions, so I was saddened but not shocked when the army asked me to testify against Major William Jeffrey Poole for being a White supremacist, for attempting to incite a violent overthrow of the US government.

But how different was he than anyone else? How different was Mom, who stayed in the Children of God throughout decades of abuse? How different am I, how different are you, how different is any human—all of us with instincts that tell us we are safer in our groups?

Why, if the cult I grew up in is "so different" from other kinds of groups, the ones we consider good, normal, and necessary in our society—our schools, our sports teams, our armies, our churches, our social clubs, our fraternities, our academic institutions, our companies, our self-help organizations—do so many of these institutions share such obvious similarities to the toxic group behavior that surrounded me growing up? Why does every struggle that applies to cult survivors trying to make it in "the System" also apply to military veterans trying to make it in the civilian world?

I see traces of the Children of God, with all its inherent cult-think and harmful behavior, in almost every group, organization, or team I have ever joined or studied. And I'm always asking myself: Where does a cult end and a culture begin? What is the difference between a *good* organization and a *bad* cult?

I don't think there is a difference, ultimately.

Maybe groups are just groups. Evil cults. Great armies. Wonderful families. Amazing countries. Pile whatever modifiers on them you want. Each one has the same inherent strengths, weaknesses, and potential pitfalls.

After my thirty-five years of studying leaders and living in cults and cultures across the globe and after my intelligence training and graduate work on group behavior, here's what I've noticed: "Good" people who do terrible things are often supported, protected, and, sometimes, empowered by organizations we love and respect. And almost always, it isn't merely a case of one or two bad apples but that the tree has rotted from within. As a society, it is incumbent on us to ask: Where are the toxins coming from?

None of it is easy to spot, these tactics that cult leaders—and many other kinds of leaders—rely upon to gain loyalty and inspire their followers. None of it happens all at once, and all of it is genuine. People don't join cults. They join churches, organizations, communities, and groups they think will solve a problem for the world or within themselves. They follow leaders, the more charismatic the better. Maybe they're driven by hope, or maybe it's fear. Maybe it is a combination of the two, strengthened by the fuel of righteousness and, often, resentment. And then the logic breaks down, but we're too tightly enthralled to these cults among us to notice.

The first rule of cults is we are never in a cult. It's always them, not us. There is always someone else to blame: the others, the outsiders, the unchosen. And as belief builds in its followers, the less likely we are to question, the easier it is to hate, harm, even kill because we are the good guys. We are right, no matter how many signs point in a different direction or how that direction shifts with the course of the wind.

■

THE WIND CREATES a melody in my heavy-duty Texas wind chime, brought from the unforgiving deserts where my parents settled, and I remember I'm supposed to call Mom for our unofficial book club. Reading has helped both of us come to terms with our own traumas. Recently, she told me that surviving the violent assault on the mountain in Ecuador was easier than delivering herself to the Uncles every night. I shared with her, finally, how those same Uncles, and others, assaulted me. When left with a history for which there are no words, we read our way toward healing. We've spent the last decade immersed in every book we can find on cults and their ways, on influence, discussing the psychology behind it, and poring over the memoirs of those who have also left their cults behind.

The women who survived.

Women like us.

I remember how Mom embraced me on my wedding day, standing on the dance floor that Tom built me after it all, whispering, "I'm proud of you," the way only a fellow survivor could. How Danielle stretched out the ten-foot train of my hand-beaded white dress that cost more than my first car. How Michaela, resplendently beautiful without a drop of sweat on her, laughed at the Americans wilting in the relentless summer Kentucky heat. How Heaven held my hand, while Merry reminded me to breathe and relax, patting my stomach. A sense of confidence and peace descended over me as we toasted, my girls gathered together, my tiny daughter already so alive in my belly.

The daughter who came into the world as dramatically as I did. Mom was there with me, and she held me in her arms when my little baby took seven minutes to take her first breath. And during those seven interminable, horrible moments—the worst thing that has ever happened to me—Mom was there. She became a fierce protector of all her children, and her grandchildren too. When my obstetrician finally handed me the most perfect baby ever, Mom said she looked like me, but we both knew that instead of fourth-generation cult, she's first-generation freedom.

■

I CAN HEAR my daughter's feet padding up behind me, and for a split second I flinch. Those ever-vigilant instincts about threat are still, and probably always will be in some form or another, present within me. But I soften my arms and relax as she climbs onto my lap. My husband says from the stairs, "Little Love, this is Mommy's quiet time."

"It's okay," I say, holding her close.

Then Tom stands behind me, places his hands on my shoulders, and squeezes gently. My daughter burrows into my lap. Soon, she will be too big for this.

But I will let her be a child for as long as possible. Even as the world outside seems full of dangers and heartbreak at every turn, I will do everything I can to make her home, her family, safe in a way mine never was. I, with Tom, am responsible for leading this little group of ours.

This group—*this* family—that I have chosen, that does not demand I be anything or anyone other than who I am, is where I can be my fullest self. This family in which I am free.

ACKNOWLEDGMENTS

As hard as this story felt to live through, it felt tremendously harder to relive. As I wrote these pages, I couldn't help but think fondly of the many, many people who got me through this journey, with all its ups and downs. The people who patiently listened to me go down countless rabbit holes for hours on end and gave me their perspectives, the mentors who encouraged me to keep writing, and those who encouraged me not to "talk less" but to "write more." To find the thread running through my life and its far-fetched but all-too-real stories, the thread that became *Uncultured*. I couldn't have done it without any of you. Thank you for being a part of my story.

To my brilliant editor, Hannah Phillips, who saw from the first moment what this book was really about—not just fearsome tales of sex cults, murder/suicides, trauma, and war stories, but that it was ultimately a saga about the danger of group behavior when it goes unrecognized. Hannah, I'm so glad you saw the potential of this story and its ability to reach . . . well, everyone, in our ever-polarizing world. My thanks to you, and the amazing team at St. Martin's Press, especially Jennifer Enderlin, Laura Clark, Tracey Guest, Paul Hochman, Allison Ziegler, Rebecca Lang, Donna Noetzel, Ginny Perrin, Diana Frost, and Henry Kaufman, for giving this book a chance.

To my literary agents, Jane Dystel and Michael Bourret, thank you for believing in me and this story. Michael, a special thank-you for being a man I know I can trust to be in my corner, for finding me life-changing opportunities, and for helping me, most importantly, to begin to learn how to say no.

To Brandi Larsen and Amy Reed, the fearsome team of women who helped me to tell my life story with the nuance and context I didn't even know I lacked, my words alone could never express my gratitude—which you both well know. When people ask me how I did it, my answer is this: When I set out to write a book about group behavior, I knew I couldn't do it without the right group. Brandi co-parented this book into life with me, from a vague and hazy psychology concept that *humans will do almost anything to be accepted by their groups*. Brandi saw both that I had a story to tell and that I was absolutely lost as to how to tell it. Without her, *Uncultured* would be still just a twinkle in my eye. And Amy, thank you for sharing your wisdom, vision, and incredible writing polish. I'm humbled and honored that you both gave so much of your time, emotions, professional expertise, ideas, and your very words to this project. Thank you for being my group.

To Scott Halter, thank you for your leadership, both at Task Force Lift and in my life since then. I'll be forever grateful for the experience of being on your team and learning from you. Thank you for encouraging me to write and to hold nothing sacred or off-limits, and for telling me to "find the thread." Thank you for being the first person I wanted to tell about this book deal, and for standing by me throughout this hard story.

To my Lieutenant Mafia: Steven, Mark, Matt & Matt, Alex, and Eric, thanks for always treating me like an equal, for standing by me the way you did, for being my friends and my first really, truly awesome unit.

To John Runkle, and all the Pathfinders of the 159th CAB OEF 2011–2012 deployment, those who made it home and those who didn't, thanks for having our backs, for being our brothers-in-arms, and for helping us to make change much bigger than just those little missions out on the sand. Thank you for your service. John, my friend, we changed the army after all.

To Auntie Jade, Ms. Raibon, Heaven, and the *countless* mentors,